JUST RESUMES™

JUST RESUMES™

200 POWERFUL AND PROVEN SUCCESSFUL RESUMES TO GET THAT JOB

Kim Marino

John Wiley & Sons, Inc.

New York ▪ Chichester ▪ Weinheim ▪ Toronto ▪ Singapore ▪ Brisbane

This text is printed on acid-free paper.

Published by John Wiley & Sons, Inc.

This publication is designed to provide accurate and authoritative information in regard to the subject matter covered. It is sold with the understanding that the publisher is not engaged in rendering legal, accounting, or other professional services. If legal advice or other expert assistance is required, the services of a competent professional person should be sought.

Library of Congress Cataloging-in-Publication Data:
Marino, Kim, 1951–
Just Resumes : 200 powerful and proven successful resumes to get that job / Kim Marino. — 2nd ed.
p. cm.
Includes index.
ISBN 0-471-16567-0 (pbk. : alk. paper)
1. Résumés (Employment) I. Title.
HF5383.M285 1997
650.14—dc20 96-29158

Printed in the United States of America

10 9 8 7 6 5 4 3 2 1

Acknowledgments

I'd like to thank my wonderfully talented clients for allowing me to include their resumes in this book. Thank you J. T. Clarke, Jane Autrey, Zackary Whitlock, Angela Schwartz, David Emmons, Calvin Salone, Irene Wasilov, Becki St. Clair, and Desiree Rohling. I'd also like to thank Colin Meaney for being instrumental in researching and helping me write the chapter about Resumes and the Internet. I'd like to express special thanks to everyone I worked with at Bernard Haldane Associates in Atlanta, GA—Trent Perry, Nancy Perry, Don Tyner, Ted Christopher, Cindy Adair, and Kelley Sparger.

Contents

Introduction

Using principles and techniques developed for a highly successful resume business, we clearly and concisely convey to you the knowledge you need to create resumes that get results. All the resumes in this book are samples from actual clients of Just Resumes™, taken from a wide range of careers and experiences. The sheer range and diversity of selections can serve as reinforcement, stimulation, and inspiration for all job seekers.

This book is designed to help open the doors that will allow job seekers to find good, challenging jobs and receive the salaries they deserve. The techniques in this book were designed to enable you to capture your most valuable assets, to see yourself in a new and exciting way—to gain that all important interview and to go into that interview feeling positive about yourself. By using this no-nonsense, step-by-step procedure, you can create a professionally designed resume that can lead to a job interview.

Resumes are always important. When the economy is expanding, new job opportunities and a fresh, new resume go hand-in-hand. Likewise, if there is a recession, job hunters need the best possible resume to improve their chances of finding employment.

These days, in fact, everyone in the working world needs a resume. College graduates exit the campus armed with a diploma in one hand and a resume in the other. This book contains suggestions for college grads who may be afraid they don't have enough experience in the "real world." Professionals venturing up the corporate ladder need a resume that effectively represents their skills and accomplishments, yet also points them toward their job objective. Those of you seeking a change of career (and there are more and more of you in that group) can greatly increase your chances of making a successful move by following the strategies outlined in this book. Housewives entering or returning to the job market can follow a number of pointers to get credit for skills and experiences, even if they don't receive a paycheck for what they have been doing.

No matter what your particular needs are, this book can show you how to create a resume that aims you toward your career goals, that captures your most valuable assets, and that can help you see yourself in a positive, re-enforcing light.

Just Resumes includes everything you need to write your own professional resume. Those in search of a resume most often need that resume for a fast-approaching interview, therefore this "how-to" guide is designed to help you produce that resume quickly and efficiently. *Just Resumes* contains 200 of the best resumes taken from the files of Just Resumes—resumes that helped clients get that interview and ultimately get that job. You will find this book an excellent guide to help you write your own resume, a reference resource for your future, and one of the best investments you'll ever make.

1

The Professional Resume

HOW TO USE THIS BOOK

This book contains 200 of the most effective resumes from the files of Just Resumes. Every resume in this book resulted in getting a job. These are real people; their resumes serve as samples to point you in the right direction toward what will become your own personal resume.

Before you begin to construct your own resume, read the text in the first three chapters. (Also read Chapter 4, 5, or 6 if it fits your specific background.) Then turn to the resume samples in Chapter 9 to get a feel for what your resume will look like. You'll use a combination of instructional text and samples to guide you. As you take these steps, review your background and the career you are aiming for. These considerations will determine which format is the best one for you. There is the traditional chronological format that highlights your jobs. The newer and adaptable functional format focuses on your skills. For those of you who need to highlight a specific job and would like to mention other related jobs you've had, the combination resume is the preferred format, combining the chronological and the functional formats. Instructions are included for creating resumes for special situations such as resumes for the artist, photographer, actress/actor, graphic artist, and contractor which highlight credits, clients/projects or freelance work. Whichever format you decide to use, the goal is to capture your strongest qualities.

Upon completing your first draft, reread the text in the first three chapters, take another look at the samples, and finalize your own resume.

THE RESUME THOUGHT PROCESS

If you've had a difficult time in the past putting together your resume, you are not alone. Most people begin the resume process with the wrong focus and either are unable to complete the project or end up with an unsatisfactory resume.

It is important to concentrate on *where* you are going, not where you have been or where you are now. By focusing on your future job objective, you can create a resume that leads in the right direction, that shows the potential employer how the past and present qualify you for that job.

WHAT A PROFESSIONAL RESUME WILL DO FOR YOU

Your resume is a custom-designed, self-marketing tool tailored to your career objectives. It's also the first link between you and the potential employer. (No wonder there's so much pressure on job seekers to create an effective resume!) A professional resume functions in four ways.

1. Focuses the interviewer's attention on *your* strongest points!
2. Gives you full credit for all your achievements, whether you were paid or not!
3. Guides the interviewer toward positive things to talk about in *you!*
4. Most importantly, lets *you* see yourself in a more focused and positive manner!

SPECIAL TIPS

Many job applications live or die in the first 30 seconds of the screening process. It's in that 30-second glance that the receptionist or applications examiner decides to either forward your resume to the next step or to reject it. But there are several things you can do to increase your chances of being selected into the group of resumes to be reviewed by the interviewer. You'll see in Chapter 9 that most of the resumes are one page in length. Because they are concise and to-the-point, the resumes clearly provide the information needed to convey your abilities and strengths. On the other hand, if you have so much experience that one page will not suffice, *do* use two pages to get the job done. Some people will use a smaller typeface to try and cram all the information on one page—an unwise decision. You don't want to make the employer's job any tougher than it is by having a hard-to-read resume.

You should have an objective on your resume, even a general objective. Faced with scores of applications each day, the person doing the initial screening needs to be able to immediately identify what position you're applying for at the company. An objective will help you look more focused, and in turn more desirable for the position than those whose resumes lack the objective.

Consider this example: A woman contacted me who had had her resume done for her by another professional resume writer. She was receiving responses from her resume but for the wrong jobs. When I looked at her materials, I saw that the objective was in her cover letter but not in her resume. By reading the resume (without an objective), I could see how she appeared qualified for several types of jobs, even though she was only interested in one. We worked together, adding a job objective and rewriting the resume so that its components pointed directly to that objective. With a revised resume, now focused on her objective, she did receive a positive response from the very company she'd written to previously, but this time for the position she desired. (See Index to Resume Samples, Product Development Manager.)

Using a job objective is not an ironclad rule; in some cases, your job title may become your objective. This especially applies to accountants, attorneys, real estate associates, psychologists, and other professionals.

As mentioned earlier, there are three basic resume formats—chronological, functional, and combination. The chronological emphasizes your previous job experience and is written in the order of the positions beginning with the most recent job working backwards. The functional style highlights your skills with a lesser emphasis on the job titles. A combination style makes use of the strengths of both the chronological and the functional. Special situation resumes such as those in the arts focus on credits, clients/projects, freelance work, exhibitions, publications, and awards. (See Chapter 3.)

Most of you will already be familiar with the chronological format, the more traditional style. Just remember that the functional, chronological, and combination resume should offer the same information, but the difference is in how the information is presented, in what is emphasized.

PERSONAL DATA

With today's equal opportunity requirements, personal data is not required, and indeed does not belong, on a resume. Sometimes a screener may not be aware of a personal prejudice, but it may turn out that the person who has the power to give your resume to the interviewer may be influenced by some personal bit of information. Unless the client insists or is in the special situation resume category, I do not put age, religion, or political affiliation on a resume (unless, of course, the client is joining the priesthood or applying for a job with a political party).

RESUME APPEARANCE

The typeface you select is almost as important as the format you use for your resume. With today's ever expanding computer typefaces, the choices can be overwhelming. To simplify the matter, opt for something that looks professional and is easy to read. A good typeface should enhance but not dominate your overall resume presentation. (See the resume samples in Chapter 9.) Avoid the temptation to use a fancy script style; more effective styles are Helvetica, Century Schoolbook, or Times Roman, all readily available.

Don't scrimp when it comes to selecting your resume paper. Color and texture are important factors in selecting resume paper. For the business world, I highly recommend a conservative look; a white, ivory, or light grey works fine. For the technical fields, such as engineering or electronics, a light grey connotes professional ability. For the medical profession, a brilliant white conveys a sense of competence (and perhaps hygienic cleanliness). Ivory works well for every profession.

Those in the arts, such as a graphic artist, photographer, or actress, can be more daring and creative and use a blue or mauve color. Bear in mind in the arts you will also be submitting a portfolio of your work and may want your artistic samples to demonstrate your creativity while choosing a more conservative look for your resume. Really, whether you're an engineer, accountant, or artist, your personal preference plays a part in this, too.

There are many different textured papers for you to choose from. Parchment paper, for example, has a light textured background woven into the paper. Classic Laid, which works well with resumes, has a heavier smooth wood-like finished look. Classic Linen has a lighter cloth-like textured look, and cotton, the most expensive, feels and looks just like cotton.

As with the typeface you choose, the resume paper should compliment your resume, *not* dominate it. Resume paper and matching envelopes are available at your local copy shop.

SUMMARY OF RESUME STYLES

- Chronological format highlights your jobs.
- Functional format highlights your skills.
- Combination format combines the chronological and functional formats to highlight selected jobs.
- Special situations: Artists, photographers, actors, and contractors highlight credits, client/projects, or freelance assignments.

RESUME DO'S AND DON'TS

- DO choose a job that you love.
- DO spend time listing all your good qualities. This is where you get credit where credit is due.
- DO include a clear and concise job objective; focus your resume on your future objective to show the employer "where I am going," not "where I have been or where I am now."
- DO include experience/skills directly related to the job objective.
- DO start each sentence with an action word.
- DO list all related experience—paid or unpaid. Include experience from school activities and committees, such as organizing fundraising events, PTA, or sorority/fraternity treasurer or social chairperson.
- DO research the position and company before the interview.
- DO keep your resume down to one or two pages.

- DO follow up the interview with a personalized thank-you letter.
- DON'T leave out the job objective.
- DON'T include material or history not related to the job objective.
- DON'T use long, repetitive explanations.
- DON'T include personal history.
- DON'T presume that the personnel screener understands skills included in the job title—tailor your job description.
- DON'T take for granted skills that you perform well as a matter of course.
- DON'T replace a job description with a job title—it's not self-explanatory. A manager in one company may not do the same activities as a manager in another company.
- DON'T forget to include your GPA under education, if you're a student or recent graduate and it's a 3.5 or higher.
- DON'T list references from whom you have not received permission or a positive response.
- DON'T send a form thank-you letter. Personalize each one.

2

Chronological, Functional, or Combination Resumes

BASIC RESUME ELEMENTS

Whether you decide to use the chronological, functional, or combination format will depend on the way you want to present your information. Your own background and your objective will determine which resume style will work best for you. No matter what the format, however, each resume should offer the same basic information.

The resume you will create, be it functional, combination, or chronological, will incorporate these basic sections:

- Name, address, and phone number
- Career objective
- Professional profile (optional)
- Educational information
- Description of work experience
- Employment history with job title, company name, location and dates of employment.

More tips. . .

- Start sentences with a vigorous action verb.
- Focus on the career objective.
- Education is placed after Professional Experience, unless you are entering the education field or you are a recent college graduate whose education is a stronger factor than your limited work experience.

THE CHRONOLOGICAL RESUME

In the traditional chronological resume, you combine the experience and the employment history under one section. Each position is listed with the dates of employment, job title, company name, city, and state, followed by a point-by-point description of job experience. Jobs are listed in order beginning with the most recent position.

The chronological resume highlights the progress in your jobs. Because of this, it works best for Professionals who are making an upward or lateral career move when your background consists of the following:

1. The entire work history shows progress with skills directly related to your job objective.
2. Each position involves a completely different job description.
3. You have a stable work history.

As an example, let's say you are an account executive for an advertising firm, and you are being considered for a position as manager of account executives or vice-president. Your previous positions, though different in nature, show a progression toward your goal: sales clerk for a department store, ad rep for a record company, entry-level position as account representative for a small ad agency, mid-level position of account representative for a larger agency, who also trained entry-level employees. A chronological resume, with appropriate job descriptions, would represent perfectly your career growth and development leading to this latest position.

THE FUNCTIONAL RESUME

A functional resume looks different from a chronological resume. In the functional format, because it highlights your skills, a great deal more space is devoted to describing your experience. Sections might include administrative skills, project development, or client relations. The actual employment history will be listed at the end of the resume and will concisely give the basic information as to job title, locations, and dates. In the functional resume:

- All the work experience is highlighted with subsections that are pertinent to the job objective.
- The entire employment history is listed at the end with job title, company name, city and state; each job is listed in reverse chronological order, but without a detailed explanation of the experience.

The functional resume works best for:

- Individuals who are changing careers
- First-time job seekers
- Housewives re-entering the job market

This resume format is best if:

1. Your entire work history goes beyond the skills and experience related to your objective.
2. You have skills related to your job objective but not necessarily in your employment history.
3. You've had several positions with the same job description.

THE COMBINATION RESUME

The combination resume allows the job seeker to highlight skills from a specific job or selected jobs and still list other work experience or employment history. It's a combination of the chronological and functional resume. For example, a combination resume was used for a client whose objective was to work in the Cultural Arts Program as the publicity writer for a university. He had been working for another university in the same kind of program, doing the same job the past two years. His prior experience included 10 years of journalism at several different newspaper publications. We highlighted his current employment experience at the university and listed his employment history of previous publications in the combination resume style. This format works great for those with the following background:

1. You've had specific job(s) directly related to your objective.
2. Each position you've held involves a completely different job description.
3. You have related jobs that are important to mention because they are indirectly related to your current objective.
4. If you're a student, points 1 and 2 apply to your background and you have jobs you'd like to mention just to show your stable work history.

RESUMES FOR THE ARTS AND OTHER SPECIAL SITUATIONS

People in the arts require an entirely different approach to resume writing. Actors and actresses need to highlight their credits. Photographers and graphic artists need to highlight their freelance work or clients/projects. Even contractors are sometimes freelancers and will have a client/project list to highlight. (See Index to Resume Samples by Job Title for a sample of your field of interest.)

This is an introduction to the particularities of the different resume formats. If you are still hazy about when to use what, relax. We'll be going into more detail about these formats in Chapter 3. When you begin to study the resume samples, you'll see the differences in each of the formatting approaches. Ultimately, what you want to use is whatever works best for you. All of these formats have gotten results.

3

The Just Resumes No-Nonsense Approach to Resume Writing

A FEW MORE POINTERS

In a professionally designed resume, you can convey a significant amount of information concisely and vigorously. Single line phrases and sentences are simple to read, straightforward, and direct the employer's attention toward your capabilities and desired experiences. If you prefer paragraph form, however, that can be quite effective. In either case, begin each sentence with an action word, such as "developed" or "implemented," describing what you did. (See List of Action Words at the end of this chapter.)

Action words energize your resume, but avoid using the same action word twice within one job description or, if using the functional format, twice in the Experience subsection. Remember, for a functional resume, you will create a subsection. The title of each subsection will depend on the skills you are highlighting as you aim toward that career objective. (See resume samples, Chapter 9.)

REMEMBER: ALWAYS THINK POSITIVE AND FOCUS ON YOUR JOB OBJECTIVE.

CREATING A FUNCTIONAL RESUME

A functional resume is designed to be selective. If your entire work history includes additional skills not related to your career objective, you'll highlight only those skills pertinent to your objective.

If you've had several positions with the same job description, you don't need to repeat yourself. Say what you did one time, which saves both space on the resume for other valuable information and time for the resume examiner. Don't worry that you might be minimizing your achievements, because you will list the jobs that cover similar experience under Employment History. (See resume samples, Chapter 9.) As you become familiar with the functional resume, you'll see how it can convey a great deal of information in a minimum amount of space. Follow this outline:

1. Personal Headline

   List your name, address, and phone number.

2. Objective

   What is your current objective? Make it brief and to the point.

   For example: An Executive Assistant position.

3. Profile

   This section is optional but useful. It's this section that my clients often refer to when they say "I can't believe this is me!" or "I hadn't thought about myself before in this light!" Your profile is a brief description or summary of working style, personality traits, and achievements that relate to your objective. These are the essence of what the employer may be looking for in the applicant.

   For example, ability to comfortably work under high-pressure situations and consistently meet strict deadline schedules. (See resume samples, Chapter 9.)

4. Education

   List your degree (B.A., M.A.), major, school, graduation date.

5. Professional Experience or Related Experience

   Here's the heart of your functional resume. Starting with the appropriate action word, describe what you do at your job. You'll use subheads to really convey your skills. (See List of Action Words at the end of this chapter.) Part of the section would look like this:

PROFESSIONAL EXPERIENCE

Project Development

- Develop highly successful marketing strategies and corporate identities.
- Design logos, brochures, and copywrite for newspaper/radio advertising.
- Achieved the highest spec ad sales rating in the history of the company.
- Increased monthly sales by 30%.

Director/Coordinator

- Coordinate, prioritize, and implement multiple projects meeting tight daily deadlines.
- Locate qualified vendors to purchase equipment under strict corporate budgets.

Remember to include any special achievements directly related to your career objective. Always focus on your strongest points that tie in to your career objective. For more details and examples, look at the functional resume samples in Chapter 9.

6. Employment History

   In this section, list your job title, company name, city, state, and date position started/ended in chronological order, starting with the most recent job and working backwards. Students and women returning to the workforce may not have a job title. I'll show you what to do about that in Chapters 5 and 6. If your job title was nondescript or if you didn't have a job title, give yourself credit where credit is due. Be descriptive: when selecting an appropriate job title that best encapsulates what you did, remember that many companies have a different title for what is essentially the same job at another company. For example, you might be called a Writer where you work, but your job may include more managerial duties than the title implies. Another company might call that same job Assistant Director.

ORGANIZING THE RAW DATA IN A FUNCTIONAL RESUME

What you do in one part of the resume can help you flesh out other sections. This is especially the case for the Professional Experience section. First list your previous employment or work history before becoming more specific in the Professional Experience section. You'll gain a better perspective on what you're going to write about. What you include under the Professional Experience heading essentially will be a description of your achievements and what you've done, taken directly from the Employment or Work History section. Remember, always focus on your career objective.

At this stage, you can afford to be expansive. Brainstorm your ideas. There really is no limit to the categories you can create. Start with an action word describing your experiences. After you've listed your achievements and experiences directly related to your career objective, sort out what you wrote. Then, create the subtitles that fit the description of your career objective.

For example, let's say you're a Restaurant Manager. You've probably gained valuable skills in restaurant and employee management, client relations, sales, marketing, and promotions.

These very labels can become the categories under Professional Experience that you will then expand upon.

With this procedure, you're accomplishing two things. First, you're putting in concrete form a description of the many (and often unstated) ways you work. Second, you're highlighting the skills the interviewer will be looking for in you.

Now that you have those skills listed as categories under Professional Experience, you can use them as subheadings. If, as in the above example, you have a subheading for Restaurant Management, you now add the details of what that role involves. Let's say something like:

Restaurant Manager

- Started up a new restaurant with three locations.
- Set up floor plans and employee stations for dining room and bar.

As you create your functional resume, visualize the employer receiving your final version. (Remember, you're aiming for that interview; keep your resume on that target; keep your achievements and experience related to your career objective.)

CREATING A CHRONOLOGICAL RESUME

The chronological resume is the old standard. Though the functional resume has certain applications, the time-tested chronological resume still is useful. Use the chronological resume when these three points apply to you!

1. Your entire employment history shows progress with skills related to your objective.

   Let's say you began your career as a book publisher proofreader, moving up to copyeditor and then became an acquisition editor. Now you're aiming for managing editor, which follows directly from your previous experience.

2. Each position involves a generally different job description.

Looking at the above example, each position—from proofreader to managing editor—incorporates different job skills and different job descriptions. A proofreader checks copy, an acquisitions editor develops book ideas, signs authors, and so on.

3. Your work history is stable.

If your job history is reflected in these points and you are aiming for a position that seems to follow from what you've previously been doing, then create a chronological resume by following these instructions:

1. Personal Headline

   List your name, address, and phone number.
2. Objective

   What is your current objective? Make it brief and to the point. For example: an Electrical Engineering position.
3. Profile

   This is a brief description or summary of your skills, personality traits, and achievements related to the objective. For example, let's say you want to be an accountant. The interviewer will look for someone who is detail oriented with the ability to meet strict deadline schedules.
4. Education

   List your degree (B.A., M.A.), major, school, graduation date.
5. Professional Experience or Related Experience

   What date did you start your present job (year starting/ending)? What's the company (name, city, and state) you presently work for?

   Describe what you did at each job. Include any special achievements you've accomplished related to your objective. Always focus on your strongest points, directly related to your career objective. Be consistent and repeat the above questions under experience for each position pertinent to your objective. Look at resume samples for more details.

Executive Vice President 1985–present

Pension Consultants Inc., Los Angeles, CA

- Managed operations involving annual sales of $2.5M.
- Designed and implemented investment advisory service.
- Increased monthly sales by 30% within first year.

For more variations on the Professional Experience theme, consult the resume samples in Chapter 9.

Once you have created the segment for your present job, repeat the procedure for each of your previous job experiences.

CREATING A COMBINATION RESUME

As discussed in Chapter 2, a combination resume brings attention to the jobs most directly related to your career objective. For some of you, certain jobs you've had deserve more emphasis than others.

A variation on the chronological and functional formats, the combination resume highlights the jobs that tie in to your objective by using the chronological style. Then it lists your other employment in the functional format. The combination has an extensive job description for a specific job or jobs, and then includes, in a different section, a job listing of your previous employment history.

To create a combination resume, follow the same instructions for the chronological resume. This time you'll highlight selected job(s) under the professional experience section that relate directly to your job objective. (See numbers 1–5, p. 23.) In addition, you will also create a section for your previous jobs at the end of your resume titled Employment History. List your job title, company name, city, state, and date position started/ended for the rest of your jobs in chronological order starting with the most recent and working backwards as in the functional resume. (See resume samples in Chapter 9.)

NOTE: IF YOU'VE HAD NUMEROUS JOBS OVER THE YEARS, YOU DON'T *HAVE* TO LIST THEM ALL.

RESUMES FOR THE ARTS

Those of you entering or currently in a profession in the arts, such as photographer, actor, actress, or graphic artist have worked on related projects for school or freelance projects for friends, family, or clients. If so, you'll want to call your work experience Clients/Projects. Simply list the name of the person, school, or company that you did the work for and briefly describe your project. For the graphic artist, for example, list your clients/projects this way:

CLIENTS/ PROJECTS:	**Kim's Boutique**—Designed and illustrated six line art promotional posters.

If you're an actress or actor, under Theatrical Experience say something like this:

THEATRICAL EXPERIENCE

Performing Experience

- Lead Role—Marvin, "March of the Falsettos," Boston University, Boston, MA.

Production/Film Experience

- Wrote a 15-minute, one-act comedy for a school production.

See Index to Resume Samples for specific examples in your field of interest.

OPTIONAL RESUME HEADINGS

All resumes have some flexibility. You may list the following skills or activities under the Professional Profile section or create titles for anything that's pertinent to your career objective and is important to you, such as:

Special Training
Office Skills
Publications
Volunteer Work
Academic Achievements
Affiliations
Special Skills
Computer Skills
Other Pertinent Information
Language Skills

See resume samples, Chapter 9.

LIST OF MORE THAN 100 ACTION WORDS

act as
active in
administer
allocate
analyze
approve
articulate
assimilate
assist
assure
augment
balance
built
chair
coach
collect
communicate
compute
conceptualize
consolidate
consult
contribute
control
coordinate
correct
correspond
counsel
create
delegate
demonstrate
design
determine
develop
direct
distribute
document

draft
edit
effect
enact
establish
evaluate
examine
execute
follow-up
forecast
formulate
forward
generate
guided
identify
implement
improve
initiate
install
institute
instruct
integrate
interface
interview
launch
lead
lecture
liaison
locate
maintain
manage
market
mediate
monitor
operate
optimize
organize
oversee
perform
persuade
plan
prepare
present
process
produce
promote
proofread
propose
provide
recommend
recruit
refer
repair
report
represent
research
resolve
review
revise
schedule
screen
secure
select
set up
specify
stimulate
strengthen
summarize
supervise
supply
systematize
tabulate
test
train
upgrade

4

Returning to the Workforce

Those of you who have been removed from the workforce for many years may be concerned that you've been out of the cycle too long to plug back in. Or you may believe you will be judged by potential employers that you lack essential experiences necessary for the business world. After all, what employer would want to hire a "mom" who has been busy raising kids for the past 10 years? But even given the courage to press ahead and seek employment, what could you possibly put in the Professional Experience section? And how can you create a resume that will compete against a man's resume?

GREAT RESULTS WITH THE FUNCTIONAL RESUME FORMAT

One of the beauties of a functional resume is that you can give yourself credit for the experiences you've gained and for the skills you've developed, even if you never received a single paycheck for what you did.

For instance, the committees you've served on, the school projects you dove into, the volunteer work you've done—these are all valuable sources of material for your resume.

Consider that PTA committee you've been involved with for several years. Yes, it's a voluntary, unpaid position, but take a few minutes to analyze what you've done on that committee, and suddenly you'll be coming up with a variety of useful skills. Write down the kinds of activities you've been engaged in for the committee (maybe you brought a speaker to the school or helped set up a recycling program), and once you've generated a list, create two or three subsections, such as:

Organization Skills
Public Speaking Skills
Teaching Skills

Place each experience under the appropriate heading. As you do this, picture the employer who is going to read your resume. What will that person be looking for? Like the other resumes in this book, your resume will include a career objective; emphasize those achievements and experiences that are related to your objective.

You might be amazed at the significant experiences you can come up with. For instance, have you helped your husband at the office or home? Did you do bookkeeping, banking, scheduling, or home selling? Did you help plan a wedding or other large social occasion?

Even the day-to-day activities can suddenly appear in a different light if you take a step back and process exactly what you do. Under the category of family/time management you have probably been scheduling appointments and travel arrangements for your children and husband, chauffering your offspring to school and afternoon activities, while still managing to have dinner on the table at 6:30 PM. Listen, you know something about deadlines and organization!

Have you ever rushed a family member off to the emergency room or nursed someone through a long illness or personal crisis? Those kinds of actions require strong interpersonal communication skills and the ability to calmly, quickly, and efficiently deal with high pressure situations.

You can use "hidden" skills such as these to your advantage in a functional resume. It's just a matter of placing those skills under the appropriate subtitle. For example:

Interpersonal Communication
People Management
Problem Solving
Time Management
Communication
Organization
Finance

If you actually have work experience but haven't been employed in many years, the functional resume also works well in this situation. First, you will be highlighting your skills under Related Experience. Then, you will be listing your work history at the bottom of the resume. (See resume samples in Chapter 9.)

But how will you fill the gap in time when you weren't in a paid job? Simple—you'll say something like this:

Home Management, Travel, Research, Santa Barbara, CA, 1985–present

or

Home Management, Travel, Studies, Bellingham, WA, 1975–90

Not only does this arrangement fill any gaps in your resume, it also explains what you've been doing, where, and when. Plus, it also proves to you that you have been accomplishing something of significance.

Here's another typical (and often overlooked) example. A client came to me for help and said, "I'd like to be a personnel counselor but I don't have any experience; I've been helping my husband and have spent the rest of my time being a mom and housewife." In putting together the resume, we discovered plenty of experience that a personnel interviewer would look for in her. (See the resume sample, Susan Michelle Ryland, p. 24.)

SUSAN MICHELLE RYLAND

Personnel Counselor—Functional Resume
Housewife/Mom Re-Entering the Workforce with Personal Experience as Committee Chairperson and Husband's Helper

The Typical Housewife/Mom Gets Credit Where Credit Is Due!

Susan is a typical example of the housewife/mom who comes for help with her resume. The first thing Susan said is, "I'd like to do something in personnel but I don't have any experience." The last thing she said is, "Wow, I can't believe that's me; I look so focused and I did so much." Well, she was so busy doing all the things described in her resume—she just hadn't formulated what is involved in being a "housewife/mom."

Summary

① First, we highlighted the personnel experience Susan earned while helping her husband hire new employees for his office on an on-call basis.

② Next, we highlighted organization experience we discovered she had from coordinating projects for three committees at her children's elementary school.

③ Then, we demonstrated Susan's public speaking experience gained as a volunteer.

④ Under Community Service, we listed the experience Susan had through helping out at her children's elementary school.

⑤ We filled in Susan's gap in time as Home Management, Volunteer, Research, Study. This answers any questions in the mind of the resume reviewer as to what she was doing and where she was during the past 10 years.

⑥ We also gave Susan an appropriately descriptive job title relating to her job objective while helping out her husband with his office needs.

Personnel Counselor—Functional Resume
Housewife/Mom Re-Entering the Work Force with Personal Experience as Committee Chairperson and Husband's Assistant

SUSAN MICHELLE RYLAND
3789 Rodeo Drive
Santa Barbara, CA 93105
(805) 569-2020

Objective: Personnel Counselor

PROFESSIONAL EXPERIENCE

Personnel Experience

- As an on-call personnel consultant for a physician's office...
  - Interviewed, screened and hired professional and clerical personnel.
  - ① Sought applicants with dedication, professionalism and experience with ability to deal in sensitive situations with competence and concern.
- Communicate effectively with employees and all types of professionals.
- Effective listener demonstrating strength in assessing people's needs and priorities.

Project Coordination Experience

- As Chairperson for the Principal Selection Committee...
  - Developed job description for an elementary school principal position.
  - Selected, scheduled appointments and interviewed candidates.
  - Recommended candidates to the board and participated in final decision.
- ② As Chairperson for the Playground Improvement Committee...
  - Contacted businesses to sponsor project through donations of materials.
  - Encouraged art teachers and students to submit ideas for improvement.
  - Located and motivated volunteers to complete this successful project, demonstrating a high degree of team work and creativity.
- As Chairperson of the Library Improvement Committee, completely renovated school library, resulting in a stimulating, bright, cheery setting that inspired children to read.

Public Speaking Experience

- ③ As docent-art tour guide, conducted tours for the Santa Barbara Museum of Art; demonstrated poise and dignity while speaking to large and small groups of people.
- As member of The Santa Barbara Theatre, participated in plays, musicals and reader's theatre of numerous productions.

COMMUNITY SERVICE

Kittridge Elementary School, Goleta, CA
④ Principal Selection Committee Chairperson
Library Improvement Committee Chairperson
Playground Improvement Committee Chairperson

EMPLOYMENT HISTORY

⑤ **Home Management, Volunteer, Research, Study**, Goleta, CA — 1980-present
⑥ **On-Call Personnel Consultant**, Jonathan Ryland, MD, Goleta, CA — 1975-80

5

Changing Careers or Moving Up

Regardless of the business climate—whether we're in the midst of a recession or a booming economy—an effective resume can help you reposition yourself. You might be in sales, management, academia, medicine, or another area and, at some point, whether by necessity or choice, you want to either advance to a higher position or make a lateral move into a related field.

You need a way of highlighting your progress and achievements in a resume that will not only be competitive but will get results. You want to show your potential employers that you are thinking in terms of a career and not just a job.

If you feel you are not advancing as quickly as you think you deserve to, a professional resume emphasizing your work history can offer you the psychological boost you need to present yourself in the best possible light. Not only will your resume show them your capabilities, it will also show *you* what you have done, allowing you to see yourself in a positive and focused manner aiming toward that goal.

MOVING UP

The best format for charting your experience if you are moving up is with the chronological format. As shown in Chapter 2, the chronological resume details your progress most clearly by highlighting your employment history. (See resume sample at the end of this chapter.)

MAKING A LATERAL MOVE

If you are making a lateral move to another company or department but essentially staying in your current field, use the functional style, which will emphasize your job skills. (Refer to Chapter 2 for directions for creating your resume.)

In all cases, remember to focus on your career objective. Highlight all the training you received and the duties you're currently responsible for. (See resume sample at the end of this chapter.)

In the past, employees tended to stay with one employer for longer periods of time, even for whole careers. People also remained in the same field for the most part. But these days, it is not at all unusual for many of us to begin in our twenties in one field and move over to another area of work in our thirties and again switch gears in our forties. A former accountant may take up real estate. An insurance representative may become a hotel manager. A teacher may become a computer consultant.

This fluidity of professional development calls for the functional resume, because you are going to be focusing on your skills, not just your employment history. You may be an accountant aiming for a change into psychology, and embedded in your past are skills and strengths that apply to that new career objective. Using the functional resume will give you more options when deciding what to highlight.

For example, let's say you are currently a professional tennis instructor and a former preschool teacher. This past year, you and your husband designed, constructed, and sold a condominium. Excited by that experience, you decided you'd like to become a real estate agent and passed the Real Estate Sales Examination. Now, how do you best present yourself?

Using a functional resume format, you'll create the heading of Related Experience. For example:

Real Estate Experience

- Assisted in the design, construction, and sale of a Los Angeles Condominium.
- Established an effective marketing strategy to promote the sale of property.
- Designed flyers and newspaper advertising; distributed flyers.
- Arranged and conducted open house.

Sales, Promotions, & Organization

- Organized and coordinated a summer tennis program for children at a private club.
- Promoted services through effective telemarketing techniques and product knowledge.
- Advised clients and members in a professional manner, securing trust and confidence.

What can often lead to a career change is the discovery about yourself that you make when you pursue a new hobby, take a class, or, as in the case above, help a friend or family member on a special project. These are more than "hidden" skills; they are true indicators of your interest that translate so well into the essence of a functional resume.

JACQUELINE ANN FRANK

Flight Attendant-Functional Resume
Changing Careers from Nanny/Teacher's Aide/Cashier

Strategy

Jacki wanted to apply for a flight attendant position. She had never worked for an airline before, but in a functional resume format, we will show how qualified she is for this position. Focusing on her career objective, we highlighted all the skills the resume screener will look for in the flight attendant position:

People skills
Cash management skills
Preparation of and serving meals
Interpersonal communication skills
Effectively deals with emergency situations
Quickly adjusts to new working and living environments

The last time I spoke to Jacki she was being flown to Chicago for an interview and is now working for a major airline. Congratulations Jacki!

Summary

① As an estate nanny, she learned how to communicate with poise and confidence while working and traveling with children and adults. She also learned how to prepare and serve meals to others with ease.
② As a teacher's aide, she demonstrated the ability to deal with emergencies quickly and efficiently.
③ As a sales representative, she showed her ability to communicate with all types of people.
④ As a cashier, she showed her ability to handle money.
⑤ The employment section shows a steady work history and progressive jobs aiming toward that position of flight attendant.

Flight Attendant—Functional Resume
Changing Careers from Nanny/Teacher's Aide/Sales Rep.

JACQUELINE ANN FRANK
301 Victoria Court
Asheville, NC 28801
(704) 254-9992

Objective: A Flight Attendant position

PROFESSIONAL EXPERIENCE

Estate Nanny

- Provided total care for 2-3 children from infant to age 6 for several prominent families since 1971.

①
- Prepared and served meals to the children.
- Planned children's activities and daily outings.
- Shopped, ran family errands and maintained light housekeeping.
- Supervised children while traveling on family vacations.

Montessori Teacher's Aide

- Assisted teacher with classrooms of 30 students ages 2-6.

②
- Set up daily classroom and outdoor activities, i.e, drama workshops, sports, arts & crafts and singing; prepared lunches and snacks.
- Motivated children to maximize participation and enjoyment.
- Learned to deal in emergency situations quickly and efficiently.

Sales Representative

- Sold educational training programs to individuals for a business college.
- Conducted sales presentations, speaking to groups with poise and confidence.

③
- Oversaw efficient, courteous and friendly service, expediting challenges students presented in a quick and creative manner.
- Interviewed prospective students, issued aptitude test and gave a tour of the school; collected enrollment fee.

Receptionist/Cashier

- Demonstrated excellent public relations skills while providing customer service at a busy retail drugstore chain.

④
- Maintained accuracy and speed while balancing daily cash transactions.
- Stocked shelves and maintained cleanliness at the end of the day.
- Worked on multiple assignments under pressured situations maintaining a highly professional and concerned manner.
- Greeted patients and scheduled appointments on a daily basis.

EMPLOYMENT HISTORY

Estate Nanny, Ms. Carla Simmons, Asheville, NC — 1989-91
⑤ **Teacher's Aide,** Montessori Center School, Asheville, CA — 1987-88
Sales Representative, SB Business College, Santa Barbara, CA — 1986-87
Receptionist, Sansum Medical Clinic, Santa Barbara, CA — 1983-84
Cashier, Longs Drug Store, Santa Barbara, CA — 1982-83

HEIDI ELIZABETH SANDLER

Escrow Officer/Department Manager—Chronological Resume
Moving Up from Escrow Officer/Assistant Manager

Strategy

Heidi's resume shows progress. We demonstrated how qualified she now is for an escrow department manager position by highlighting each job and job title over the past 10 years of experience in the chronological resume format.

Summary

① Heidi's job title becomes her job objective in this resume style.

② First, we highlighted the work attributes Heidi acquired that the resume screener will be looking for in a management employee.

③ With a vigorous action verb, we showed all the management duties she already is held responsible for as the assistant departmental manager for the main branch and one branch office.

④ Here she shows stability and continued growth as an escrow officer for another title company.

⑤ Having been an escrow assistant she demonstrates her well-rounded ability to understand other department employee job functions.

⑥ As Escrow Secretary, she further shows her progress and ability to understand the duties of the entire escrow department.

HEIDI ELIZABETH SANDLER
210 Chelsey Road
Toluca Lake, CA 95102
(818) 324-8900

① **ESCROW OFFICER/MANAGER**

PROFESSIONAL PROFILE:

②
- Success oriented with high energy and positive attitude.
- Highly organized with attention to detail and the ability to service several transactions simultaneously.
- Special talent for assessing client needs and gaining trust.
- Supervise employees with professionalism, diplomacy and tact.

PROFESSIONAL EXPERIENCE:

1989-present — AMERICAN TITLE COMPANY, Toluca Lake, CA
Escrow Department Assistant Manager

③
- Assist manager with escrows for the main office and one branch office, working closely with lending institutions nationwide.
- Process millions of dollars in all types of escrows: exchange...residential...refinance...loan escrows...mobile homes
- Set up and deliver seminars and presentations for real estate offices in the San Fernando Valley area.
- Guest speaker for San Fernando Valley real estate offices.
- Hire, train and supervise a staff of 15 employees.
- Conduct motivational meetings for all staff members.
- Brought in a high volume of business through word-of-mouth, thorough industry knowledge and a large personal client base.

1980-1988 — SAN DIEGO TITLE COMPANY, San Diego, CA
Escrow Officer/Foreclosure Officer

④
- Key member in the conversion of manual office systems to computerized escrow office procedures.
- Processed foreclosures, maintaining strict deadlines on a daily basis.
- Handled large volumes of all types of escrows in San Diego County.
- Developed and maintained a large personal customer base.

1979-1980 — SAN DIEGO BANK & TRUST, San Diego, CA
Escrow Assistant

⑤
- Assisted the escrow officer in processing escrows at the main office.

Winter-Fall '79 — LAKE TAHOE TITLE COMPANY, Lake Tahoe, NV
Escrow Secretary

⑥
- Assisted the escrow assistant and escrow officer in processing escrows.
- Gained valuable knowledge through company seminars and on-the-job training.

6

Resumes for the College Student and Recent Graduate

You studied hard in school for four years, graduated with honors, and yet, when it came time to enter the job market, the first request the interviewer made was "to see a copy of your resume."

A good resume, one that represents your hard earned skills and accomplishments, will help you bridge the gap between college and the work world.

Some college graduates are frustrated because they feel they don't have enough previous employment experience to allow them to find a decent job. They hear so much about the importance of practical experience. Others may fear that they're good but their grade point average may keep them from being considered by the companies they really want to work for.

There are solutions to these and related problems that are addressed in this chapter.

For the majority of college students, a functional resume highlighting skills is the ticket to getting that interview. Most college students do not have enough experience to warrant using a chronological resume. However, a student who has had several unrelated paid jobs and has also had internships and/or volunteer committee or other work experience can list those unpaid though valuable assets under Experiences in the flexible combination resume.

STUDENTS, GRADUATES, AND THE TWO-PAGE RESUME

As in the case of most professional resume writers, students and recent graduates should be able to create a one-page resume. But some graduates may have an abundance of related experience requiring a two-page resume. That is all right. It is better to have a well-written and properly formatted two-page resume than a poorly written, crowded one-pager. Don't use a smaller typeface in hopes of getting all the information on one page. Such a tactic will hinder rather than improve your job chances. No employer wants to bother with a hard-to-read resume.

Here are a couple of pointers for those of you with a two-page resume.

- Add *More* or *Continued* at the bottom of the first page.
- Place your name and *Page Two* at the top of the second page.

YOUR GPA AND YOUR JOB FUTURE

A high grade point average (GPA) is certainly an asset, but it is not a necessity for finding a good job. It is true certain corporations have a 3.5 or above GPA requirement, and many management trainee programs with major retailing chains require at least a 2.9 for recent graduates or students. But the key word here is *students.* Once you've been on the job for three years at another company, you are no longer a recent graduate and will not be treated as such if you apply to some of the businesses that previously wouldn't look at you. With three years of job experience, you will probably not be asked for your college transcripts unless applying for a job in the field of education. Your GPA will not follow you around for the rest of your life.

When you are interviewing with companies that visit your campus, you will find listed in their promotional material which ones have that 3.5 or above GPA requirement. Or you can ask your school's Career Counseling Center for the information. If you GPA is lower, apply for a position at the many fine companies that do not have that requirement. Then, after three years of professional work experience, if you still wish to do so, try again with the corporation you originally wished to work with.

COLLEGE GRADUATES STEPPING ONTO THE CORPORATE LADDER

Some college graduates have previous paid employment experience involving skills that directly relate to the jobs they're applying for. For example, during college, let's say you had a part-time job as an assistant at a public relations firm during your last two years of college, and now, as a graduate, you are seeking a position with a larger publicity firm in another city. You would use the chronological format to detail the job experiences that point you in the direction of your future position. The chronological resume format works best in this situation because it emphasizes the jobs you have held while those positions directly lead toward your career objective.

WHAT IF YOU HAVE NO PAID EMPLOYMENT EXPERIENCE?

Many college students do not have any paid employment experience that ties into their job objective. That might seem like an insurmountable barrier, for as we all know, many companies won't hire someone until he or she has experience in the field. But how do you obtain experience if no one will hire you?

Don't give up. I've found that most of my clients, even students, have some sort of related experience to write about in their resume for that upcoming job or they wouldn't be interested in applying for it.

Think back over your school years. Perhaps you worked on school projects related to your job objective. Or, what about those committees you've been an active member of. And don't forget volunteer work in your field. Also include any special achievements that are directly related to your career objective.

In a functional style, here's a resume for a second-year college student with only school project experience who wanted to find part-time work in an architectural firm.

Under Education we listed related classes taken, and under Related Experience we made up the appropriate subheading as shown below:

Objective:	A position leading to a career in *architecture.*
Education:	**BA Degree, Architecture,** 1993 *University of Nebraska,* Lincoln, NE *Related Courses:* Freehand Prospective Drawing Design Graphics, CAD CAM Designing, Environmental Design, Architecture 5
Related Experience:	

Residential Architectural Projects

- Designed a poolhouse on the CAD CAM computer system.
- Developed design and drew a set of plans for a 200-square-foot beach-house.
- Designed a two-story townhouse with a family room addition.

You certainly don't have to be an architectural student to apply this method to your situation. Business majors who have been interns, journalism students who wrote for the school newspaper, environmental studies majors who helped institute a city-wide recycling program—all of you can demonstrate to your potential employers that you do have the experience to move into paid employment.

For those of you with internship experience and unrelated or somewhat related, previous employment (fast foods, sales clerk, etc.), try the combination resume format, which was discussed in Chapters 2 and 3. Basically, you will highlight your internship or selected job(s) as in a chronological format under the Related Experience heading and place your other jobs under Employment History at the bottom of the resume as in the functional format.

This method helps to solve the Catch-22 problem in which a company won't hire you unless you have experience and it seems impossible to gain experience unless you get hired. By pinpointing your projects and volunteer work, you can demonstrate to employers and to yourself that you do have what it takes to obtain that valued first job!

FIRST-YEAR STUDENT VERSUS RECENT COLLEGE GRADUATE

Most of you soon-to-be graduates are seeking *full-time* work. But what if you're a first- or second-year student seeking *part-time* employment in your field of study? Go for it! The key word here is *part-time* employment. To some employers, a first-year student means stability. Employers feel there's a good chance students will plan on staying with the company throughout their school years. That could mean 2–4 years of employment for you.

CYNTHIA A. FRANCHESCA

Marine Biologist—Functional Resume
College Student with School Project Experience

Strategy

Cynthia is a typical example of the college student who needs help with her resume. As with the Housewife/Mom clients, the first thing Cynthia said was, "I don't know what we're going to write about. I don't have any experience." And after we finished her resume she said, "Wow, I can't believe that's me. I didn't realize I had that much experience." Students are gaining experience through their special projects but don't realize it's material for their resume because they didn't get paid for the work they did. We focused Cynthia's entire resume on her school projects.

Summary

① Cynthia's education goes first and before her experience because it's a stronger asset than her experience. Her Bachelor of Science degree is in Marine Biology, the same field as her job objective.

② Cynthia did an intensive field study in marine biology so we created a separate section under related experience to highlight the knowledge and skills she gained.

③ Cynthia organized and coordinated related studies and research projects that we also highlighted under related experience by creating a subtitle and describing her experiences starting with a vigorous action verb.

④ In the Professional Profile section, we listed all the work attributes Cynthia gained while working in her unrelated jobs that are still important in the eyes of the resume reviewer for her position of marine biologist.

⑤ Cynthia's paid work experience demonstrates skills she gained in other areas while financing her education so we listed it at the bottom of the resume under employment history.

Marine Biologist—Functional Resume
College Student with School Project Experience

CYNTHIA A. FRANCHESCA

222 Tool Street
Santa Barbara, CA 93101
(805) 222-8080

Objective: A position in Marine Biology

EDUCATION

BS Degree, Marine Biology, 1992
Northridge State University, Northridge, CA

(1)

Washington Institute of Marine Biology
University of Washington, Seattle, WA
Summers 1980-81

RELATED EXPERIENCE

Marine Biology Experience

- Researched and collected data for a 1-week study on the Santa Cruz Island.
- (2) Investigated existence and population of invertebrae in the Caprillidae family in Morro Bay.
- Gained thorough knowledge of identification of marine species while studying at the Washington Institute of Marine Biology. Projects included:
  - Preparing study skins of marine birds.
  - Reconstructing bone skeletons of marine fish and mammals.

Organization/Coordination

- Coordinated and wrote marine biology research projects.
- (3) Designed a study of kelp flies in a marine biology research project; located species and measured quantity.
- Photographed coverage through a microscope of an animal behavior study.
- Organized projects for an aviation company working closely with engineers and customers; involved blueprints, correspondence and manual updates.

PROFESSIONAL PROFILE

- Highly organized, dedicated with a positive attitude.
- Handle multiple assignments under high pressure and (4) consistently meet tight deadline schedules.
- Excellent written, oral and interpersonal communication skills.
- Thrive on working in a challenging work environment.

EMPLOYMENT HISTORY

Cashier, Von's Grocery Store, Los Angeles, CA	1988-present
(5) **Documentation Clerk**, Hughes Aircraft, El Segundo, CA	Summer 1987
Assistant Manager, Hi-Valley Development Inc, Seattle, WA	Summers 1985-86

7

Resumes and the Internet

With more people turning to the internet for information, the advantages of an on-line job search continue to increase. It is far more efficient for an employer to type in a few qualifications for a position and let the computer select the appropriate resumes from a data bank than to wade through a stack of loose resumes. The standard resume is no longer adequate for the new search process. This is the dawning of the electronic resume.

There are three approaches to posting your resume in an electronic form: rethinking your current resume to make it computer-friendly, designing your own web page, and going to a paid resume service. We will discuss the first method.

OVERVIEW OF THE SCANNING PROCESS

Many human resource departments use computers to file resumes they receive from applicants. Generally, a standard paper resume is electronically scanned and OCR (optical recognition software) converts the information into a form that the computer understands. This information is then stored in a data bank for later retrieval. You can increase your visibility and your success by making your resume easy to read and easy to find. This book will enable you to do both.

> *NOTE:* A STANDARD RESUME UNLESS CONVERTED TO A SPECIALIZED LANGUAGE (ASCII OR HTML) MAY APPEAR VERY DIFFERENT WHEN RECEIVED VIA E-MAIL.

THE ELECTRONIC RESUME

The electronic resume is computer friendly, which means that it is easily read, understood, and transmitted through a computer. You must revamp your traditional resume's visual appearance; certain elements that look appealing to the human eye on paper can confuse a computer scanner converting these graphics into digital information for storage.

The resume must include "key words" to succeed in the internet's data bank. Key words are used in subject searches. For instance, if an employer were looking for an accountant, he or she would type accountant, accounts payable/receivable, audit, and Lotus 1-2-3. A list of candidates would appear. If that list was too long, it could be streamlined by including additional key words in the search criteria.

In electronic resumes, *nouns* are important, not action verbs. A successful electronic resume includes as many key words from your specific industry as possible since you want as many "hits" with the system conducting the search as possible. The more hits you make the better, because adjustable tolerance levels glean the resumes that don't contain enough key words. Your resume is selected because it contains a certain number of specified key words, whereas someone else's is passed over because it does not.

Key words may take the form of experience, skills, or job title. Here are a few examples:

- 5 year design experience
- HTML programming
- Senior Attorney

Electronic Resume Do's and Don'ts

- DO use nouns instead of verbs or "action words." Computers conduct subject searches, and each noun in your resume is a potential subject.
- DO maximize your use of key words: words associated with specific jobs, experience, education, or skills.
- DO place your name by itself on the first line of your resume.
- DO keep your language simple. Depending on the computer system conducting the search, certain words may not be in its vocabulary.
- DO keep the use of abbreviations to a minimum. Common abbreviations like MBA, BS, and so on are fine.
- DON'T be afraid to maximize your use of industry jargon. It reflects positively on your resume and assists in a key word search.
- DON'T clutter your resume! A computer uses white space to recognize the different sections of your resume.
- DON'T feel limited to one page. Depending on your work experience, you may use two, three, even four pages.
- DON'T use graphics or shading on your resume. The possibility of scanner error is too great.

▶ DON'T use colored paper. Don't use italics or underlining—again you are striving for clarity; any unnecessary frills will be to your detriment.

Example of an Electronic Resume

The following numbers correspond to the numbers in the margin of the sample electronic resume. Each number demonstrates an important electronic resume principle.

① John's name appears on the first line by itself, followed by his address and phone number.

② In the job objective section, John included as many key words or optional job titles as possible. Nouns best illustrate his abilities and familiarities with his industry. These key words become his job objective.

③ The skills section appears above the body of his resume and briefly summarizes his abilities.

④ John used boldface to highlight his headings while avoiding underlining and italics. Here, under the summary section, is a detailed breakdown of his past responsibilities or a more specific look at his applicable skills.

⑤ To break up the uniformity of his resume and make it easier for the computer and employer to read, John used extra white space.

⑥ Notice that John highlighted the education section without use of underlining or italics.

⑦ Under the "career history" section, John used lots of key words and avoided underlining or italics. This section details where he worked, when he worked, and what he did for each employer.

⑧ Here he uses a synonym, "Associated Press" for the "AP" listing in the summary section. If an employer searches under either key word entry, John has his bases covered.

Sample Electronic Resume

① **JOHN GRISWOLD**
10 West Street
New York, NY. 10104
(212) 555-1212

② **EDITOR, EXECUTIVE EDITOR, METROPOLITAN EDITOR, NEWS EDITOR.**

③ **Skills:** Supervision, directing, editing, writing, layout.

④ **Summary:**
Detail-oriented professional with editing and supervising experience in newspaper organization, layout, content, style, and production.

Editing: news, editorial, sports, features, arts, opinions writing organization, article sizing, style, grammar, AP style.

Supervisor: hire, train, supervise, direct copy reading staff.

⑤

Excellent written and verbal skills, team player with ability to function and oversee all levels of production. Detail-minded, with a good eye for balance and organization. Outstanding trouble-shooting skills.

Computer literate. Proficient in Quarkxpress, Pagemaker, Printshop, Word, Wordperfect, and Excel on both MAC and PC systems.

⑥ **Education:**

MA, Journalism, University of Idaho, 1979
BA, English, University of Indiana, 1974

⑦ **Career History:**

1989–present
EDITOR, Magazine of the West, Somewhere, CA.
Oversaw all aspects of editing for a magazine with a distribution of over 800,000. Supervised a staff of 30.

1984–89
COPY EDITOR/COPY WRITER, Bylines Newspaper, Midtown, OR.
Chief copy editor of a local newspaper. Adjusted articles to fit
⑧ format of the Associated Press. Edited style, grammar, and length of articles.

1980–84
REPORTER, Local Tribune, Alphaville, CA.
Contributing reporter for small newspaper. Responsible for weekly columns on food and dining, as well as other creative articles.

Additional Tips

- ▶ Including specific skill words from a job advertisement is a sure way to increase your chances of being selected from a data bank.
- ▶ Use written figures instead of numbers whenever possible.
- ▶ It is advisable to prepare a different resume for each job you apply for.
- ▶ Choose either the chronological or functional resume format to emphasize your qualifications.
- ▶ Choose a point size between 10 and 14 for your type. To highlight your name you may use up to 24 points. Make sure the typestyle you use is plain and easy to scan.
- ▶ Justify everything to the left, avoiding the use of columns. Computers scan from left to right and may be thrown off track by columns.
- ▶ Faxed copies tend to blur—use an original, laser-printed resume.
- ▶ Use the electronic resume whenever computer scanning might be involved. This does not mean abandoning the standard, human-friendly resume—the well-prepared job seeker should carry both versions.

SURFING JOB SITES

On the internet, there are sites specifically for posting resumes, locating resumes, and some sites that are a combination of the two. Many web sites have a fill-in-the-blanks resume form that is automatically posted on a job board, but which will not give you the obvious advantages of a resume that is custom designed. Keep in mind that there are specialty sites for engineers, actors, doctors and just about everyone else. The best way to search is probably under the category "skills required," but you may also search using geographical location or job title criteria.

JOB POSTING SITES ON THE INTERNET

The following is a list of a few popular web sites for your job search. This list is not intended to be exhaustive, as new web sites appear daily. Use the list as a springboard or starting point from which to conduct a more specialized job search. With a little resourcefulness, you can locate a site or network that is suitable for your needs.

▶ **America's Job Bank**	job.search.html
▶ **American Employment Weekly**	branch.com/aew.html
▶ **Career Magazine**	www.careermag.com/
▶ **Career Mosaic**	www.careermosaic.com
▶ **Career Wise**	www.transkey.com

▶ **Help Wanted.com**	helpwanted.com
▶ **Inet Employment Network**	garnet.msen.com:70/1/vendor /napa/jobs/
▶ **Job Web**	www.jobweb.org
▶ **Jobtrak**	www.jobtrak.com
▶ **Monster Board**	www.monster.com
▶ **NCS Jobline**	ncs@jobline.com
▶ **Online Career Center**	www.occ.org
▶ **Recruiter Online Ntwk**	www.onramp.net/ron
▶ **Skill Search**	www.internet-is.com/skillsearch

- www.woodtech.com/~clong/paradise.html
- www.internetuniv.com/career/nsendresume.html

8

The Cover Letter and Thank-You Letter

ABOUT COVER LETTERS

Most resumes are not complete without a cover letter, which introduces you and your resume to the employer. Providing essential information not found in the resume, cover letters are needed whenever you mail your resume to an employer. They can be personalized or generalized, but are written specifically to go with the individual's resume. You can create an effective cover letter in three paragraphs.

1. The first paragraph states why you are writing, that is, what position you're applying for and whether you saw an advertisement or heard about the position or company through a referral or simply by reputation.
2. The second paragraph is a brief summary stating why you feel qualified for the position. What makes you different? If adding the Professional Profile section in a resume will make an otherwise one-page resume into two pages, use it in a cover letter instead. Never use it for both or repeat verbatim what is said in the resume.
3. The third paragraph is the closing statement saying where you can be reached and thanking the employer. See the following cover letter sample.

SAMPLE COVER LETTER

Dear Executive Search Committee:

I am writing in response to your advertisement in The Wall Street Journal, dated September 19, 1991, for the position of Trust Administrator.

I have successfully managed over $750M in the short to intermediate area. With over 10 years experience working with living and probate accounts, I've demonstrated thorough industry knowledge in trust management. I am

confident I will make a significant contribution to your firm now, and an increasingly important one in years to come.

Enclosed is my resume for your review. I am available at the address and phone number above at your earliest convenience. Thank you for your time and consideration.

Sincerely,

Darcy Lansing

ABOUT THANK-YOU LETTERS

A thank-you letter is sent after you've had an interview for a position you're interested in. The thank-you letter should be mailed the day of the interview; it should be brief and personalized. Follow this three-paragraph procedure:

1. In the opening paragraph simply thank the interviewer, and re-emphasize your interest in the position.
2. In the second paragraph remind the employer why you are a good candidate for the position. Try to remember something specific in the interview to be mentioned.
3. The closing paragraph again adds a thanks and states that you look forward to hearing from the interviewer.

It might seem unnecessary to send a thank-you letter so quickly after the interview, but doing so will reinforce in the interviewer's mind just how serious and enthusiastic you are about the position. That very act can separate you from the other applicants, giving you the extra something that leads to your being hired.

SAMPLE THANK-YOU LETTER

Dear Mrs. Hamilton:

Thank you for spending so much time with me yesterday. I am very excited about the prospect of seeking a new position in the financial marketplace.

I am aware of your excellent reputation and aggressive commitment to the financial industry and I would be proud to be a member of your management team.

If you have questions, feel free to call me at any time. I look forward to hearing from you.

Sincerely,

Donald Carpinter

9

200 Highly Successful Resume Samples

This chapter consists of resume samples from the client files of Just Resumes. There are many careers represented. Each resume focuses on particular individual goals. You will see a variety of formats to choose from in functional, chronological, combination, and artist styles. There's an index for the resume samples on page 257. The resumes are listed in alphabetical order and categorized by job title.

Look at each resume carefully. Think about how your own background applies to the job or internship you'd like to obtain.

> *REMEMBER:* IT'S IMPORTANT THAT YOU'VE ALREADY READ CHAPTERS 1, 2, AND 3 BEFORE REVIEWING THE RESUME SAMPLES IN THIS CHAPTER. THIS WILL GIVE YOU THE OVERALL PERSPECTIVE YOU WILL NEED TO WRITE AN EFFECTIVE RESUME.

Accountant, Corporate—Functional Resume
Experienced Recent Graduate Moving Up from Sr. Accounting Assistant

PAUL BLACK
999 College Avenue
Santa Barbara, CA 93105
(805) 555-1111

Objective: A Corporate Accounting position.

PROFESSIONAL PROFILE

- Highly organized, dedicated with a positive attitude.
- Work under strict deadline schedules with attention to detail.
- Financed education with experience in computerized accounting and management.

EDUCATION

BA Degree, Business Economics, 1991
University of California, Los Angeles

ACCOUNTING SKILLS

Profit and loss statement, balance sheet, trial balance, general ledger and supporting journals, accounts receivable, payroll, bank reconciliation, strong computerized accounting skills.

EXPERIENCE

STRUCTURAL ACCOUNTING SYSTEMS, Los Angeles, CA 1985-1991

Financial Statements & Computer Skills
- Prepared financial statements under cash and accrual accounting methods for sole proprietorships, partnerships, S and non-profit corporations.
- Converted manual accounting systems to a computerized accounting system for clients.
- Designed custom spreadsheet programs for internal use as well as for clients.

Billing, Payroll & Client Relations
- Prepared billing and maintained accounts receivable for private water companies and homeowners' associations.
  - Learned to interpret customer's needs efficiently; solve potential problems in a diplomatic & courteous manner, under sometimes sensitive situations.
- Generated payroll checks and reports.

Management & Organizational Skills
- Reported directly to the owner of the company.
- Assisted in establishing a successful structure for a growing company.
  - Trained and supervised employees, maintaining a professional manner.
  - Helped prioritized work schedules and delegated assignments.

Accountant, Entertainment—Functional Resume
Recent Graduate with Related Experience

KATIE A. ADLER
222 Soho Court
San Francisco, CA 94117
(415) 558-0002

Objective: An Accounting position in the Entertainment Industry.

EDUCATION

BA Degree, Business Economics, December 1990
University of California, Santa Barbara

ACCOUNTING SKILLS

Profit and loss statements, income statements, accounts payable, payroll, bank reconciliation, general ledgers and journals balance sheets, trial balance, accruals, contract monitoring, computerized accounting on Lotus 1-2-3 and Excel.

RELATED EXPERIENCE

Accounting Experience

- Process accounts payable for 18 mental health clinics throughout Santa Barbara county.
  - Order county services, equipment and supplies working with purchasing department.
  - Prepare accruals and liquidate encumbrances at fiscal year end.
  - Assist manager in balancing budget reports.
  - Developed a computerized filing system for accounts payable resulting in a quicker and more efficient process for locating vendors.
- Maintained computerized bookkeeping for clients of a small business management firm.
  - Prepared bank reconciliations, payroll and daily sales totals.

Entertainment Experience

- Host a popular weekly rock-n-roll radio program.
  - Oversee 35 rock disc jockeys; represent them in the scheduling process.
  - Serve on review committee; judge shows looking for quality, style and technical abilities.
  - Determine the weekly Top 35 Artist List and report to trade journals.
  - Add new records into radio library on a weekly basis.
- Buy the best selection of independent label tapes, cd's, records and accessories for a small upscale music store in Santa Barbara.

EMPLOYMENT HISTORY

Accounts Payable, County of Santa Barbara, (Mental Health)	1989-90
Buyer, Sound Factory Records & Tapes, Santa Barbara, CA	1988-90
Rock Disc Jockey Leader, KCSB, 91.9 FM, Santa Barbara, CA	1988-90
Bookkeeper, EKW Systems, Santa Barbara, CA	1987-88

Accountant, Junior—Chronological Resume
Recent College Graduate with Related Accounting Work Experience

LESLIE A. LIEBERMANN

Current Address
4999 College Road
Goleta, CA 93117
(805) 222-0800

Permanent Address
1111 Marina Avenue
Concord, CA 94333
(222) 888-8888

Objective: Entry Level position leading to a challenging Accounting career.

PROFESSIONAL PROFILE

- Highly organized, dedicated and committed to professionalism.
- Work well under pressure with attention to detail.
- Excellent written, oral, interpersonal communication skills.
- Active member of the Philanthropy Committee and Scholarship Committee.

ACCOUNTING SKILLS

Profit and loss statements...income statements...accounts payable ...payroll...bank reconciliation...general ledgers and journals... balance sheets...trial balance...strong computerized accounting. Coursework: Individual, Partnership & Corporate Tax Accounting... Intermediate Accounting...Micro & Macro Economic Theory...Auditing.

PROFESSIONAL EXPERIENCE

Bookkeeper/Data Entry, Gustin & Associates, San Francisco 1987-present

- Maintain computerized accounts for small businesses on the IBM PC computer.
  - Prepare income statements, bank reconciliation, general ledgers, journals, balance sheets and trial balance, meeting demanding deadline schedules.
  - Interface with clients to analyze business needs and maintain better records.
  - Enter data on IBM System 34 computer using a custom financial software program.

Personnel Assistant, Martin Corporation, San Francisco, CA Summer 1988

- Assisted management with personnel recruitment and orientation meetings.
  - Involved answering phones, filing and accurate recordkeeping on a daily basis.

Customer Service Representative, San Francisco Chronicle, San Francisco, CA 1984-86

- Created solutions in the customer complaint department on a daily basis.
  - Developed phone skills, expediting challenges customers presented quickly and creatively.
  - Excellent problem solver, dealing with irate customers in a professional and diplomatic manner under highly pressured situations.

EDUCATION

BA Degree, Business Economics, June 1990
University of California at Berkeley
Accounting GPA: 3.8 Overall GPA: 3.6

ROBERT REYNOLDS

422 Peachtree Road
Atlanta, GA 30305
(404) 815-1320

Objective: Account Executive

AWARDS AND RECOGNITIONS

Quarterly Revenue Award, A One Service Personnel, 1996
Monthly Objective Award, Creative Loafing, 10 consecutive months, 1989-90

EMPLOYMENT HISTORY

Account Executive, A One Service Personnel, Atlanta, GA 1990-present
Account Executive/Project Manager, Creative Loafing, Atlanta, GA 1985-90
Sales Associate, Entertainment USA, Miami, FL 1980-85

PROFESSIONAL EXPERIENCE

Sales, Marketing and Analysis

- Generated 69 percent of new business territory for a $12MM international personnel corporation.
- Developed a marketing plan for a $12MM personnel corporation to justify repositioning advertising and recruiting efforts into niche markets that maximizes revenue and minimizes operating costs.
  - Analyzed competitors' advertising and marketing efforts and costs.
  - Investigated recruiting, staffing and customer service process.
  - Contacted competitors' clients to determine their needs and services available.
- Conducted market research for an entertainment firm and created a highly effective strategic marketing plan that consistently increased annual profits by 200 percent.

Project Management

- Managed all aspects of a publishing project for an annual supplement insert.
  - Hired freelance writers and photographers; worked closely with in-house graphic designers; Developed production budgets.
  - Assisted designers with layout and makeup of innovative advertising and sold space to local businesses through powerful, motivational sales presentations.

EDUCATION

- **BA Degree: Communications,** 1985
  Jacksonville University, Jacksonville, FL

Accounting Clerk, Sr., Banking—Chronological Resume
Recent College Graduate with Internship Experience, Moving Up

JODY SUK SONG
PO Box 2341
Goleta, CA 93117
(805) 964-2222

OBJECTIVE: **An Accounting Clerk II position leading to a career in Banking.**

EDUCATION: **BA Degree, Business Economics**
University of California, Santa Barbara
Graduation: 1991

Education Abroad, Summer 1990
Yonsei University, Seoul, Korea

EXPERIENCE:

1990-present SANTA BARBARA FEDERAL S&L, Santa Barbara, CA
Accounting Intern (1990-present)
- Developed custom spreadsheet programs using Lotus 1-2-3 for finance and analysis of 100 branch offices in California.
- Analyze, research and maintain daily accrued interest reports for demand deposit accounts.
- Prepare and organize various statements for accounting staff.
- Assist accountants with outages and reconciliation projects.

Cash Reserve Specialist (1988-89)
- Reviewed customer applications and solved potential problems for 100 California branch offices.
- Prepared and posted computerized payments to customer's cash reserve accounts.
- Answered customer account inquiries quickly and efficiently.
- Assisted branch personnel with proper cash reserve procedures.

1986-87 TRI-COUNTIES REGIONAL CENTER, Santa Barbara, CA
Systems Operator
- Maintained client information using IBM System 36.
- Prepared monthly and daily reports for hospital staff.

1985-86 CAPELLO AND FOLEY LAW FIRM, Santa Barbara, CA
Document Control Clerk
- Assisted paralegals with document preparation.

JOHN PAUL SMITTY

2201 Lenox Circle
Clemson, South Carolina 29632
(864) 654-2210

Objective: Acquisitions Negotiator

QUALIFICATIONS

Project Management ..Innovative Sales and Trade Negotiations
Contract Administration ..Regulatory Compliance ..Problem Solving
Business Analysis ..Training, Workshops/Seminars ..Interpersonal/Communication Skills
Information Mapping Methodology ..Fluent Oral/Written German ..Computer Literate

PROFESSIONAL EXPERIENCE

Acquisitions Negotiator/Business Process Analyst 1989-96
Land Corporation, Houston, TX

Acquisitions Negotiator

- Initiated, negotiated and secured management approval for the first sale of a non-producing lease for Land Corporation.
  - Received $2MM immediate profit with the potential for additional $10MM in overriding royalties for a 640 acre lease which was about to expire.
- Negotiated the first sale of non-producing leasehold acreage in the State of Texas.
  - Received $10.2MM for a property not scheduled for development.
- Resolved deadlock and negotiated exchange of properties with another Fortune 500 corporation.
  - Enabled corporation to proceed with mine plans and government approval for multi-million dollar coal gasification project.

Business Process Analysis/Development

- Research, wrote and presented *Farmout Risk Analysis* for a new division manager resulting in a better understanding of the legal ramifications and impact of farmouts on division mission.
- Developed a Trade Process Form, used by division professional staff that improved staff efficiency and status reporting.
- Analyzed trade process and developed division guidelines for evaluation and approval as part of a 5-member team.
- Developed and wrote Policy and Procedure Manuals for two small real estate companies.

EDUCATION

Master of Business Administration, 1989
Houston Baptist University, Houston, TX

Actor/Producer—Artist Resume

AARON LEVIN
PO Box 40146
Santa Barbara, CA 93140
(805) 569-0003

PROFESSIONAL PROFILE

- Experienced actor and producer in theatre arts since 1982.
- Positive, success oriented, goal achiever.
- Actor of the Year, cum laude in French; top 10% of graduating class in high school.

THEATRICAL EXPERIENCE

Production Experience

- Assistant Stage Manager, "The Last Meeting of the Knights of the White Magnolia," Santa Barbara City College.
- Professional Pianist, "Music for All Times," self-employed.
- Musical Director, "An Evening of Awards," an original production featuring Broadway show tunes produced by Sinai Drama Society, Denver, CO.
- Assistant Director, "Angel Antics," the annual Drama Club variety show of East High School, Denver, CO.
- Director, Musical Director, "Bye Bye Birdie," Sinai Drama Society, Denver.
- Technical Assistant, "Angel Antics," East High School, Denver, CO.
- Technical Assistant, "The King and I," Sinai Drama Society.

Performing Experience

- Lead role-Marvin, "March of the Falsettos," Boston University, Boston, MA.
- Supporting lead-Japeth, "Two By Two," Town Hall Arts Ctr, Littleton, CO.
- Supporting lead-Lurvy, "Charlotte's Web," Shwayder Theatre, Denver, CO.
- Lead role-Emile De Becque, "South Pacific," East High School, Denver, CO.
- Singer, "The Acapellas," a six-person group performing unaccompanied vocal music.
- Lead role-Adam, "The Appletree," a musical comedy, East High School.
- Lead role-Curly, "Oklahoma," East High School, Denver, CO.
- Lead role-Sky Masterson, "Guys and Dolls," East High School, Denver, CO.
- Lead role-Will Parker, "Oklahoma", Sinai Junior Drama Society.
- Lead role-Frank Butler, "Annie Get Your Gun," Sinai Drama Society.
- Understudy-all male roles, "Mame," Sinai Drama Society.

EDUCATION

Theatre Arts, in progress
Santa Barbara City College, SB, CA

Theatre Arts, 1988
Boston University, Boston, MA

Actress—Artist Resume

RAVELL ERENBERG

333 Moreno Road
Santa Barbara, CA 93103
(805) 569-0964

Birthdate: 9-27-72
Ht/Wt: 4' 10"; 95 lbs
Hair/Eyes: Auburn, Green

EDUCATION:
- Santa Barbara City College - advanced student
- Santa Barbara High School - class of 1990

THEATRE EXPERIENCE:

1990 California Arts Scholar in Theatre, Cal State Summer School for the Arts.

1989-90 Advanced acting and production classes at Santa Barbara High School Theater Arts Department.

1989 "Our Town", Assistant Director, SB High School Theater Department.

"The Imaginary Invalid" (role of Louise), directed by Robert Weiss, Ensemble Theatre, Santa Barbara.

1988-89 Enrolled in theater classes at Santa Barbara City College and an actor's workshop with professional acting coach, Paula Russell.

1988 "Romeo and Juliet" (role of Page to Paris), directed by Robert Weiss, Ensemble Theatre, Santa Barbara.

1987 "The Dark at the Top of the Stairs" (role of Sonny), directed by Sandra Muir, Santa Barbara High School Theater Department.

"Orestes" (role of Hermione), Santa Barbara City College Studio Theater.

"The Myth of Perseus" (role of Eurygania), Santa Barbara Summer Stock Theatre, Lobero Theater, Santa Barbara.

"The Sound of Music" (role of Brigitta), Goleta Valley Community Center.

1986 "Dovetail" (role of Evan), directed by James O'Neil (Cal Arts '80) An Alternative Theatre Production, Santa Barbara City College Studio Theater.

"Peace Child", Lobero Theater, Santa Barbara.
"Peace Child", Arlington Theater, Santa Barbara.

1985 "A Christmas Carol" (role of Belle's Daughter), directed by Robert Weiss, Ensemble Theatre Production, Lobero Theater, Santa Barbara.

La Belle, Class for Young Actresses.

Actress—Housewife/Mom Re-Entering the Job Market

BRENDA BERNHARDT
Actress

63 Brittany Road
Santa Barbara, CA 93103
(805) 962-6467

Age Range: 40-60
Height/Weight: 5' 5", 165 lbs
Hair/Eyes: Auburn Frosted/Brown

FORMAL ACTOR'S TRAINING

Commercial Workshop, Winter 1990
Jack Rose Agency/Nance Management
Hollywood/Santa Barbara, CA

Professional Acting, W. Hollywood
Players Ring/Players Circle

THEATRICAL EXPERIENCE

Commercial Experience

- "Alphasonics." Played the part of a business person giving a testamonial on the benefits of subliminal tapes aired on four cable TV stations, 1990.

Production/Film Experience

- 60-year old frumpy, confused bank robber, "Make It Real," a 10-minute, action/comedy film shown at the closing ceremonies of the 1990 Santa Barbara International Film Festival.
- Team member in writing a script as part of a weekend workshop titled "Make a Movie," sponsored by the 1990 Santa Barbara Int'l Film Festival.
- Wrote, directed and produced original one-act children stage productions.
  - Narrator, story-teller for "The Beginning of the Brownies/Girl Scouts."
- Wrote a 15-minute, one-act comedy for a school production.

Theatre Experience (Elementary-High School)

- Supporting Role-Karen & Inga, "On the Night of January 16th," Fairfax High School, West Hollywood, CA.
- Improv, Cold Reading, One-Act Plays, Scenes, Players Ring & Players Circle, Hollywood.
- March Hare, "Alice in Wonderland." Los Angeles, CA.
- Supporting Role-Mary, "The Children's Hour." Dramatic three-act play, Los Angeles, CA.
- Assist. Master of Ceremonies, "talent showcase," Los Angeles, CA.
- Tap Dancer, danced "Tea for Two" in a 2-minute talent showcase, Los Angeles, CA.
- Johnny Ray. Played Johnny Ray's Cry (Lip-sync), in a exaggerated comedy routine.
- Lead Role, Queen Esther, "Queen of Israel" school production, Los Angeles.
- Created numerous routines for auditions and talent shows.

SPECIAL TALENTS

Scuba diving...golf...tennis...costume design banker...secretary...photographer...ice skating...model...fashion coordinator.

ZOE WHEELER
Doctor of Oriental Medicine
Licensed Acupuncturist
1257 Olive Street
Summerland, CA 93108
(805) 682-1470

PROFESSIONAL EXPERIENCE

Private & Group Detox-Acupuncture

- Administered in-house acupuncture and herbal treatment for the Skid Row population of 60-150 clients per day.
- Monitored clients with breathilizer and urine testing.
- Provided continued recovery treatment and referral service, working with law enforcement, social services and counselors throughout the community.
- Treated individuals and provided home detox care to private patients.
- Gained life experience participating in family members' drug addiction/recovery process.
- Received "Outstanding Accomplishment" from the Mayor of Los Angeles for participation in the Turnaround Program - January, 1988.

Foreign-Group Therapy/Counseling

- Provided crisis intervention, brief and long term counseling to:
  - individual adults -adolescents -couples -groups
- Dealt with clients of racial and economic diversity.
- Conducted group therapy series utilizing Peer Counseling or Bioenergetic techniques.
- Founding member of a 300 person skill training-work cooperative in London.

EDUCATION

SAMRA Univ. of Oriental Medicine, LA, CA
Doctor of Oriental Medicine, 1986
Bachelor of Science Degree, 1983
Graduate Studies, Beijing, China, 1986
Qi Gong, Acupuncture

SPECIAL TRAINING

- California Acupuncture License #CA 1589 since 1983
- National Acupuncture Detox Assoc, Certified 1986
- Hypnotherapy Certification Board of California, 1983
- First Int'l Qi Gong Conference, Shanghai, China, 1986
- Acupuncture Detox Training Program, Lincoln Hospital of Bronx, New York, in Los Angeles, CA, 1982 & 1986

EMPLOYMENT HISTORY

Licensed Acupuncturist, Health Spectrum, Santa Barbara, CA 1989-present
Volunteer Acupuncturist, Turnaround (Detox Facility), LA, CA 1986-89
Clinic Director/Acupuncturist, Wheeler Holistic Clinic, LA, CA 1985-86

SANDRA T. WALSH

111 Peachtree Street
Atlanta, GA 30307
(404) 872-1112

Objective: Administrative Assistant

OFFICE SKILLS

IBM ..Word Perfect ..Lotus 1-2-3 ..Filing ..Purchasing
Collections ..Data Entry & Computerized Reports ..Customer Relations
Excellent Multi-line Phone Skills ..Appointment Scheduling
Accounts Receivable/Payable ..Payroll ..Typing Speed: 110 wpm

EMPLOYMENT HISTORY

Administrative Assistant, ABS Services, Atlanta, GA	1989-present
Executive Assistant, Arthur and Associates, Atlanta, GA	1985-89
Receptionist, Bellington USA, Atlanta, GA	1980-85

PROFESSIONAL EXPERIENCE

Office/Administrative Skills

- Typed, edited and proofread correspondence, memos and spreadsheets/reports on the IBM computer using Microsoft Word and Lotus 1-2-3.
- Improved automated office systems that resulted in more timely and cost efficient order processing procedures for the catalog mail order company.
- Set up, maintained and updated patient files for a busy chiropractic clinic.

Client Relations

- Performed as executive receptionist during a major expansion for the corporate headquarters of a multi-million dollar corporation.
  - Answered customer inquiries and directed calls on a computerized 35 phone system for the Board of Directors, Personnel and Sales Departments.
  - Scheduled appointments and meetings with vendors and private investors nationwide on a daily basis.
- Liaison between office and production staff, warehouse, dispatch and the customers of a small gourmet and specialty food distributor.
- Negotiated contracts with vendors nationwide and filled orders to purchase catalog items as catalog coordinator for a service-oriented mail order company.
  - Trained 30-50 customer service reps on how to work with customers in a professional manner while receiving incoming phone orders and returns.

Administrative Assistant/Supervisor—Combination Resume
Moving Up within the Same Organization

HANNA I. RICHARDS

17704 East Valley Road
Irvine, CA 92715
(714) 250-6000

Objective: Supervisor/Administrative Assistant

EDUCATION

UCI Training: Personnel Action Forms...Year-end Closing (Fiscal)...Supervisory Skills Workshop... Gen'l Ledger Workshop....Powerful Communication Skills for Women...How to Supervise People.

CURRENT EMPLOYMENT EXPERIENCE

UNIVERSITY OF CALIFORNIA, Irvine, Physics Accounting Dept. 1984-present

Administrative Assistant II (1987-present)

- Coordinate and implement purchasing and accounting activities.
- Fully responsible for maintaining and executing the recharge system.
- Design and formulate new spreadsheet programs for budget/expense reports and recharge summaries using Lotus 1-2-3 and Excel.
- Track departmental purchases with an account budget of $600K, assuring compliance with University policies/procedures and union contracts.
- Prepare a series of statistical reports from the recharges as well as general and payroll ledgers for the Chairman and MSO; assist administrative staff with payroll.
- Schedule travel arrangements and maintain department files.

Principal Clerk (1986-87)

- Responsible for all the above.

Senior Clerk (1984-86)

- Processed invoices and tracked departmental expenses on a daily basis.

PROFESSIONAL PROFILE

- Gained extensive knowledge of campus administrative policies and procedures through six years of university experience.
- Ability to supervise employees and work well with all levels of management.
- Work on multiple projects under pressure situations and meet strict deadlines.

PREVIOUS EMPLOYMENT HISTORY

Clerk, Irvine City School District — Fall 1983
Court Clerk, Municipal Court of Orange County — 1979-82
Accounting/Payroll Clerk, The Southland Corporation — 1977-79

MARYANN S. DOYLE
324 East 72nd
New York, NY 10038
(212) 799-4002

Objective: An Advertising Manager for a Daily Newspaper

PROFESSIONAL EXPERIENCE

Public Relations/Advertising Sales

* Contact clients at location sites on a daily basis to counsel, advise and assess specific needs for advertising services of the daily newspaper.
  - Outstanding ability to solve problems under highly pressured situations in a professional and concerned manner.
* Member of staff Newsletter and Recreation Committees. Plan and coordinate internal social events, promotional projects and the entire newsletter.
* Marketing Committee Member at the Santa Barbara YMCA.
  - Compose press releases and public service announcements to publicize special events for this nationwide non-profit organization.
  - Successfully gain radio media and local business sponsorships.

Project Development

* Develop highly successful marketing strategies and corporate identities.
  - Design logos, brochures and copywrite for newspaper/radio advertising.
  - Establish excellent rapport with sales representatives throughout the advertising and publications industry locally and nationwide.
* Achieved the highest spec ad sales rating in the history of the art department of the daily newspaper publication. Increased monthly sales by 20%.

Director/Coordinator

* Coordinate, prioritize and implement multiple projects efficiently; consistently meet tight deadline schedules under daily pressure situations.
* Locate qualified vendors to purchase equipment and supplies under strict corporate budget requirements.
* Quality Assurance Board Member; monitor daily paper and magazine quality.
* Became main source of information for Pagemaker on the Macintosh computer.
* Interview, train and supervise creative staff members.

EDUCATION

BA Degree, Graphic Communications, 1985
University of Florida, Gainesville, FL

EMPLOYMENT HISTORY

Ad Director, The Daily Paper, New York, NY	1988-present
Commercial Artist, Orange Coast Magazine, Florida, CA	1987-88

RORY LANDERS HOLBROOK
PO Box 1234
Los Angeles, CA 90025
(213) 344-1111

ANNOUNCER

PROFESSIONAL EXPERIENCE:

RADIO
- Extensive Announcer experience on morning/afternoon drive times with Big Band, Swing, Jazz, Lite Rock, Country music and News.
- Write/prepare commercials, promos and psa's for production.
- Prepared and delivered short, in-depth and lengthy newscasts.

TELEVISION
- TV Board operator and switcher as well as editing and extensive voice-over narrations in television production broadcasts.

FREE-LANCE
- Perform frequent production voice over narrations for industrial films, presentations and commercials.
- Emcee and Deejay a variety of assignments for private organizations and public groups.

EMPLOYMENT HISTORY:

1988-91 — **Announcer,** KLIT, Santa Barbara, CA.
Lite-Hits music station

1985-88 — **Announcer,** KBLS/KKSB, Santa Barbara, CA.
Big Band, Swing, Jazz music station

1984-85 — **Announcer,** KZTR, Ventura, CA
Lite-Rock music station

1983-84 — **Announcer,** KRUZ, Santa Barbara, CA
Easy Listening music station, part-time

1983-84 — **Announcer/Board Operator,** KVON/KVYN, Napa Valley, CA
Vintage Sounds music station, AM/FM

1977-83 — **Announcer/Producer,** Broadcast Services, San Francisco, CA
Sub-carrier, multi-format station

Announcer, Radio Personality—Functional Resume
Changing Careers from Private Club Entertainer/Host/Model

RACHEL D. DARCY
209 Centinnel Drive
Montecito, CA 93108
(805) 966-2222

Objective: An Announcer/Radio Personality position

PROFESSIONAL PROFILE

- Six year member of the Academy of Ballet in Victoria BC, Canada.
  - Studied Ballet, Jazz Dance and Russian Character.
- Danced in ballet, jazz and modern dance productions at Santa Barbara City College.
- Participated in a commercial at Brooks Institute.

PROFESSIONAL EXPERIENCE

Entertainer/Host

- Host and entertainer at Club Med Corfu in Greece.
  - Hosted Friday Night Sports Awards Show.
  - Created comedy show/bits. Performed in dance, comedy productions and fashion shows.
- Participated in comedy bits on KTYD Morning Show, a popular rock and roll music station.
- Performed in talent and fashion shows for various companies and agencies through the La Belle Modelling & Talent Agency in Santa Barbara, CA.

Radio Operations/Electrician

- Operated radio news, weather, traffic control for Ventura Harbor Patrol.
- Responded to emergency situations. Searched and rescued visitors on beach, land and sea.
  - Involved police and fire response, first aid, reports, computer warrant identifications, range qualifications trimonthly, vessel assignments, fee collections, vessel towing, operating and public relations.
- Set up electrical hookups & maintained dock box for City of Ventura.

EDUCATION

Theater Arts, Dance, Drama, Music
Santa Barbara City College, Santa Barbara, CA
Theater & Commercial Acting & Modelling
La Belle Model & Talent Agency, Santa Barbara, CA

EMPLOYMENT HISTORY

Host/Entertainer Aerobics Instructor, Club Med, Corfu, Greece 1988-90
Teacher/Model, La Belle Modelling & Talent Agency, Santa Barbara, CA 1986-88
Harbor Patrol Officer, City of Carpinteria, Carpinteria, CA 1985-88
Apprentice Electrician, City of Ventura, Ventura, CA 1984-85

JOHN PAUL KERRY, AIA

999 Rhodes Avenue Santa Barbara, California 93110 (805) 569-7777

Objective: Architect

PROFESSIONAL EXPERIENCE

FRANKLIN DESIGNS 1989-present
Financial and Project Manager
Organize and administer projects for the interior design department of a 50 man architectural practice.

JOHN PAUL KERRY, Freelance 1988-89
Architect
Designed a single-family residence in Pennsylvania and miscellaneous remodels in San Francisco and Santa Barbara.

LEONE ARCHITECTS 1985-88
Project Architect/Associate
Designed and coordinated multi-family Type V housing developments in Colorado, Redwood City, Vallejo and an office building in Palo Alto.

SANFORD & ASSOCIATES 1979-85
Project Architect
Designed multi-family housing and mixed use developments, both HUD and privately funded projects of medium to high density (12 to 50 units per acre.) Performed construction administration for a $100M Tiburon waterfront development.

CITY OF SANTA BARBARA, CALIFORNIA 1977-78
Plan Reviewer
Enforced BOCA and city building codes; issued building permits.

UNIVERSITY OF MICHIGAN 1974-77
Associate Architect
Designed and supervised construction for renovation work including the Kelsey Museum of Archaeology, Bentley Historical Library and numerous laboratory facilities.

EDUCATION

School of Architecture and Design
University of Santa Barbara
Bachelor of Science, 1973
Master of Architecture with Distinction, 1974

ADRIENNE LEAH SHANNON
PO Box 5640
Santa Barbara, CA 93190
(805) 569-1111

Objective: An Architect position

PROFESSIONAL PROFILE

- 9 years experience in architectural design.
- Highly organized, dedicated with a positive attitude.
- Ability to communicate well with clients and professionals.
- Detail oriented, problem solver and team player.

PROFESSIONAL EXPERIENCE

Commercial Architectural Projects

- Developed preliminary concept design of entire remodel and additions to the Santa Barbara Museum of Art as part of a 5-member team.
  - Involved model work, drafting, ink overlays and organization of working drawings in this $3.5M project.
- Developed preliminary concept design for an art pavilion at the Huntington Museum and Art Gallery in Pasadena, CA.
- Project Architect; drafted and developed working designs for the Ventura Fire Department.
- Revised the drawings for GM Delco Corporation in Goleta, CA.

Residential Architectural Projects

- Developed conceptual design and layout for multi-million dollar projects.
  - Designed entire 2-acre estates with guest houses, servants quarters and pool houses in Montecito, Hope Ranch and Santa Barbara, CA.
- Designed development of an entire 100-acre ranch.
  - Included ranch house, office, stables, barn, guest quarters for employees and servants.
- Designed a 5-acre avocado ranch.
  - Developed all the working drawings for a traditional Spanish-style house.

EDUCATION

Degree: Bachelor of Environmental Design, 1979
University of Colorado, School of Environmental Design and Architecture. Accredited by the NAAB

EMPLOYMENT HISTORY

Architect, Daniel & Benny Enterprises, Santa Barbara, CA	1986-present
Architect, XYZ Affiliates, Santa Barbara, CA	1986-88
Project Architect, Freelance, Santa Barbara, CA	1982-86
Head Draftsperson, The ABC Architects Inc, FAIA, Montecito, CA	1979-81

Architect Assistant—Functional Resume
College Student with Related School Project Experience

MARK STEVEN MORENO

Permanent Address	Campus Address
333 Jerry Ave	234 East Apache
Los Angeles, CA 10001	Tempe, AZ 85222
(213) 555-1222	(602) 921-2305

Objective: A part-time position leading to a career in Architecture

PROFESSIONAL PROFILE

- Four years experience in line drawing.
- Learn quickly, creative in conceptual architectural design.
- Lifetime interest; willing to learn all aspects of architecture.
- Communicate well with customers and professionals.
- Detail oriented, problem solver and team player.
- Take directions and follow through to completion.

EDUCATION

BS Degree Architectural Design, 1992
Arizona State University, Tempe, AZ

RELATED EXPERIENCE

Residential Architectural Projects

- Designed a poolhouse on the CAD CAM system.
- Successfully developed conceptual design and drew the whole set of plans for a 2000 square foot beachhouse.
- Designed the development of a three-story townhouse.
- Created the conceptual design for a family room addition.

Customer & Employee Relations

- Assisted the owner of a company to set up an entirely new retail store.
  - Involved inventory control, shipping & receiving, pricing, setting up lighting fixtures, clothing racks and assembling furniture.
- Interfaced with customers interpreting their needs in a professional and courteous manner.
- Assisted employees simultaneously in all phases of a busy fast food restaurant. Maintained opening procedures and cash management.
- Developed excellent communication skills with employees and customers.

EMPLOYMENT HISTORY

Telecommunication Sales, Tempe America, Tempe, AZ	Spring 1989
Data Entry/Sales/Warehouse, Cousin's Children Store, LA, CA	1985-88
Cashier/Cook, In & Out Burger, Los Angeles, CA	1984-85

Art Historian—Combination Resume
Recent College Graduate with Related Work Experience

HANNAH SAPIR

234 Gayley Avenue
Westwood, CA 90024
(213) 360-1234

OBJECTIVE

An Art Historian/Research position for a museum

EDUCATION

BA Degree - Art History, 1991
University of California, Los Angeles

WORK EXPERIENCE

UCLA Daily Bruin, 1989-present
Staff writer. Review local art exhibitions and conduct personal interviews with artists for the Arts and Entertainment Section.

UCLA Art Museum Docent and Educator, 1988-89
Tour Guide. Guided tours of exhibitions at the museum to students and adults. Involved in the art education/outreach programs entailing instructing children from kindergarten through third grade in painting and sculpture.

Contemporary Arts Forum Home Shop, Fall 1988
Lecturer. Volunteered every Sunday for one month at the installation by Joseph Kosuth. Developed an understanding of Kosuth's work and provided such information to viewers.

Earthwatch Expedition, August 1987
Archeologist. Selected to participate in a one-month expedition conducted by the University of Arizona in Winslow, AZ. The expedition involved excavating a native American Indian site. Learned valuable skills archeological techniques and knowledge in native Indian arts with emphasis in pottery.

AWARDS/MEMBERSHIPS

- UCLA Art History Affiliate Award 1989
- Dean's Honor List 1987-89 (3 times)
- UCLA Art History Honors Program
- Outstanding College Students of America
- Golden Key National Honors Society
- Museum of Contemporary Art, Los Angeles

EMPLOYMENT HISTORY

Waitress, Hamburger Hamlet, Westwood, CA 1987-90
Waitress, Yesterday's Bar & Grill, Westwood, CA 1983-87

Associate Director, International Affairs—Functional Resume
Non-Profit Organization

Anthony Cantellio

9941 Springs Road
Atlanta, GA 30306
(404) 820-4444

Objective: Associate Director of International Affairs

PROFESSIONAL EXPERIENCE

WORLD USA, Atlanta, GA — 1988-present
Associate Director of International Affairs

International Affairs

- Analyzed and assessed the effectiveness of the Somali Refugee Program which resulted in new approaches for future relief programs.
- Designed and secured $200K in funding for the Mozambique Refugees.
- Wrote and submitted three successful project proposals for governmental funding.
  - Received $1MM from US government for immunization campaign in Zambia.
  - Obtained $1MM funding from Australian government for health issues.
- Negotiated World Bank agreement to collaborate with non profit organizations in the funding of new program activities for low income communities in Zambia.

International Business/Trade Development

- Collaborated in field operations with United Nations Children's Fund, United Nations Development Program, Food and Agricultural Organization.
- Developed extensive network of business contacts with government officials and business, religious and civic leaders worldwide.

Organizational Development/Program Management

- Instituted a program for Zambia that attracted a more highly-qualified personnel and increased retention by providing a more attractive compensation program.
- Ensured immunization campaign in Zambia that reached 92% coverage of target population, the highest coverage in the world.
- Streamlined Zambia and Mauritania field operations manual, increasing time/cost effectiveness.

Executive Management

- Functioned as team leader and liaison between African operations and offices in the USA, Canada, Australia, United Kingdom, Germany and New Zealand.
- Traveled to major US cities and met with corporate CEO's, business, foundation and religious leaders and successfully raised funding for operations in Africa.
- Spoke as motivational speaker to live audiences and on television, radio and newspaper media.

EDUCATION

MBA: International Business, 1988
Harvard University, Boston, MA

Athletics Director—Combination Resume
Moving Up, Community Service and Work Experience

WALTER E. MURRY, MS

97009 Resort Road
Portland, OR 97201
(503) 760-3333

Objective: Athletics Department Director

PROFESSIONAL ACTIVITIES

Faculty Supervisor, PCC Quad Rugby Program
Active Member, PCC Student Athletic Assistance Program
Committee Member, PCC Employee Wellness Program
Academic Advisor, Portland City College (PCC)

CURRENT EMPLOYMENT

PORTLAND CITY COLLEGE, Portland, OR 1983-present

Founder/Director

- Established and supervise the Health Appraisal and Exercise Sciences Lab program at Portland City College.
- Program includes health promotion, fitness testing and development of a comprehensive health and fitness program for students and articulation with area high schools and colleges.

Student Health Services Coordinator

- Promote student health and fitness.
- Established a highly successful college-wide fitness testing program.
- Supervise the wellness program for college faculty and staff.
- Active participant in the Student Athlete Assistance Program.

Instructor

- Teach college students Health, Adapted Physical Education, Senior Fitness, Exercise Sciences and Physical Education Activities.

EDUCATION

MS Degree, Physical Education, 1982
Cal Poly State University, San Luis Obispo

California Teaching Credential, 1972
University of California, Santa Barbara
Minor: Athletic Coaching

BA Degree, Business Economics 1970
University of California, Santa Barbara

CREDENTIALS/CERTIFICATIONS

- Adapted Physical Education Credential, 1989
  Cal Poly State University San Luis Obispo
- California Community College Supervisor Credential, 1989
- Exercise Test Technologist Certification, 1986
  American College of Sportsmedicine
- Adapted Aquatics Credential, 1984
- California Community College Teaching Credential, 1983
  Emphasis: Special Education
- California Teaching Credential (Life), Secondary Level, 1972

PROFESSIONAL ORGANIZATIONS

- Member, American College of Sportsmedicine
- Member, California Association for Health, Physical Education, Recreation & Dance
- Member, California Association of Post-Secondary Educators of the Disabled

PROFESSIONAL PAPERS

- Electromyographic Study of Abdominal Exercises.
- The Cardiovascular Fitness Value of Jazzercise Using Telemetry.
- Biomechanical Analysis of Bat and Ball Velocities in Baseball.
- The Effect of Locomotor Activities on Strength Gains of Adolescent Boys.
- Comparative Measurement of Body Composition During Pregnancy Using Bioelectrical Impedance, Skinfold Measurements & Hydrostatic Weighing.

PREVIOUS EMPLOYMENT

Post-Graduate Internship, UC San Diego Rehab. Program — Spring-1982
Phys. Ed. Coach, Santa Barbara High School District — 1973-81

Athletics Sales/Marketing Representative—Chronological Resume
Recent College Graduate with Related Work Experience

JENNIFER P. PACCINO
510 Court Drive
Petaluma, CA 94903
(415) 555-9999

OBJECTIVE: Seeking a progressive Athletic company offering an excellent training program leading to a challenging Sales/Marketing career.

PROFILE:
- Success oriented with high energy and positive attitude
- Strong sense of responsibility and self motivation
- Good written, oral and interpersonal communication skills
- Problem solver and team player with proven leadership qualities

EDUCATION: **BA Degree - Communication**, 1990, GPA 3.7
University of California, Los Angeles

RELATED EXPERIENCE:

1985-90 **SUPERVISOR/SALES COORDINATOR**
Intramural Sports Program, UC Los Angeles, CA.
- Increased student participation three consecutive years.
- Conducted weekly motivational meetings with sales staff.
- Successfully negotiated contracts with management of local businesses to sponsor college sporting events.
- Coordinated fund raisers, design and distribute brochures and create newspaper advertising for promotions and sales.
- Successfully organized leagues and structure playoffs.
- Conducted meetings with athletics involving rules and regulations, safety standards and team motivation.

Winter 1988 **SPORTS PROMOTIONS INTERN**
California Sportswear, Long Beach, CA
- Worked directly under the President of the corporation to promote sporting good clothing and tournaments worldwide.
- Wrote bid proposals and negotiated contracts with international advertising firms and magazine editors.
- Developed success themes and organized international volleyball tournaments to be played in Japan.

Spring 1988 **MARKETING REP. INTERN,** UCLA, Athletic Dept, CA.
- Successfully increased participation, obtained sponsorship from the entire Los Angeles business community. First time ever in the history of the program to receive outside participation.
- Sold radio and newspaper advertising to sponsorships.
- Set up fund raisers with alumni members to promote major sporting events.

JOSHUA PAUL ALDO
Attorney at Law
PO Box 91302
Santa Barbara, CA 93190
(805) 569-0002

Objective: Staff Attorney

EDUCATION:

JD Degree - 1965
Southwestern University, School of Law
Los Angeles, CA

BA Degree - Economics - 1960
Loyola University, Los Angeles, CA

EXPERIENCE:

1988-present **LEGAL CONSULTANT**, Santa Barbara, CA
Provided legal advice and opinions to clients concerning EEC commercial business transactional matters.
- Specialize in import/export, franchising and real estate acquisitions.
- Involved repeat European travel to Austria, Germany and Portugal.

1976-80 **GENERAL PRACTITIONER**
John, Mahoney & Jones, Santa Barbara, CA
Represented clients throughout the Santa Barbara Tri-County area in gov't contract, general business, land use and construction law.

1971-76 **MANAGER OF CONTRACTS & ADMINISTRATION**
LTC Systems, Santa Barbara, CA
Negotiated multimillion dollar programs with the Department of Transportation, American Motors and Chrysler. Reported to the director.
- Contracts involved innovative automobile technology.
- Required extensive travel throughout the United States.
- In charge of hiring, training, supervision and delegation of assignments to all administrative personnel; 11 employees.

1968-71 **SR. CONTRACT ADMINISTRATOR**
JDL Company, Goleta, CA
Negotiated and administered multimillion dollar governmental contracts and associated int'l licensing agreements.
- Contracts involved sophisticated electronic countermeasure and aviation communication equipment.
- Coordinated all division patent applications and legal claims with corporate legal department.

Auditor—Functional Resume
Housewife/Mom Re-Entering the Job Market

BRITTINY A. SAWTELLE
690 10th Street
Boulder, CO 80302
(303) 449-1123

Objective: An Auditor position.

PROFESSIONAL PROFILE

- Highly organized, dedicated with a positive attitude.
- Ability to handle multiple assignments in highly pressured situations and consistently meet tight deadline schedules.
- Thorough and committed to professionalism; thrive on opportunities to assume responsibility.

PROFESSIONAL EXPERIENCE

Proposal Audit/Incurred Cost Audit

- Successfully perform audits of small and intermediate contractors throughout Santa Barbara as an active member of the mobile team.
  - Evaluate proposals to determine reasonableness, accuracy and compliance with government regulations.

Labor Floor Check

- Review contractor's labor charging and allocation system to determine the adequacy of contractor's labor policies, procedures and internal controls.
  - Recommend improvements to comply with government regulations.

Accounting System Review

- Analyze contractor's accounting systems and internal controls to determine adequacy of accumulating and segregating costs for government contracts.

EDUCATION

BS Degree, Business, Accounting Emphasis
University of Colorado, Boulder, CO, 1987

AA Degree, Business Economics, 1984
Kingsborough Community College, Brooklyn, NY

EMPLOYMENT HISTORY

Home Management, Travel, Study 1988-90
Auditor, Boulder Bank & Trust, Boulder, CO 1982-88
Sales Representative, Joslyn College Division, Ft Collins, CO 1975-82

GARTH A. FRANKLIN
9087 Falcon Lane
Atlanta, GA 30034
(404) 872-4949

Objective: Internal Auditor

QUALIFICATIONS

Internal Auditing ..Financial Planning and Analysis ..Budget Analysis
Operation's Management ..PC Windows Applications
Tax Accounting ..General Accounting ..Cost Accounting

EMPLOYMENT HISTORY

Internal Auditor, City of Atlanta, Atlanta, GA — 1993-present
Internal Auditor, USA Corporation, Atlanta, GA — 1991-93
Senior Accountant, Grant Thornton,, Atlanta, GA — 1989-91
Experienced Accountant, Arthur Andersen & Co., Atlanta, GA — 1987-89

PROFESSIONAL EXPERIENCE

Internal/External Auditing

- Managed, analyzed and implemented highly successful internal audits for Fortune 500 corporations and small businesses of Big 6 public accounting firms in the Southeast.
- Examined year-end physical evaluation of electrical inventory and discovered unrecorded inventory valued over $550K.
- Conducted an audit of a real estate management company and discovered funds due to the City in excess of $100K.
- Directed audits of business licenses and detected unreported revenues of $20K.
- Uncovered unrecorded payments of property taxes for the City of $50K.
- Brought in two new clients and audit fees of $150K through strategic planning and implementing and delivering sales presentations of services.

Cost Accounting

- Reviewed and implemented successful cost accounting analysis for Fortune 500 corporations and small businesses of Big 6 public accounting firms throughout the Southeast.
  - Analyzed changes in product design, raw materials, manufacturing methods and services provided to determine effects on cost.
  - Analyzed actual manufacturing costs and prepared periodic reports comparing standard costs to actual production costs.

EDUCATION

BS Degree: Accounting, 1987
Florida Agricultural and Mechanical University
Passed CPA Exam: 1988

Auto Dealership General Manager—Chronological Resume

DOUGLAS B. YOUNG
335 Sierra Vista
Montecito, CA 93108
(805) 969-3816

Objective: Auto Dealership General Manager

EXPERIENCE:

1986-91

SALES MANAGER
Ventura Porsche Audi, Ventura, CA.
Purchased dealership from Ralph Masterson in 1986. Operated at a monthly loss for prior two and a half years. In two months, we showed our first profit and remained profitable throughout the year.

- Ranked in top 25% in Audi sales for entire western region.
- Improved from 18th position in Porsche sales to 8th position and became one of four dealers in the region showing an increase in sales in 1988 over 1987.
- Exceeded reg'l/nat'l average of EHG sales market penetration.
- Showed a 30% growth in service and parts sales since purchase.
- Award winner for "Service Excellence" in 1986. First place award winner in California and second place for the entire western region in 1987.
- Received "Highest Customer Satisfaction" ratings by JD Power and Associates for Porsche service in June 1988.

1984-86

MANAGER
Sunnyvale Porsche Audi, Sunnyvale, CA.
Accepted position with Texas base automotive group to manage their newly acquired California dealership. At the time of purchase, the dealership was selling only 20-25 new cars monthly. Analyzed problem areas to fully develop and implement successful sales programs, advertising and marketing programs, customer sales and service follow-up programs.

- Responsible for ranking fifth place in total sales volume in the entire western region for the year of 1985.

1972-84

MANAGER TRAINEE
Alpine Porsche Audi, Colorado Springs, CO.
Trained in all phases of dealership operations. Created departments budget plans, annual objectives with monthly reviews. Built a very financially strong dealership. Planned and implemented highly successful in-house programs and community relation programs.

- Elected Secretary/Vice President of Colorado Springs Auto Dealers Association.

NOEL ALLEN RANCHARD
9021 68th Street
Dallas, TX 75227
(214) 631-2039

Objective: Automotive Manager/Mechanic

PROFESSIONAL EXPERIENCE

RANCHARD MOTOR COMPANY, Dallas, TX 1974-present
Automotive Manager/Mechanic of the only independent company in the county specializing in mechanical and collision repair.

Mechanical Repair Facilities

- Specialize in repairing all phases of foreign and domestic automobiles.
  - Diagnose functional sensing units through a state-of-the-art computer engine management system.
  - Troubleshoot faulty units through performance checks.
- Perform engine and transmission overhauls.
- Replace wiring harnesses.
- Evaluate and complete brake repair and cooling system overhaul.
- Recharge and repair air conditioning; offer complete restoration service.

Collision Repair Facilities

- Specialize in repairing all phases of Ferrari, Mercedes, Porsche and BMW foreign and domestic cars.
  - Perform paint work, color matching, metal finishing and frame service.
- Offer complete glass replacement service.

PROFESSIONAL ORGANIZATIONS

Member, Automotive Service Councils
Member, Chamber of Commerce, Dallas, TX
Approved Member, Automobile Club of Texas
Executive Director, Texas Concour d'Elegance
Board Member, ROP, a body shop training organization sponsored through the Dallas school system.

EDUCATION

BA Degree, Business Administration, 1990
University of Texas, Austin, TX

Bank Manager—Functional Resume

STANLEY JONATHAN THOMAS
309 San Antonio Drive
Petaluma, CA 94952
(707) 765-2341

Objective: Bank Manager

PROFESSIONAL PROFILE

- 20 years experience with thorough knowledge of banking rules & regulations, policies & procedures and operations.
- Received extensive training sponsored by United California Bank. Involved all phases of lending/banking operations.
- Served as Military Policeman and Chaplain's Assistant in the US Army 1967-69. One year in Vietnam, honorable discharge.
- Currently in the Certified Credit Union Executive program.
- Gained valuable personal and business contacts.

PROFESSIONAL EXPERIENCE

Management & Administration

- Oversee operations at six offices of the Petaluma Federal Credit Union. Assist the President/CEO in the details of operations on a daily basis.
  - Serve as source of information concerning needs of various departments.
  - Insure quantity and quality of work performance.
- Rewrote and updated a Policy Manual for the Board of Directors of the entire credit union.
- As a Licensed Insurance Agent, oversee Credit Union Service Organization.
- Attend Board of Directors meetings.

Business Development & Promotions

- Assist in the development of a disaster preparedness computer system.
- In charge of field of membership expansion; work closely with employee groups and organizations to insure the approval of memberships.
- Assist in developing plans for Hertz-type sales, new car dealer sales and used car "Swap Meet" sales for members.
- Spokesman for television commercials.

Personnel/Human Resources

- Assist in administration of salary and personnel policies, selection, training and performance appraisals.
- Review personnel needs and assure adequate staffing of branch offices.
- Insure effective and timely communications between all offices.
- Standardize all operating procedures. Assure uniformity of operations and compliance with bylaws and Federal Regulations.

- More -

EDUCATION

BS, Business Administration, 1967
San Francisco State College, San Francisco CA

AA, Liberal Arts, 1965
Valley Community College, Santa Rosa, CA

CIVIC/COMMUNITY RELATIONS

- **Chairman**, FOA, Credit Union Executives Society, 1988/89
- **President**, Northern Coastal Development Corp, 1986-89
- **President**, Petaluma Chamber of Commerce, 1985-86
- **Vice President**, San Francisco United Way, 1984
- **Board Member**, San Francisco Rotary Club, 1984

EMPLOYMENT HISTORY

Operations Manager, Petaluma Federal Credit Union, 1984-present
Bank Manager, Mid State Bank, Santa Rosa, CA, 1981-84
Bank Manager/Sr Loan Officer, Santa Rosa Community Bank, 1977-81
Loan Officer/Assistant Manager/Auditor, United California Bank, 1969-77

Biologist—Chronological Resume
Recent College Graduate with Related Work Experience

SCOTT RAYMOND LANSING

9912 Media Road, Los Angeles, California 93111 (213) 964-3599

OBJECTIVE: **An entry level Biologist position.**

EDUCATION:

Biological Sciences/Biochemistry, 1987-88
University of California at Los Angeles

Marine Science Program, Certified 1985-87
Los Angeles City College, Los Angeles

PADI Certification - Rescue Diver, 1986
CPR/AR Red Cross Certification, 1986

SUMMARY OF EXPERIENCE:

UNIVERSITY OF CALIFORNIA, Los Angeles, CA — Winter 1988
Chemistry Storeroom Assistant
- Maintained supply of chemicals for graduate research.
- Assisted graduate students for the set-up of chemical apparatus.
- Responsible for liquid Nitrogen/Acetone accessibility and tank operation.
- Validated cost center codes for input into computer.

LOS ANGELES CITY COLLEGE, Los Angeles, CA — 1986-87
Mathematics Tutor
- Evaluated material for classroom of 20 students.
- Counseled students on an individual basis to promote effective learning skills.
- Graded exams and homework material to evaluate student progress.
- Available for tutoring on a one-on-one basis outside of classroom instruction.

SEA WORLD, San Diego, CA
Safety & Maintenance Technician/Tour Guide — Summers 1984-85
- Prepared Hydrofoils for daily readiness.
- Performed hydraulic, oil, fuel, coolant system and transmission testing to assure proper functioning of engine and boat.
- Evaluated systems check and passenger safety via log entries for each trip.
- Answered questions pertaining to sea life and boat operation.
- Guided visitors to park exhibits.

HONORS
- Won Chamber of Commerce Sports and Attractions Committee Award.

Biotech Research Assistant—Functional Resume
Recent Graduate with Related Volunteer and School Project Experience

FANNIE HELEN BURTON
1925 Moores Mill Raod
Atlanta, GA 30179
(312) 459-2301

Objective: A Research Assistant for a Biotech firm

EDUCATION

BS Degree, Bio-Psychology, Summer 1990
Georgia State University, Atlanta, GA

RELATED EXPERIENCE

Related Courses
Physiological Psychology...Psychopharmacology...Hormones & Behavior..Sensory Processes...Pharmacology...Pharmacology Lab...Experimental Psychology Lab...Physics...Biology...Chemistry...Organic Chemistry...Statistics.

Bio-Psychology Research Lab
- Researched and collected data for a Ph.D. graduate student's Master Thesis.
  - Set up and performed laboratory experiments on a daily basis for a year.
  - Injected laboratory animals, measured oxygen consumption and body temperature change to investigate the effects of drugs on thermogenesis.
- Gained valuable knowledge of research and surgery techniques in a bio-psychology lab setting including...
  - stereotaxic surgery, cannula implants, electrolytic lesions, adrenalectomy.
- Trained and supervised other volunteer research assistants with the entire lab set up and proper experimental procedures.

HONORS/ACTIVITIES

Member, Psi-Chi, National Psychology Honor Society
Member, Alpha Lambda Delta, Freshman Honor Society
Personnel Officer, Chi Omega Sorority UG
Alumni/Out-of-House Relations, Chi Omega Sorority, UG

WORK HISTORY

Research Volunteer, Georgia State University, Atlanta, GA	1988-present
Waitress/Shift Leader, Cajon Station, Atlanta, GA	1987-88
Library Assistant, Georgia State University, Atlanta, GA	1986-87

Bookkeeper—Functional Resume
Housewife/Mom Re-Entering the Job Market

KAREN J. PETERS
222 Blanca Lane
Santa Fe, NM 85702
(505) 471-0489

Objective: A Bookkeeping position with a reputable firm.

EDUCATION

- **California Teaching Credential**, 1983
  California State University, Chico, CA
- **BS Degree, Education**, 1969
  Brigham Young University, Provo, UT

OFFICE SKILLS

Ten key by touch...accounts receivable...accounts payable... general ledgers and journals...payroll...bank reconciliation... balance sheets...trial balance...computer skills...Microsoft Word and Word Perfect word processing...excellent phone, customer and employee relation skills...typing: 55 wpm.

PROFESSIONAL EXPERIENCE

Management & Bookkeeping

- Assisted in establishing a structure for a growing company.
  - Set up and maintained bookkeeping procedures for accounts receivable, payable and general ledgers.
- In charge of managing three very service-oriented McDonald's Restaurants.
  - Prepared detailed labor cost and analysis, weekly statistical reports and analyzed annual profit and loss statements.
  - Conducted monthly motivational and educational staff meetings.
  - Performed weekly accounting procedures for accounts receivable, payable and inventory control.
  - Hired, trained and supervised 60 employees at each location.

Community Relations & Promotions

- Developed in-house theme campaigns that successfully promoted sales.
- Promoted fundraisers through local business sponsorships and donations.

EMPLOYMENT HISTORY

Home Management, Travel, Studies	1984-present
6-7 Grade Teacher, Richmond School District, Susanne, CA	1979-84
Manager, McDonald's Corporation, Seattle, WA	1977-79
K-2 Grade Teacher, Granite School District, St George, UT	1969-77
Bookkeeper, Cal Liquid Gas Corp, Sacramento, CA	Summers 1965-75

Bookstore Sales Clerk—Chronological Resume

NANCY CAROL HOWARD
PO Box 921
Santa Barbara, CA 93190
(805) 965-1112

Objective: A Bookstore Sales Clerk position.

PROFESSIONAL PROFILE:

- Highly organized, dedicated with a positive attitude and a real passion for the printed word.
- Special talent for assessing people's needs and priorities.
- Outstanding ability to communicate with all types of people and developing rapport.
- Excellent written, oral and interpersonal communication skills.
- Problem solver/team player with proven leadership qualities.
- Work well with fellow employees, flexible and dependable.

PROFESSIONAL EXPERIENCE:

1985-present **BOOKSTORE SALES CLERK**
Choices Bookstore

- Sell books, magazines and accessories at this local bookstore.
- Developed a loyal customer base with thorough product knowledge, excellent sales ability and superior customer service.
- Set up in-house displays that quickly promoted book sales.
- Assist manager with ordering books and inventory control.
- Maintain accuracy with daily cash transactions.
- Assist in general upkeep of the store.

1980-85 **INNKEEPER**
Simpson House Inn

- Demonstrated extensive amount of public relations while interfacing closely with guests at this Victorian Bed & Breakfast Inn.
- Greeted guests when they arrived.
- Prepared gourmet food tray of wine and cheeses.
- Socialized with guests and provided them with a pleasant, homey atmosphere during this social hour.
- Delegated kitchen responsibilities to prepare breakfast for guests.
- Maintained upkeep of the Inn on a daily basis.

Brewmaster—Functional Resume

DANIEL C. BENNATTI
999 Dry Gulch Road
Santa Barbara, CA 93101
(805) 965-0000

Objective: A Brewmaster position.

PROFESSIONAL EXPERIENCE

Brewmaster Experience

- Brewed a wide variety of beers from recipes and original all-grain formulas. lager...light ales...dark ales...stouts...porters...honey meads.
- Prepared lager beers; processed 75 barrel batches for a brewing company.
- Developed concepts and formulated new beer brewing recipes with the flexibility to follow company recipes with little or no supervision.
- Thoroughly familiar with all aspects of enzyme action, microbiology and engineering of beer brewing procedures.

Gourmet Food Preparation/Menu Selection

- Planned and prepared creative gourmet food dishes.
  - Italian...American...Mexican...Continental...Californian...Oriental.
- Developed standard menu selections and daily specials.
- Set up catering and banquet menus, food preparation and service for up to 150 guests. Proficient saute and grill cook under pressured situations.
- Developed special talent for creating a quality restaurant atmosphere.

Kitchen Management/Organization

- Successfully set up an entire kitchen for a new 300-seat restaurant.
  - Established efficient procedures and par levels for all pasta dishes.
- Oversaw daily kitchen operations at two busy restaurants.
  - Trained and supervised kitchen staff of 2-12 employees in a highly professional and effective manner.
- Maintained inventory, quality and cost control, opening/closing procedures and purchasing.

EDUCATION

Master's Candidate, Food Science
University of California, Davis

BS Degree, Engineering Science, 1984
University of Texas, Austin, TX

EMPLOYMENT HISTORY

Assistant Brewmaster, Old City Brewing Co, Austin, TX — 1988-89
Chef, 35th Street Deli & Bakery, Austin, TX — 1988-89
Line Cook/Pasta Chef, Chianti's, Ft Lauderdale, FL — 1985-87

ANNIE A. FREEMAN

1023 Falcon Lane
Atlanta, GA 30034
(404) 870-1149

Objective: Budget Analyst

EMPLOYMENT HISTORY

Budget Analyst, Melita International, Atlanta, GA — 1991-present
Budget Analyst, BellSouth Corporation., Atlanta, GA — 1989-91
Budget Analyst, Arthur Andersen & Co., Atlanta, GA — 1987-89

PROFESSIONAL EXPERIENCE

Budget Analysis

- Examined and implemented successful budget analysis for Fortune 500 corporations and small businesses of Big 6 public accounting firms throughout the Southeast.
  - Monitored the operating budgets by reviewing periodic report and accounting records to determine if allocated funds have been spent as specified.
  - Prepared annual budgets by providing advice and technical assistance, working closely with financial directors and CFO's.
  - Reviewed financial requests by employing cost-benefit analysis, assessing program trade-offs and exploring alternative funding methods.
  - Consolidated departmental budgets into operating and financial budget summaries and submitted preliminary budgets with recommendations to senior management.
  - Developed procedural guidelines and policies governing the development, formulation and maintenance of budgets.
  - Projected future revenues and expenses by analyzing computerized records of historical operations, trends and costs.
- Reviewed proposed operating and financial plans--proposed program increases or new initiatives, estimated costs and expenses and capital expenditures needed to finance these programs for the City.
- Received Certificate of Excellence in Budget Reporting for organizing and coordinating departmental budgets into effective operating and financial budget presentations for a multimillion dollar governmental organization.

EDUCATION

BS Degree: Accounting, 1987
University of Georgia, Athens, GA
Passed CPA Exam: 1988

JUNE S. WATLEY
432 Riverview Drive
Atlanta, GA 30303
(404) 872-3333

Objective: Business Analyst

EMPLOYMENT HISTORY

USA Corporation, Atlanta, GA — 1992-present
Business Analyst

Resource U.S.A., Inc., Atlanta, GA — 1988-92
Business Analyst

PROFESSIONAL EXPERIENCE

Business Process Analysis/Development

- Research, wrote and presented Farmout Risk Analysis for a new division manager resulting in a better understanding of the legal ramifications and impact of farmouts on division mission.
- Developed a Trade Process Form, used by division professional staff that improved staff efficiency and status reporting.
- Analyzed trade process and developed division guidelines for evaluation and approval as part of a 5-member team.
- Developed and wrote Policy and Procedure Manuals for two small real estate companies.

Industrial Relations

- Served as liaison and developed strong working relations with governmental agencies and industry partners.
  - Coordinated review and approval process of large volumes of contract requests that substantially decreased turnaround time and enhanced corporate image with smaller industry partners.
  - Ensuring timely submission of reports from corporation to state governing boards.

EDUCATION

- **Master of Business Administration**, 1992
  Emory University, Atlanta, GA
  GPA: 4.0

- **BS Degree: Economics**, 1988
  University of Georgia, Athens, GA

Business/Systems Analyst, Sales Support—Functional Resume
Financial Software Corporation

DIANNE R. RAYANNE

1267 Virginia Avenue
Atlanta, GA 30306
(404) 815-0987

Objective: Business/Systems Analyst, Sales Support

QUALIFICATIONS

Business/Systems Analysis ..Project Management
Sales Support ..Business Solutions ..Product Development Management
SCSI BIAS ..SPS Paragon Commercial Services ..MicroSoft ..Lotus SmartSuite

EMPLOYMENT HISTORY

Business Systems Analyst, Software Technology Inc., Atlanta, GA — 1988-present
Senior Systems Consultant, Dean Witter, Discover, & Co., Riverwoods, IL — 1980-88

PROFESSIONAL EXPERIENCE

Business/Systems Analysis

- Defined user requirements for accounts receivable product enhancements for a $1.6mm financial services corporation through client interviews and industry research.
  - Analyzed proposed program enhancements/fixes to mainframe systems.
  - Carefully orchestrated multi-step, complex plans to certify program changes.
  - Worked with systems users to review testing results and resolve issues.
  - Created formal documentation for users regarding system features.
  - Conducted system walk-throughs for the users.
  - Monitored system performance to ensure that corporate goals are met.

Sales Support/Business Solutions

- Delivered powerful sales presentations for three multimillion dollar financial services corporations.
  - Developed and conducted educational workshops for clients nationwide.
  - Served as sales support for business analysis, solutions and technical expertise.
- Appointed customer service representative for the corporations highest profile client.
- Awarded highest customer satisfaction rating of 50 customer service representatives.
- Received Employee of the Month award for superior sales support role.
- Selected to be the first employee to service clients on the Help Desk, the front line contact for technical and business issue resolutions.
- Represented corporate product lines at bi-annual national tradeshows.

EDUCATION

BS Degree: Computer Science, 1988
University of Georgia, Athens, GA

Carpenter, Motion Picture Studio—Combination Resume

JAMES N. ANDREWS
3459 Wagon Road
Orlando, FL 32819
(407) 352-0009

Objective: A Carpenter position with Universal Studios

TECHNICAL THEATRE EXPERIENCE

OLD GLOBE THEATRE, San Diego, CA 1982-present

Lead Carpenter, (1986-88)

- Special skills include Welding Rigger and Electrics.
- Worked on the Festival Stage in the following:
  Comedy of Errors, Night of the Iguana, Pumpboys & Dinettes, Spokesong, Tartuffe, Much Ado About Nothing, Talley's Folley, Greater Tuna

Staff Carpenter (1982-88)

- Worked on the following sets: Skin of Our Teeth, Henry IV, Into the Woods, Macbeth, Antony and Cleopatra, Arsenic and Old Lace, Scapino, Catsplay, Richard III... Vikings...Kiss Me Kate, Twelfth Night, Wings, The Rivals, Taking Steps, Angels Fall, Strange Snow, The Miser, Fallen Angels, Mass Appeal

SAN DIEGO REPERTORY THEATRE, San Diego, CA 1980-82

Set Carpenter/Rigger

- Division Street, Death of a Salesman - (also worked as a Rigger) and Mother Courage, designed by Ron Ranson.
- Home, True West and A Christmas Carol, designed by Chuck McCall.
- Tintypes, designed by Steve Lavino.
- Elephant Man, Talley's Folly, School For Wives and Working, designed by Bob Green.

Stage Manager

- Working, (second run), directed by Sam Woodhouse.
- Petrified Forest, directed by Tavis Ross.
- Bonjour la Bonjour, directed by David Hay.

Running Crew

- Working, directed by Sam Woodhouse.
- A Christmas Carol, directed by Doug Jacobs.

PREVIOUS EMPLOYMENT HISTORY

Carpenter, Catamaran Hotel Jazz Club, San Diego, CA 1977-79
Theatre Arts Major, Cuyahoga Community College, Cleveland, OH 1974-76
Set Designer/Carpenter, Sheraton Hotel Dinner Theatre, OH 1973-74
Carpenter, Followspot, Running Crew, Musicarnival, Cleveland, OH 1972-73

ANDRIA S. BARTELLO
PO Box 23459
Goleta, CA 93117
(805) 968-2229

Objective: Catering Manager

PROFESSIONAL PROFILE

- Experienced in all phases of hotel catering management.
- Highly organized, dedicated with a positive attitude.
- Outstanding ability to communicate with all types of people.
- Service several transactions simultaneously while meeting demanding deadlines.

PROFESSIONAL EXPERIENCE

SANTA BARBARA HOTEL & RESORTS, Santa Barbara, CA 1988-present
Catering Manager

<u>Management & Organization</u>

- Manage, supervise and train catering and conference room functions to employees of a 71 room, ocean front hotel in Santa Barbara, California.
  - Work directly with food and beverage directors, chefs, sales, front desk management and accounting departments.
- Supervise and schedule 30 volunteers for a Humane Society Benefit.
- Developed financial analysis for a five year profit/loss margin.
- Process monthly forecasts, end-of-the-month and weekly reports.

<u>Food & Beverage/Catering</u>

- Catered and coordinated business luncheons, private parties, weddings, conferences and special events for 10-300 guests.
- Served as waitress, hostess, busperson, dishwasher and bartender.
  - Involved opening and closing procedures and cash management.
- Served food and beverages at the 1988/89 Hospice Ball.

<u>Marketing/Sales/Customer Relations</u>

- Successfully generate and maintain business for future events.
- Member, NAMA Marketing Competition Team in 1986. Developed a successful marketing plan and theme campaign. Introduced two proposals and an entire advertising campaign.
  - Researched product and competition, resulting in a new target market.
- Organized, set up and exhibited booths for the Santa Barbara Hotel and University of California, Santa Barbara.

EDUCATION

BA Degree, Health & Nutrition, 1980
<u>University of California</u>, Santa Barbara, CA

Chemical Dependency Counselor—Functional Resume
Recent College Graduate with Personal and Internship Experience

WESTON BOSWELL
5098 3rd Avenue
Montecito, CA 93108
(805) 966-0002

Objective: Chemical Dependency Counselor

PROFESSIONAL PROFILE

- Active member of Alcoholics Anonymous.
- Active member of 12-step Programs dealing with codependent relationships.
- Member of Support Group Network.
- Member, California Association of Marriage and Family Therapists.
- Member, American Group Psychotherapy Assn.
- Personal Psychotherapy for four years, including Rogerian, Family Therapy and Psychodynamic Psychotherapy.
- Attended 5 day Evolution of Psychotherapy training seminar.

PROFESSIONAL EXPERIENCE

Chemical Dependency Counseling & Assessment

- Counsel couples, individuals, families and adult children of alcoholics during their participation in a 12-step program.
- Primary educator on predictable course of early recovery for clients.
- Instruct on indicators of potential relapse. Designed and implemented a more effective treatment program, focusing on coping styles pertinent to the individual's social support system, workplace and family.
- Coordinate intakes, referrals, correspondence and case records.
- Supply community referral resources.
- Provided crisis intervention, brief and long term counseling to:
  -individual adults -adolescents -couples -families -groups

EDUCATION

MA Degree, Clinical Psychology, 1991
Western University, Santa Barbara, CA

BA Degree, Political Science, 1988
University of California, Santa Barbara, CA

EMPLOYMENT HISTORY

Counselor Intern, Cottage Hospital, Santa Barbara, CA — 1988-90
General Manager, Ocean Dance Co. Inc, Santa Barbara, CA — 1982-88
General Manager, Randy's Diner, Santa Barbara, CA — 1978-88

Chemist, Polymer—Chronological Resume
Moving Up to a Specialized Chemist Position

ELIZABETH KIM
550 River Rock Road
Baton Rouge, LA 70809
(504) 227-9004

POLYMER CHEMIST

EXPERIENCE:

Coatings technology
Polyurethane based adhesives for composites
Silicone primers for aircraft transparencies
Aircraft transparencies
Polyurethane liners
Composite laminates
Laminate procedures

EMPLOYMENT HISTORY:

1987-present

STAFF CHEMIST
Southern Research & Development, Baton Rouge, LA
* Research and develop adhesion modification of the polycarbonate and composite aircraft transparency products.
* Evaluate suitability of polyarylates and polyestercarbonates as outer ply and structional materials in transparencies for high speed aircraft (ATF).

1985-87

CHEMISTRY TUTOR
San Antonio College, San Antonio, TX
* Tutored students in general and organic chemistry studies.

EDUCATION:

BS Degree, Chemistry, 1987
University of Texas, Austin, TX

INSTRUMENTATION: G.C., A.A., I.R., H.P.L.C., U.V.

COMPUTER SKILLS:

Proficient in Lotus 1-2-3, Multimate and ChartMaster computer software programs.

Child Development Counselor—Chronological Resume
Recent College Graduate with Related Internship Experience

LORI L. HAYLEY

2345 College Drive, Washington, DC 90210 (212) 222-9090

OBJECTIVE: Desire further education and training in Child Development.

EDUCATION: **Bachelor of Arts - Psychology with Honors**
Georgetown University, Washington, DC
Graduation: June 1990 GPA: 3.9

ACADEMIC HONORS: Dean's List of Scholastic Excellence
1987 to 1989 (7 times)

EXPERIENCE:

1988-89 **GROUP HOME RESIDENTIAL INTERN**
The Home Group, Fairfax, VA

- Provide counseling and support for emotionally disturbed and/or juvenile delinquent female residents of a teenage group home.
- Assist staff in program planning and implementation.
- Attend weekly supervision meetings conducted by a licensed Marriage, Family & Child Counselor.

1987-89 **RESIDENTIAL AID**
The Child's Foundation, Fairfax, VA

- Assisted with behavior modification and independent living programs.
- Implement programs for developmentally disabled males ages 15-23.
- Increased effective counseling and conflict intervention skills.

1985-86 **PRE-SCHOOL TEACHER**
The Children's Center, Fairfax, VA

- Prepared children with necessary developmental skills.
- Acquired planning and scheduling techniques.
- Increased communication skills through the use of conflict negotiation with children ages 2-1/2 to 6 years old.

CHRISTINE LOIZEAUX
Choreographer...Teacher...Filmmaker
PO Box 24019
Santa Barbara, CA 93121
(805) 569-0547

Objective: Choreographer

PROFESSIONAL EXPERIENCE

Teaching
- Associate Professor of Dance for 14 years, Grand Valley State University, Michigan.
- Pioneered the Dance Department for Thomas Jefferson College, GVSU.
- Designed the curriculum, created and administered a dance major for the Performing Arts Centre, GVSU.
- Developed the dance program for The School of Communications, GVSU.
- Taught classes in modern dance technique, ballet, choreography, film/video dance, performing and directing.
- Organized and performed in the Outdoor Environmental Dance Events.
- Extensive teaching of creative dance to ages 5-65 throughout New York and New Jersey in schools, community centres, universities and churches.

Choreography
- Creator of more than 65 original dance works.
- Performed in theatres, outdoor festivals and libraries throughout New York, New Jersey, Michigan and England.
- Collaborated extensively with visual artists, filmmakers for sets, lighting design, costume and props.
- Worked with composers writing original music for my dances and films.

Administration
- Created and administered the dance department, GVSU.
- Established and administered a winter term exchange program for visiting dance artists from New York City.
- Directed the resident dance company of GVSU; student Advisor.
- Directed Christine Loizeaux Dance Company in New York City.
- Started Dancers Workshop in New York City.

Grants/Awards
- Selected as an outstanding choreographer from the National Association of Regional Ballet, Craft of Choreography Conference.
- Michigan Council for the Arts, 2 creative artist grants.
- Centre for New Television, NEA grant; recipient of 6 awards for dance films.

- More -

PROFESSIONAL EXPERIENCE (Continued)

Film

- Directed and produced 12 dance film/video works.
- Collaborated with public television to create 2 original dance works for broadcasting.

EDUCATION

- **BA, Dance & Graphic Arts**
  Bennington College, Vermont

- Pratt Graphic Art Centre, New York City

- Dance Study on East Coast and England with the following:
  Martha Graham, Jose Limon, Erick Hawkins, Donald McKayle, Leon Danelion, Alfredo Corvino, Maggie Black, Richard Thomas, Nina Fonaroff, Dan Wagoner, Alvin Ailey, Mary Anthony, Zena Romett, Sally Stackhouse, Lavinia Williams

DANCE REVIEWS

The New York Times
Dance Magazine
The Herald Tribune
Ann Arbor Press
Grand Rapids Press

AFFILIATIONS

Member, American Dance Guild
Member, Dance Alliance, Santa Barbara

EMPLOYMENT HISTORY

Creative Movement for Adults, Music Academy of the West, Santa Barbara, California	1990
Movement Awareness for Adults, Dance Warehouse, Santa Barbara, CA	1989
Master Composition, Pomona College, Pomona, California	1988
Creative Dance for Adults, Harbor House, Maine	1987
Associate Professor of Dance, GVSU, Michigan	1971-85
Modern Dance, Birch Wathen School, New York, NY	1968-71
Creative Dance for Children, Chatsworth Ave. School, New York	1966-71
Modern Dance & Ballet, Drew University, New Jersey	1967-68
Modern Dance & Ballet, Fairleigh Dickinson University, New Jersey	1966-67

Chyron Operator—Functional Resume

ROSS A. KALLMAN
PO Box 876
Goleta, CA 93117
(805) 968-4444

Objective: A Chyron Operator position.

PROFESSIONAL EXPERIENCE

Graphic Operations Skills

- Performed computerized graphic operations for the Oakland Athletics baseball sporting events.
  - Operated a 3M D-8800 character generator for pre-games and live-games.
  - Designed graphic pages of statistics for in-house video screen.
- Created graphic pages of job listing for UC Santa Barbara.
  - Operated the VP2 Chyron in pre-production for live broadcasting.

Production Skills

- Video taped the Women's Intercollegiate Basketball Team; used as a tool for the head coach to review team for improvement.
- Archived tapes in the news and sports department for later retrieval.
- Assisted in developing conceptual ideas of upcoming game promotions for the Oakland Athletics; ideas were used for in-house video screen.

Media Relation Skills

- Integral member in the Friday Football Focus Show; a show highlighting high school football sporting events in the Santa Barbara Tri-county area.
  - Monitored editing to determine best plays for viewing on KEYT TV, Channel 3.
- Wrote press releases for the university athletics department.
  - Formulated statistics for media guides and game notes.
  - Interfaced closely with radio, television and newspaper sporting news media throughout the community.

EDUCATION

BA Degree, Sociology, 1988
University of California, Santa Barbara

EMPLOYMENT HISTORY

Chyron Coordinator, Oakland Athletics Baseball Company	1989-present
Media Relations Representative, Athletic Department, UCSB	1988-89
Production Assistant, Kerr Learning Resources, UCSB	1987-1989
News & Sports Intern, KEYT Television, Santa Barbara, CA	1985-87
Team Manager, Athletic Department, UCSB	1984-85

City Planner—Chronological Resume
Lateral Career Change from Planner

ANITA S. GARCIA
PO Box 1235
Lancaster, CA 93536
(805) 942-2347

Objective: City Planner

PROFESSIONAL EXPERIENCE:

PLANNER, Land Concepts, Lancaster, CA 1979-present

- Prepare submittal packages for city and county agencies throughout the county.
  - Research land use and ownership for prospective projects.
  - Prepare zone change, tentative map, and general plan amendment applications, including environmental impact analysis.
  - Draft base maps and design preliminary site plans.
- Revise and resubmit plans, working closely with draftsmen, surveyors, clients as well as planners of city & county agencies.
- Draft job proposals and reviewing cost analysis.
- Handle multiple assignments throughout the development process and consistently meet demanding deadline schedules.

PLANNING ASSISTANT, (Planning Department) 1977-79
Knappman & Associates Civil Engineers, Lancaster, CA

- Established a better system for organizing planning materials, building ordinances and area maps.
- Submitted and delivered plans.
- Prepared land use and ownership maps.
- Assisted with minor drafting assignments.
- Position required excellent communication skills and cooperation with fellow employees, clients, county and city agencies.
- Learned basic knowledge of planning policies and procedures in a business environment.

LAW OFFICE ASSISTANT, Kramer & Williams, Valencia, CA 1976-77

- Assisted five attorneys and secretarial staff.
- Filed legal documents at Superior and Municipal Court.
- Researched legal information for cases under submission.

EDUCATION

BA Degree, Engineering, 1979
University of California, Santa Barbara

Client's Rights Advocate, Developmentally Disabled—Functional Resume
Making a Lateral Move with Community Service and Volunteer Experience

MICHAEL P. ANDERS
2991 York Drive
Memphis, TN 38126
(901) 774-3450

OBJECTIVE

A Client's Rights Advocate for the Developmentally Disabled

RELATED EXPERIENCE

Individual/Systemic Advocacy

- Provide advocacy for the protection of civil, legal and service rights of persons with developmental disabilities residing within the Tri-Counties area as Board Member for the Developmental Disabilities Board, Area IX.
  - Review legislative issues.
  - Provide written comment to elected officials, local and state agencies.
  - Investigate alleged violations of client's rights.
  - Work with Executive Director and local agencies for resolution.
  - Participated in team review of local provider.
  - Interviewed consumers regarding satisfaction with service system.
- Provide advocacy to protect systemic rights of persons with developmental disabilities in California as Organization of Area Board's Representative.
  - Review systemic issues affecting consumer rights; provide input to state agencies.

Consumer Representation

- Represent and advocate for families of children with developmental disabilities as member of California Interagency Coordinating Council.
  - Develop and write statewide newsletter for families and professionals.
  - Establish network of family representatives for input to state planning.
- Advocate for persons with developmental disabilities in the Individualized Educational Planning Meetings and Mediation; inform families of rights and attend IEP meetings.
  - Identify challenges to resolution of IEP, provide due process information.

Advocacy & Collaboration Trainer/Educator

- Provide advocacy training for families-professionals in the Tri-Counties.
  - Set up and coordinated Tri-County phone network to support legislative information as Governmental Affairs Chair for Assn. for Children and Adults with Learning Disabilities.
- Provide parent-professional collaboration training.
  - Developed and coordinated family-professional conference as member of the Santa Barbara Down Syndrome Association.
  - Facilitated parent-professional teams in needs assessment/planning for involvement with Department of Developmental Services, Local Planning Areas Family Professional Teams.

- More -

PROFESSIONAL EXPERIENCE (Continued)

Educational/Family Consultant

- Provide parent-professional collaboration consultation for Department of Education, California Early Intervention Technical Assistance Network; Personnel Development Infant Preschool Programs.
  - Establish Institute for family-professional collaboration.
  - Write and review material for Institute.
  - Plan and facilitate the family-professional Institute.
- Provided educational consultation for St. Vincent's Residential Program.
  - Developed and implemented training program for residential instructors.
  - Provided resources and instruction.

EDUCATION

MA, Special Education, in-progress
University of California, Santa Barbara

BA, English, Penn State University, Univ. Park, PA, 1967

SPECIAL TRAINING

- Learning Handicapped Specialist Teaching Credential, Life
- Single Subject Teaching Credential, English, Life
- Community College Basic Skills Credential, Life

PROFESSIONAL AFFILIATIONS

- Association for Children and Adults with Learning Disabilities (ACLD) - California, Santa Barbara Chapter
- Council on Exceptional Children - Mental Retardation Division, Early Childhood Division
- National Down Syndrome Congress

EMPLOYMENT HISTORY

Substitute Teacher, Maricopa County Schools, Austin, TX 1973-75
Res. Group Home Coordinator, Children's Industrial Home, Bellingham, WA 1972
Special Education Resource Teacher
Camp Springs Elementary School Bellingham, WA 1970-71
Special Education Day Class Teacher, Severely Emotionally Disabled
Edgemeade School, Seattle, WA 1969-70

LUKE DURHAM
519 W. Alamar #12
Houston, TX 93105
(801) 224-6785

Objective: Part-time Computer Analyst position

PROFESSIONAL PROFILE:

- Success oriented and outgoing with a positive attitude
- Strong sense of responsibility and self motivation
- Good written, oral and interpersonal communication skills
- Problem solver and team player with proven leadership qualities
- Rapidly analyze and recognize problems and find solutions
- Strong organizational skills with attention to detail
- Creative, flexible and efficient work habits.
- Thorough knowledge of developing company cross training programs.

EDUCATION: **MA Degree - Clinical Psychology, 1990**
Antioch University, Houston, TX

BS Degree - Electrical Engineering, 1988
Western Washington University, Bellingham, WA

QUALIFICATION SUMMARY: **MANAGEMENT CONSULTING/TRAINING SKILLS**

- Analyzed departments needs and designed systems and procedures.
- Set up workshops and trained new policy/procedures to employees.
- Designed mini computer systems, wrote requests for proposals.
- Evaluated and selected vendors to purchase hardware and software.
- Worked with vendors to design custom software to meet their specific needs.
- Developed seminars to prepare employees for training on computer.
- Trained/cross trained entire company all phases of computer system.

EMPLOYMENT HISTORY:

Consultant, Houston Computer Corp, Houston, TX	1990-present
Consultant, Puget Sound Company, Seattle, WA	1986-89
Systems Mgr, KD Engineering, Seattle, WA	Summer 1985

Computer Instructor, College Level—Functional Resume
Housewife/Mom Re-Entering the Job Market

CLAUDIA DIANE SOPHIA
702 Dry Lake Avenue
Santa Barbara, CA 93110
(805) 569-0004

Objective: College Level Instructor

EDUCATION/CREDENTIALS

BA Degree, Psychology, 1971
University of California, Santa Barbara

Community College Instructor Credential, 1989

Lifetime Limited Service Credential
Architectural Engineering Related Technologies

PROFESSIONAL EXPERIENCE

Computer Instructor

- Teach Computer Assisted Drafting and Design (CADD).
  - Instruct classes of 24 students in computer lab with 12 stations twice a week.
  - Deal effectively with multicultural and handicapped students.
  - Currently teach intermediate and advance AutoCAD systems and will be teaching beginning AutoCAD, Summer of 1989.
- Taught CADVance and PCAD software programs to college level students as well as the following college level drafting courses: Blueprint Reading... Freehand Drafting...Mechanical Drafting...Electronic Drafting.

Computer Drafting & Consulting

- Develop conceptual design of mechanical and architectural projects.
- Produced existing layout from blueprints to AutoCAD.
- Set-up customized versions of the AutoCAD system for various companies throughout Northern and Southern California.
  - Developed an effective employee training manual.
  - Provide training seminars and workshops for company employees.

EMPLOYMENT HISTORY

Home Management, Family, Study, Travel	1980-present
Instructor, Santa Barbara City College, Technologies Div.	1975-80
Teacher, Santa Barbara Elementary School District	1970-75

Computer Technician, Career Change—Combination Resume

JARED M. WELLINGTON
1129 Mt. Vernon Lane
Camarillo, CA 93010
(805) 653-4567

Objective: A Computer Technician

COMPUTER SKILLS

Software: MS DOS...UNIX...Dbase III...AUTOCAD Lotus 1-2-3...Word Perfect...ProWrite...Quatro pro...Procomm...Wordstar

Hardware: IBM...Hewlett Packard...Gould...DFS V.

PROFESSIONAL EXPERIENCE

HALLIBURTON GEOPHYSICAL SERVICES, Houston, TX 1983-present
Navigator

Computer Hardware/Software & Electrical Experience

- Installed the HP computer system to perform navigation on a 275 foot ship.
- Set up IBM computers for three-dimensional data collection.
- Troubleshoot and repair entire systems to component level.
- Develop customized computer programs using BASIC for several in-house projects resulting in more efficient productivity.
- Design spreadsheets to keep track of navigation.
- Created and wrote the manual for the navigation system used companywide.
- Gained thorough knowledge of Word Perfect and Professional Write, Lotus 1-2-3, Quatropro, AUTOCAD, Dbase and all versions of DOS.
- Locate and solve computer software/hardware problems without supervision.
- Perform a wide range of electrical AC/DC wiring on several sea vessels.

Employee Training & Supervision

- Train and supervise crew members one-on-one with computerized navigation procedures.
- Served as crew leader for 12-hour shifts on a daily basis.
- Managed crew members and management staff; responsible for shore contact during a two-month trip offshore.

EMPLOYMENT HISTORY

Observer, Seiscom Delta United, Singapore 1982-83
Observer, Western Geophysical, Singapore 1981-82
Field Manager, National Encyclopedias, San Diego, CA 1977-80

DAVID B. WEINSTEIN
5394 Star Pine Road
Carpinteria, CA 93013
(805) 684-5884

Objective: A position in Construction Management.

PROFESSIONAL EXPERIENCE

Commercial Projects

Cottage Hospital...St. Francis Hospital...Tahatchipee Prison...Vandenberg Air Force Base...China Lake Naval Facility...Santa Barbara School District...Diablo Canyon Nuclear Power Plant...HUD housing projects.

Project Management/Vendor Relations

- Established and managed two successful construction companies.
  Single family dwellings...spec houses...commercial building
  - Hired, trained and supervised a crew of 10-25 employees.
  - Complete projects on-time while meeting strict budget requirements.
  - Located qualified vendors and negotiated contracts with subcontractors.
  - Hired, scheduled and supervised subcontractors; developed and enforced effective company policy, procedures and project safety regulations.
  - Acquired zoning variance and building permits.
  - Purchased, expedited materials/equipment; maintained quality control.
  - Carried out daily on-site supervision, maintaining safety standards.

Client Relations

- Liaison between contractors, engineers, architects and clients, solving potential problems and meeting realistic demands at a fair price.
- Effectively negotiated cost estimation with clients.
- Maintained daily contact with clients at location sites.
- Established new business and successfully developed a personal client base through excellent customer relations, hard work and word-of-mouth.

EDUCATION

- **California Real Estate License,** 1990
- **Real Estate Development,** UC Santa Barbara, 1988

EMPLOYMENT HISTORY

Construction Manager, XYZ Construction Company, Carpinteria, CA	1978-present
Project Manager, ABC Roofing Incorporated, Carpinteria, CA	1975-78

RICHARD DALLAS BENJAMIN
9001 Stagecoach Road
Santa Barbara, CA 93110
(805) 966-0001

Objective: Controller

PROFESSIONAL PROFILE

- 20+ years experience in general, cost accounting, auditing, budgeting, management; all phases of computer conversions.
- Rapidly analyze/recognize company problems and solutions.
- Highly organized, dedicated, thorough in completing projects.

PROFESSIONAL EXPERIENCE

Cost Accounting

- Implement cost accounting systems.
  - Established complete integrated accounting package for entire corporations.
  - Tracked cost for multi-million dollar contracts.
  - Reduced costs for small businesses and large corporations.

Accounting & Budgeting

- Converted manual accounting systems to efficient computerized office systems for several companies throughout the Santa Barbara community.
  - Designed, installed and implemented effective budgeting systems under cash and accrual accounting methods.
  - Successfully tracked and reduced costs for multi-million dollar contracts.

Auditing

- Audited multi-million dollar subcontractors accounting records and facilities for government contracts.
- Analyzed problem areas and successfully developed programs to improve operations of local bank and entire restaurant chain.

Management & Administration

- Reported directly to the President. Accounting, Data Processing, Procurement Analysis & Review Departments reported directly to Controller.
  - Increased sales from $1M to $2.5M.
  - Hired, trained and supervised 2-40 employees.
  - Set up and conducted monthly motivational staff meetings.
- Established and implemented daily training programs to educate management and staff on new accounting office procedures.

EMPLOYMENT HISTORY

Controller, ABC Business Inc, Santa Barbara, CA — 1985-present
Controller, GDF Security Services Inc, Santa Barbara, CA — 1978-85
Staff Accountant, DPZ Technology, Goleta, CA — 1970-78

Copy Editor, Senior—Chronological Resume
Moving Up from Copy Editor

DEIRDRE A. LYNDS
671 Laurel Lane
Montecito, CA 93108
(805) 687-4567

Objective: Senior Copy Editor position

EXPERIENCE:

1986-1990 **COPY EDITOR**, Daily Nexus Newspaper, UC Santa Barbara
Began as an Assistant Editor and was promoted to Editor through dedication, long hours, weekend work and the ability to work under constant deadlines. Edit all stories for news, editorial, sports, feature, arts and others. Position required strong writing organization and style skills, as well as faultless grammar, spelling and knowledge of style conventions of the Associated Press. Hire, train, supervise and direct copyreading staff.

- Won Recognition of Editorial Contribution Award, 1988

GRAPHICS/PRODUCTION. Responsible for daily assembly of entire paper. Required precision and versatility with graphics equipment as well as graphic creativity. Ability to read design layout; knowledge of pica and columnar measuring systems, point sizes, typefaces, half-tone/line shot techniques and equipment.

- Achieved Most Outstanding Production Staff Member, 1987

1985-86 **PROOFER/TYPESETTER/PRODUCTION**, Goleta Sun, Goleta, CA
Proofread entire paper. Edited opinion columns, news service material, operated extensive computer typesetting and paste-up of all corrections. Developed in-depth familiarity with specific guidelines associated with editing of opinion material.

Relevant Skills
- Computer - Compugraphic, WordStar, MacIntosh
- 10-key by touch
- Multi-line phones
- Scheduling/Dispatching
- Typesetting

EDUCATION: **BA Degree, Graphic Art**
University of California, Santa Barbara
Graduated: December 1988 GPA: 4.0

Director, International Business and Trade Development—Functional Resume
Nonprofit Organization

Harry J. Adulah

1994 Parkway Drive
Atlanta, GA 30305
(404) 877-2020

Objective: Director of International Business and Trade Development

QUALIFICATIONS

International Affairs/Relations ..International Business/Trade Development
Leadership ..Negotiations ..Program Management ..Organizational Development
Research ..Budgeting ..Financial Analysis ..English ..French ..Swahili

PROFESSIONAL EXPERIENCE

WORLD INTERNATIONAL, Los Angeles, CA 1979-present
Director of Business Trade/Development

International Business/Trade Development

- Established new offices for international operations of a highly successful, $300MM non-profit organization throughout Senegal, Mauritania, Chad, Mali and Gambia.
  - Increased funding by $15MM that improved education, health care, food distribution, water accessibility and agricultural production and created a positive impact to millions of people throughout West Africa.

International Affairs

- Served as Country Representative for Zambia and Chad.
  - Responsible for approximately $20MM in program resources in Zambia.
  - Operated effectively in Chad during its' civil conflicts of the 1980's.
- Participated at conferences worldwide for political, economic and development issues.

Organizational Development/Program Management

- Reorganized operations in Mauritania and Ethiopia.
  - Human Resource ..Finance ..Field Programs ..Administration/Transport ..PR
- Developed and executed global management and technical training programs that enhanced capabilities and dedication of staff.

Executive Management

- Served as Executive Assistant to Vice President of Africa throughout Kenya, Ethiopia, Uganda, Tanzania, regional support and technical groups.
  - In charge of portfolio in excess of $30MM per year.

EDUCATION

- **Ph.D.: Business Administration**, 1979
  University of London, London, England
- **MA: African History**, 1976
  University of London, London, England

Director, New Media Development—Functional Resume

DAVID MIRANDA

1190 Hillsbury Street
Atlanta, GA 30305
(404) 873-2440

Objective: Director of New Media Development

QUALIFICATIONS

International Business/International Relations ..Negotiations
Sales and Marketing Analysis ..Operation's Management ..Project Management
Organizational Development ..New Business Development/Start up

AWARDS AND RECOGNITIONS

TNT Award of Special Recognition, TNT VP of Operations, 1995
First Place, Northeast Florida Programming Competition, 1987

PROFESSIONAL EXPERIENCE

DIRECTOR, NEW MEDIA DEVELOPMENT 1992-present
Turner Network TV Europe, Atlanta, GA

International Business/New Media Development

- Managed the United States Creative Services office for the TNT Europe launch team.
  - Created the organizational structure and project management systems for TNT Europe that currently serves as a model for TNT Asia.
  - Monitored and managed creative and employee budgets of over $3MM.
  - Hired, trained, scheduled and supervised production staff; met strict deadlines to... screen movies ..create movie logs ..develop clip reels in edit sessions ..produce commercials ..supervise scripts.
  - Developed television commercials for network launch with European producers and international consultants.
  - Designed and implemented more efficient reports, spreadsheets and acquisitions.
- Established a Quality Team System of communications between the London Corporate Headquarters and the United States office.
  - Discussed administrative and technical issues in the U.S. office that improved quality levels of work produced under tight deadline requirements.
  - Updated daily and weekly movie and commercial schedule changes.
  - Developed valuable business relationships with foreign advertising agencies and production companies throughout Europe.

EDUCATION

- **MBA: International Business**, 1995
  Mercer University, Atlanta, GA
- **BS Degree: Political Science**, 1992
  Jacksonville University, Jacksonville, FL

JANE PIATROWSKI
194 Lenox Road
Atlanta, GA 30305
(404) 870-3320

Objective: Director of Operations

QUALIFICATIONS

Operations Management ..Negotiations
Sales and Marketing Analysis ..Project Management
Organizational Development ..New Business Development/Start up

AWARDS AND RECOGNITIONS

Quarterly Revenue Award, Children's Entertainment, 1996
Monthly Objective Award, Children's Entertainment, 10 consecutive months, 1994-95
Leader/Organizer, Taskforce Lobbying Group, University of Georgia, 1992
First Place, Northeast Florida Programming Competition, 1987

PROFESSIONAL EXPERIENCE

DIRECTOR OF OPERATIONS 1986-present
Children's Entertainment, Miami, FL

Business Development/Start Up

- Established a highly successful entertainment company for children that became the largest children's entertainment company in NE Florida.
  - Developed valuable business relationships with clients such as... Revlon ..Independent Life ..Young Life and Florida National Guard.

Operations/Project Management

- Hired, trained and supervised administrative and event staff.
- Developed standard operating procedures based on industry demand.
- Conducted daily on-site supervision to ensure consistent service and quality.
- Negotiated contracts with clients and agents.

EDUCATION

- **MBA: International Business,** 1995
  Emory University, Atlanta, GA
- **BS Degree: Political Science,** 1986
  University of Georgia, Athens, GA

Engineer, Design—Chronological Resume
Recent Graduate Moving Up from Engineering Aide

NICOLAS ANTHONY
2367 Gold Hill
Nederlands, CO 80534
(303) 345-6789

Objective: A Design Engineer position.

EDUCATION:

BS Degree, Physics, March 1991
University of Colorado, Boulder, CO

AA Degree, Engineering, 1985
Santa Barbara City College, Santa Barbara, CA

AS Degree, Aviation Maintenance, 1984
Santa Barbara City College, Santa Barbara, CA

JOB EXPERIENCE:

1989-present RESEARCH WEST CORPORATION, Boulder, CO
Engineering Aide I
- Assist engineers in design, testing, and implementation of instrumentation for various energy measurement experiments.
- Design and fabricate apparatus for materials testing on vacuum.
- Start up and maintenance of class 100 clean room.
- Perform mechanical design using computer aided drafting (CAD).
- Programmed computer using FORTRAN and BASIC languages.
- Setup electrical tests i.e., oscilloscopes, meters, power supplies.

1986-89 AVIATION CORPORATION, Carpinteria, CA
Aircraft Inspector
- Performed heavy inspections (C and D checks) on the following aircraft: DC-10 (-30, -40) 727 -200, DC-9 (-10, -30, -40, -50).
- Inspect installations and modifications of structural, electrical, and hydraulic systems on DC-10 (-30, -40), 747-SP, MD-80.
- Performed heavy maintenance on McDonnell Douglas DC-10 aircraft, including engine and flight control replacements.
- Repaired and modified aircraft systems and components.
- Trained and supervised apprentice mechanics.

1980-86 WEST COAST AIRLINES, Santa Maria, CA
Quality Control Inspector
- Inspected aircraft repairs and required inspection items (RII).
- Accomplished checks on aircraft and engines.
- Designed tooling for maintenance applications.
- Performed nondestructive testing methods including magnaflux, eddy current and dye penetrant; trained new inspectors.

Engineer, Electrical—Chronological Resume
Recent College Graduate with Internship Experience

JULIAN P. WASHINGTON

Current Address
111 Dry River Street
Santa Barbara, CA 93111
(805) 683-2222

Permanent Address
8888 Westland Drive
Saticoy, CA 90004
(805) 644-1111

Objective: An Electrical Engineering position.

EDUCATION:

MS Degree, Electrical Engineering
University of California, Santa Barbara
Graduation: June 1990.

BS Degree, Electrical Engineering, 1988
University of California, Los Angeles

Honors

UCLA Alumni Scholarship
Ralph Bunche Scholarship
GEM Fellowship
GOF Fellowship
Adolph Coors Scholarship
UCLA Chancellor's Scholarship

PUBLICATIONS: Lithium Ion Mobility Enhancement in Silicon, published in *Engineering Today*, Fall 1989 issue, Volume 9.

COMPUTER SKILLS: Skilled computer programmer in PASCAL and BASIC languages.

EXPERIENCE:

MOTOROLA GEG, Scottsdale, AZ — Summer 1988
Engineer Internship
- Tested for failure of filters, capacitors, inductors and power supplies.
- Wrote controlling program on HP computer system in BASIC.
- Calculated power requirements of certain IC chips.

IBM CORPORATION, Norwalk, CA — Summer 1987
Systems Engineer Internship
- Assisted with large system maintenance.
- Delivered effective product demonstrations to business groups.
- Developed forecast model on PC to assist the branch sales staff.

AFFILIATIONS:

National Society of Black Engineers
Institute of Electrical and Electronics Engineers
Toastmasters International

Engineer, Electrical—Chronological Resume
Recent College Graduate Moving Up from Engineering Assistant

DARCY AMANDA FAUST
330 Ocean View Drive
Seattle, WA 98105
(206) 624-0068

Objective: An Electrical Engineering position

EDUCATION: **BS Degree, Electrical Engineering**
Western Washington University, Bellingham, WA
Graduation: Spring 1990.

WORK EXPERIENCE:

Summers 1988-89 CITY OF BELLINGHAM, Bellingham, WA, (Summer 1989)
(Department of Public Works-Bureau of Street Lighting)
Electrical Engineering Assistant
- Prepare lighting system design in coordination with Cal-Trans, Bureau of Engineering and other agencies.
- Perform calculations, utilizing plans and material specifications.
- Determine locations for street lighting facilities.
- Meet with the public and employees of other agencies to discuss various aspects of design and operation.

CITY OF BELLINGHAM, Bellingham, WA, (Summer 1988)
(Department of Water and Power)
Electrical Engineering Assistant
- Worked in new business section concerning power distribution.
- Designed drawing specifications for customer power upgrade.

Summer 1987 SEATTLE NAVAL SHIPYARD, Seattle, WA
Electrical Engineering Trainee
- Analyzed power requirements and ensured the adequacy of power generation equipment.
- Designed the arrangement and installation of electrically operated machinery and equipment.
- Prepared drafting, layout and detailed design using manual drafting tools and CAD CAM computer system.
- Researched manuals and technical specifications.

Summer 1986 US NAVY, National City, CA
(Naval Ship Weapon Systems Engineering Station)
Electrical Engineering Trainee
- Observed simulation system and provided knowledge for design.
- Delivered and assisted in program installation on board Naval ships. Programmed computer weapon systems.
- Designed an interface unit for a more efficient computer system.

Engineer, Electro-Mechanical—Chronological Resume

DAVID L. ROLAND
90387 Cherry Hill Court
San Marcos, CA 92404
(714) 780-0999

OBJECTIVE: An Electro-Mechanical Engineering Designer position.

EDUCATION: **AA Degree - Mechanical Engineering**, San Marcos College

SPECIAL TRAINING:
- Computer Vision Design and Drafting Systems (CADDS).
- Automated drafting and manufacturing Systems (ADAM).
- Anvil 4000 CAD (VAX Database) IBM PC, Apple PC.
- Fundamentals of InfraRed Detector operation and testing.

MILITARY: US Navy (E5). Trained in celestial and electronic navigations. Maintain navigation PUBS and related equipment. Honorable Discharge, 1960

USNR Mobile Construction Battalion (Seabees). Engineering Aide (E5). Civil Engineering included plane surveying, planning and estimating. Architectural design and drafting. Reserve 1968-78

US Air Force Reserve (Master Sergeant). Squadron Career Counselor. Reserve 1978-89.

EXPERIENCE:

1984-present **ENGINEERING DESIGN SPECIALIST**, San Diego Research Center, San Diego, CA. Design and develop complex electro-mechanical components and systems working within parameters. After preliminary investigation, submitted ideas for changes in scope of a design in meetings with responsible personnel from other departments. Performed necessary calculations to insure the integrity of the design, functionally and environmentally. Analyze for appropriate selection of commercial components and utilized them in the design of systems. Familiar with military specifications applicable to equipment and hardware.

1983-84 **SR ENGINEERING DESIGNER**, Airborne Company, San Marcos, CA. Research and design layout on antenna, radar and transmitter projects. Performed production and manufacturing investigations on form, fit and make design review presentation to project engineer and chief engineer. Planned and estimated milestone requirements on assigned projects.

THOMAS J. LESTER
PO Box 10990
Goleta, CA 93190
(805) 966-0009

OBJECTIVE: A Design Engineer Management position.

EDUCATION:

- **BS Degree, Management**, Pepperdine University, Malibu, CA
- **Business Administration**, Long Beach College, Long Beach, CA
- **Design Engineering**, Cerritos College, Cerritos, CA
- **Design Drafting**, Fullerton College, Fullerton, CA

EXPERIENCE:

1975-present ENGINEER RESEARCH & DEVELOPMENT INC, Goleta, CA

Design Engineer (1988-Present)
Engineering involvement to compile technical data and complete conceptual design in response to RFPs and customer requested changes to hydraulic filtering devices. Served as manager for configuration control with responsibility for the management and control of technical data being input to a MIS data base using Hewlett Packard 3000 computing system. The technical data available was a compilation of 30-years of corporation engineering data which was converted to a common base and used to establish the system data base.

Assistant Process Engineer (1984-88)
Maintained quality control records for ferrous and non-ferrous investment castings manufactured for aerospace applications.

Project Engineering Analyst (1980-84)
Assigned to the Flight Laboratory Division, conducting program planning including estimating, scheduling, and agency coordination for DC-10 certification testing on pylons and landing gears. As a PERT Analyst, served as DC-10 project coordinator between the flight test division and the project office.

Engineering Scientist (1975-80)
Designed and conducted structural tests on DC-9, DC-10, and A-4 airframes and missiles launch racks, ejection seats, flight control systems, and fuel cells. Served on RFP teams for the NASA Space Shuttle project, the US Air Force Airborne Tanker Project, and the project team involved in reequipping the Navy Blue Angels with Douglas A-4 aircraft.

LARRY S. SWANSON
PO Box 999
Goleta, CA 93117
(805) 964-0001

OBJECTIVE
Electro-Mechanical Engineer Manager

PROFESSIONAL PROFILE

- Rapidly analyze problems; recognize cost-effective solutions.
- Special talent for assessing company needs and priorities.
- Supervise employees in a professional and diplomatic manner.
- Developed valuable contacts with vendors in the electronics industry nationwide.

PROFESSIONAL EXPERIENCE

ENGINEERING DESIGN CONCEPTS 1980-present
Senior Electro-Mechanical Engineer/Acting Manager

Project Management
- Develop conceptual designs as part of a product design team for all company projects.
  - Schedule projects from concept to completion.
  - Select qualified personnel and equipment resources.
- Create detailed design including part specs, wiring and cable design and documentation.
- Work on multiple projects effectively while maintaining strict budget requirements and tight deadline schedules.

Staff Management
- Supervise designers and drafters.
- Member of a weekly discussion and action group who resolves Engineering Department scheduling issues, conflicts and to establish more efficient departmental procedures.

Engineering Design
- Develop innovative concepts and designs of computer networking equipment.
  - Design projects to military and commercial specification.
  - Create functional specifications, working closely with Marketing, Sales, Manufacturing and Customer Service Departments.
- Analyze cooling requirements, shock and vibration.
- Design products to meet foreign and domestic safety regulations and EMI requirements (including TEMPEST).

EDUCATION
BA Degree, Engineering, 1978
University of California, Santa Barbara

THOMAS GEORGE BRONTE
PO Box 2341
Sunnyvale, CA 94087
(408) 245-1111

Objective: Mechanical Engineer

PROFESSIONAL EXPERIENCE

SUNNYVALE MISSILES & SPACE CO, Sunnyvale, CA 1980-present
Mechanical Engineer (1989-present)

- Created a database from information gathered throughout propellant processing of the US Navy's fleet ballistic missile system.
- Developed a 35 variable predictive model of motor performance from propellant processing database.
- Presented the modeling methodology to the US Navy's top propulsion representative and major subcontractors (Hercules and Morton Thiokol)
- Assisted managing propulsion assets in conjunction with subcontractors.

Junior Engineer (1985-89)

- Developed a preliminary discriminant model of motor performance.
- Performed technical analysis of numerous subcontractor proposals.
- Provided technical support during negotiation of subcontractor proposals.

Engineering Assistant (1980-85)

- Participated in engineer studies to review electrostatic discharge safety.
- Assisted engineering staff in daily activities of managing solid propellant rocket motors.

CENTER FOR ROBOTIC SYSTEMS, Sunnyvale, CA Summer 1979
Engineering Intern

- Conceived a direct drive gripper for computer controlled robotic arm.
- Developed arm for class 1 clean room capability and one micron repeatability.
- Capable of many tasks including assembly of microelectronics.

COMPUTER SKILLS

- Hardware: IBM XT & AT, Apple Macintosh SE
- Software: Lotus 1-2-3, dBase III, Power Point & Microsoft word

BS, Mechanical Engineering, 1980
University of California, Los Angeles

MAX RYAN MICHAELSON

Current Address
6222 Riverview Road, Apt E
Boulder, CO 80524
(303) 251-1278

Permanent Address
20341 Raymond Street
Portland, OR 97039
(202) 315-9346

Objective: A Mechanical Engineering Internship

EDUCATION

BS Degree, Mechanical Engineering, June 1991
University of Colorado, Boulder, CO

RELATED EXPERIENCE

Printer Operator Technician

- Operated Xerox 9700 Laser printers for a computer company.
  - Repaired complex mechanical computer systems and printers, meeting strict deadline schedules on a daily basis; performed data entry on the IBM PC computer.
- Learned to work on multiple assignments under pressured situations while maintaining a positive attitude.

Communication & Organization Skills

- Picked up tapes, printed information/delivered tapes from Denver to Boulder, CO.
  - Liaison and main source of information between clients and management staff at two locations for a very service-oriented company.
  - Maintained excellent communications with managers of major corporations to meet tight deadline requirements.
- Prepared displays & software packages for national trade show exhibitions.
- Gained vital organizational and communication skills.

Public Speaking & Promotions

- Led tours throughout the UC Boulder campus to high school students and parents.
- Successfully promoted dorm attendance & activities for 1000 dorm students.
  - Interviewed students and reviewed personal information forms to evaluate and determine living situations.
  - Guided tours and provided assistance to students for the facility.
- Learned to speak in front of large and small groups of people in a highly professional manner with poise and dignity.

EMPLOYMENT HISTORY

Office Assistant, Tropicana Gardens, Boulder, CO — 1989-present
Tour Guide, UC Boulder, (Relations with Schools Dept) — Spring 1988
Printer Operator/Technician, X-Tec Systems, Boulder, CO — 1984-87

Environmental Affairs Officer—Chronological Resume

BRUCE C. ROTH
PO Box 1230
Santa Barbara, CA 93101
(805) 966-0002

Objective: Environmental Affairs Officer

PROFESSIONAL PROFILE: Experienced in research...planning...fieldwork...water resources ...public works...toxic and hazardous substances ...analysis of data...decision-making...problem solving...highly dedicated with proven ability to excel in a variety of situations...communicate effectively with the public, staff and all levels of management.

EXPERIENCE:

1985-91 **ENVIRONMENTAL AFFAIRS OFFICER**
Borough of Montvale, Montvale, NJ

- Reviewed proposed construction plans and sites to detect possible undesirable environmental impacts.
- Detect and remedy environmental health problems through resources from the Environmental Commission and Public Works.
- Provided the community with improved recreational facilities.

1983-85 **ENVIRONMENTAL AFFAIRS COORDINATOR**
Offshore Transport Inc, Santa Barbara, CA

- Member of an immediate response team which fulfills an oil spill and emergency contingency plan for the Santa Barbara Channel.
- Deploy and maintain all equipment aboard a water pollution control vessel.

1980-83 **MAINTENANCE WORKER**
City of Santa Barbara, Santa Barbara, CA

- Installed, replaced and repaired water mains, meters, fire hydrants and related water services equipment.
- Read, understand and prepared detailed maps and drawings.
- Interpreted technical manuals, read schematics and blueprints.
- Exercised thorough knowledge of water treatment health factors.
- Qualified in 1987 for the American Waterworks Association Grade I Water Distribution Operations Certificate.
- Performed diversified public works operations.
- Maintained parks, roads, waste water facility and equipment.
- Compiled EPA lists of toxic and hazardous substances.

EDUCATION: **BS Degree, Human Ecology,** 1984
University of California, Santa Barbara

Environmental Law Internship—Functional Resume
Law Student with Related Volunteer Work Experience

MICHAEL R. LUNDY
2000 Green Forest
Mariposa, CA 96002
(405) 999-0002

OBJECTIVE

An Internship leading to a career in Environmental Law

EDUCATION/LICENSE

- **JD**, Santa Barbara College of Law, 1987-in progress
- POST Certified Law Enforcement Training, 1976-87
  State Dept of Parks & Recreation Training Center
- California Real Estate Salesman's License, 1986

RELATED EXPERIENCE

Legal Research & Writing

- As a union officer, represented the legal rights of State Park Rangers in labor issues; coordinated and conducted labor management meetings.
  - Investigated, wrote and processed grievances through all department management levels statewide.
  - Negotiated collective bargaining contracts as part of a 6-8 member team.
- Served as prosecutor for a US military court marshal.
  - Gathered and presented evidence at trial.
  - Investigated & wrote findings of an aircraft accident with senior officers.
- Researched/wrote a request for conscientious objector status, granted 1969.

Environmental Education

- Guided field trips throughout the San Diego Zoo for second grade students of the San Diego County School District.
- As zoo bus guide, wrote and presented 4-7 lectures daily.
- Taught fourth grade students in the zoo's summer school program.
- As ranger, prepared and presented educational campfire programs.
  - Led nature walks & interpreted natural & cultural resources of the park.
  - Educated grades K-9 students on natural resources and their protection.

AFFILIATIONS

Local Chapter Director & Vice President, 1981-85
State Park Peace Officers Association of California

EMPLOYMENT HISTORY

Park Ranger, California Dept of Parks & Recreation, Yosemite, CA — 1975-present
RE Agent, Coldwell Banker Referral Network, Mariposa, CA — 1986-present
Teacher/Guide, Los Angeles Zoological Society, Los Angeles, CA — 1971-75

Escrow Assistant—Chronological Resume
Making a Lateral Change from Title Assistant

JOYCE DIANE APPLETON
PO Box 222
Santa Barbara, CA 93111
(805) 967-2222

Objective: An Escrow Assistant position

PROFILE:

- Success oriented with high energy and positive attitude.
- Highly organized with attention to detail and the ability to service several transactions simultaneously.
- Good written, oral and interpersonal communication skills.
- Work well under pressure with the ability to deal with all types of people with diplomacy and tact.
- Problem solver/team player with proven leadership qualities.
- Gained valuable personal and business contacts in the finance industry throughout the Santa Barbara Tri-County community.

EDUCATION: **Finance/Real Estate**, Santa Barbara City College, ongoing.

EXPERIENCE:

1989-91 **TITLE ASSISTANT**, Western Title Company, Santa Barbara, CA

- Prepare legal and vestings quickly and efficiently.
- Edit and process pre-liminary reports and title policies using IBM computer.
- Open 100 title orders on a monthly basis.
- Set up recordings and coordinate demands and closings.
- Compose, type and proofread correspondence, indemnity requests and endorsements on the word processor.
- Answer phones, expediting challenges customers present in a quick and highly professional manner.
- Familiar with computerized and lot book search procedures.

1984-89 **LOAN PROCESSOR**
Goleta Valley Teachers Federal Credit Union, Goleta, CA

- Maintain several millions of dollars in annual sales at this two person, busy branch office. Work closely with title companies, county offices and appraisers throughout the community.
- Originated over 150 real estate 2nd Trust Deed documentation annually, completing projects on time and under budget.
- Effectively counsel, evaluate and inform members of credit options. Verify members employment and credit histories.
- Key member in converting new computerized office systems. Set up computerized loans and entire Visa program.
- Actively involved in successful campaigns, promoting loans and credit card accounts to generate new business.

Escrow Officer—Functional Resume
Moving Up from Assistant Escrow Officer

JOY L. WEISSMAN
PO Box 4564
Santa Barbara, CA 93101
(805) 966-1111

Objective: **Escrow Officer**

PROFESSIONAL PROFILE

- Experienced supervisor with superior customer relations.
- Proven ability to run a smooth efficient operation.
- Resourceful; skilled in analyzing and solving problems.
- Highly organized, dedicated with a positive mental attitude.
- Excellent written, oral and interpersonal communication skills.
- Supervise employees with professionalism, diplomacy and tact.
- Gained valuable business and personal contacts throughout the Santa Barbara business community.

PROFESSIONAL EXPERIENCE

Supervision & Organization

- Trained/supervised 2-10 employees, maintaining excellent staff relations.
- Developed an entire loan department for this busy nationwide corporation.
- Key member in the conversion of a new computerized office system.
- Serviced several transactions simultaneously under highly pressured situations and demanding deadlines.
- Demonstrated professionalism, tact and diplomacy while working closely with staff and customers under highly pressured situations.

Public Relations & Promotions

- Maintained and promoted multi-million dollars in annual sales.
  - Actively involved in coordinating many successful marketing campaigns.
  - Designed effective brochures and flyers working closely with realtors, lenders, brokers and private investors to promote loans, property and sales in the Tri-county.
  - Developed strong phone skills, expediting challenges that customers present in a quick and creative manner.

EMPLOYMENT HISTORY

Assistant/Jr. Escrow Officer, Executive Title Co., Goleta, CA	1985-86
Escrow Secretary, Heron Developments, Goleta, CA	1981-83
File Clerk, Stanton Realtors, Goleta, CA	1980-81

Executive Assistant—Combination Resume

DENISE SANDERS
9821 Willis Road
Santa Barbara, CA 93103
(805) 682-0000

OBJECTIVE

A people-oriented Executive Assistant position.

OFFICE SKILLS

CPT Word Processor...IBM Computer/Word Perfect 5.0...Fax Telex...Calculator...Bank Reconciliations...Superior Phone and Customer Relation Skills...Office Manager...Excellent Spelling and Grammatical Skills. Typing Speed: 150+ wpm.

CURRENT PROFESSIONAL EXPERIENCE

ROB S. DERRICK, Attorney at Law, Santa Barbara, CA 1983-present
Office Manager/Administrative Assistant

- In charge of office management for a sole practitioner, demonstrating efficiency and confidentiality under pressure situations.
- Type, edit and finalize legal documents and correspondence on the CPT word processor with speed and accuracy.
- Maintain and reconcile bank accounts.
- Interface with clients, answer phones and order all office supplies.

EUROPEAN RESTAURANT, Inc., Santa Barbara, CA 1977-83
Executive Assistant

- Assisted the President, Financial Vice President and Vice President/ General Counsel at corporate headquarters of a restaurant chain.
- Typed financial statements and minutes of meetings of shareholders and board of directors.
- Worked daily with public, directors, investors and managers.
- Scheduled appointments, coordinated and prepared billing for travel arrangements including private limousine and airplane transportation.
- President was also owner of an NBA basketball team; interfaced with other NBA teams; typed player contracts and arena leases.
- Prepared reports and interfaced daily with bank computer.
- Hired, trained and supervised clerical staff.

PREVIOUS EMPLOYMENT HISTORY

Service Rep., Mortgage Investment Securities, Santa Barbara, CA 1977
Executive Assistant, Enrico Mexican Restaurants, SB, CA 1973-75
Executive Secretary, Sandy's Restaurants, Inc., SB, CA 1969-73

JILLIAN LUSTIG (805) 962-1111
305 Riverside Drive
Santa Barbara, CA 93103

Objective: An Executive Assistant position.

PROFILE:
- Success oriented and outgoing with a positive attitude.
- Strong sense of responsibility and self motivation.
- Good written, oral and bilingual communication skills.
- Problem solver/team player with proven leadership qualities.
- Highly organized with attention to detail.
- Work well under pressure, diplomatically and tactfully.

QUALIFICATION SUMMARY: Over 20 years experience working with high level executives in International Relations, Astronautics, Architecture Design, Agriculture, and Retail Furniture Industries. Emphasize strong cost effective organizational skills with excellent employee and client relations on an international level.

PROFESSIONAL EXPERIENCE:

1983-91 **EXECUTIVE ASSISTANT**
Danica House of Santa Barbara, Santa Barbara, CA
- Maintained international and domestic accounts for three major corporations at a busy one person office.
- In charge of office management, scheduling extensive foreign travel arrangements, meetings and operating FAX machine.
- Prepared multi computerized general ledgers.
- Composed and typed correspondence on the word processor.
- Worked closely with attorney's, accountants and diplomats.
- Represented Consulate at Scandinavian social/cultural events.
- Processed passports and Visa applications, language translations, legal matters and maritime business.

EMPLOYMENT HISTORY:

Executive Assistant, Continental Corp., Goleta, CA	1980-83
Administrative Assistant, Sanwa Bank, Santa Barbara, CA	1976-80
Receptionist, Berlington Corp., Goleta, CA	1975-76

Executive Sales/Marketing Assistant—Functional Resume
Recent College Graduate with Related School Activity Experience

MOLLY RACHEL KANTRELL
567 Gold Hill Road
Boulder, CO 80309
(303) 492-0736

OBJECTIVE

A growth-oriented Executive Sales/Marketing position

SKILLS

ORGANIZATION

- Delegated jobs to work committees, planned and managed all activities, and set standards for the smooth running of a sorority as the president.
- Composed press releases, assembled press kits and collected data for an advertising campaign for the Boulder Museum of Art.
- Implemented programs designed to promote scholastic achievement within college sorority, resulted in presentation of Scholastic Excellence Award by the Panhellenic Council.
- Scheduled and assisted in fundraising events, assembled press clippings and wrote press releases for the Heart Association as an intern.

COMMUNICATION

- Acted as a liaison between active and alumni members and promoted sorority activities both within the chapter and in various other settings through public speaking events as an executive sorority officer.
- Worked with customers assisting them with their cameras and photographs, and informed the public about upcoming sales and new merchandise as a camera shop sales associate.
- Implemented new Public Relations programs, working closely with the Boulder Museum of Art Public Relations/Development Dept.
- Operated communication systems between office volunteers and staff of the Heart Association as an intern.

EDUCATION

BA Degree, Communication Studies, 12-89
University of Colorado, Boulder, CO

HONORS AND EXPERIENCE

- **President/Vice-president**, Chi Omega Sorority, 1987-89
- **Outstanding Senior Award**, Chi Omega Sorority, June 1989
- **Sales Associate**, Cañada Camera Shop, Boulder, CO, 1983-87
- **Grants & Public Relations Intern**, Boulder Museum of Art, 1989
- **Public Relations Intern**, Boulder County Chapter, American Heart Association, 1988

Executive Secretary—Chronological Resume
Making a Lateral Change from Court Reporter

MARYANN S. MARSDEN
5678 Los Altos Drive
Goleta, CA 93117
(805) 966-2002

Objective: An Executive Secretary position

PROFILE:

- Success oriented and outgoing with a positive attitude
- Strong sense of responsibility and self motivation
- Good written, oral and interpersonal communication skills
- Problem solver, team player with ability to work independently
- Accurate and efficient in medical and legal terminology
- Strong organization skills with attention to detail

EDUCATION:

Certified Secretary - Santa Barbara Business College - 1971

Certified Shorthand Reporter - Canada College, Oxnard, CA.
Received California State License - 1980

OFFICE SKILLS:

Typing, transcription, computer skills, recordkeeping, excellent phone skills and machine shorthand. Typing Speed: 60 wpm; Machine Shorthand: 225 wpm

EXPERIENCE:

1980-present **COURT REPORTER**, Rudy Martinez & Associates, Santa Barbara

- Transcribe accurate word-for-word testimony in court and in depositions.
- Demonstrated tact and diplomacy, working closely with attorneys and clients under pressure situations.

1971-80 **SECRETARY**, Goleta Valley School District

- Assisted Santa Ynez Valley Union High School Student Body.
- Promoted and supervised student ticket sales for social and athletic events as well as fund raising campaigns.
- Developed phones skills efficiently and professionally, expediting challenges presented in a quick and creative manner.
- Maintained accurate record of accounts and cash management.
- Ordered textbooks for the entire school district.
- Purchased office supplies within budget requirements.
- Prepared financial reports, meeting tight deadline schedules.
- Gained valuable personal contacts with students and parents throughout the Santa Ynez Valley and Santa Barbara area.

Exotic Animal Trainer—Chronological Resume

SUSAN A. COX
5112 Parkridge Lane
Thousand Oaks, CA 90266
(818) 342-9099

OBJECTIVE: A career expanding my Human Relations skills, working with Marine Mammals and other Exotics.

PROFESSIONAL PROFILE:

- Highly organized, dedicated with a positive attitude.
- Excellent oral and written communication skills.
- Ability to cultivate relationships with people of various professional and personal backgrounds.
- Speak with poise and confidence in front of groups of people.
- Served as guest speaker on local TV station representing Exotic Animal Program and guest lecturer for community organizations.
- Participated in televised broadcasts and photography layouts for various media events.

EDUCATION:

- BA Degree, Behavioral Psychology, in-progress
  California State College, Northridge, CA
- Designated Subject Credential, 1988
  Cal Lutheran, Thousand Oaks, CA
- AS Degree, Exotic Animal Training & Mgmt, 1987
  Moorpark College, Moorpark, CA
- Psychology/Business Administration, 1986
  Ventura Community College, Ventura, CA
- Cert. of Achievement, Exotic Animal Care & Handling
  Moorpark College, Moorpark, CA, 1985

EXOTIC ANIMAL EXPERIENCE:

1985-present EXOTIC ANIMAL TRAINING & MGMT PROGRAM, Moorpark College
Community Education Coordinator/Instructor
Provide diet planning and implementation, veterinary care and first aid for 150 species of birds, mammals and reptiles. Supervise and manage students in wildlife care and maintenance. Instruct and assist students with training and upkeep of behaviors on marine and terrestrial exotics and domestics. Update animal inventory including medical records and Int'l Species Inventory System. Prepare reports, permits and license requests. Guide public relation tours and correspond with the media, public and

- More -

EXOTIC ANIMAL EXPERIENCE: (Continued)

private organizations. Serve as instructor for Animal Training and Advanced Education and Entertainment in Animal Parks. Organize and execute educational animal presentations for public and private organizations. Programmer and MC for public educational services. Coordinate and implement animal assisted therapy programs for the mentally and physically handicapped. Represent staff at conferences, seminars, lectures and workshops. Serve as office assistant/liaison for director of EATM Program.

June 1988 SAN DIEGO ZOO'S WEGEFORTH BOWL
Trained with head trainer of seals and sea lions.

May 1988 DOLPHIN QUEST, The Big Is., Hawaii
Assisted with capture of wild dolphins in the Florida Panhandle. Included transport, medical work-ups, initial care and training.

1985-86 MARINELAND OF THE PACIFIC, Rancho Palos Verdes, CA
Volunteer Assistant
Assisted with basic care and medical work-ups. Observed techniques of trainers and veterinarians working with seals, sea lions, walruses, dolphins, penguins and sea birds.

1983-85 EXOTIC ANIMAL TRAINING & MGMT PROGRAM, Moorpark, CA
Zookeeper
Responsible for all aspects of exotic and domestic animal care including diet preparation/distribution, record keeping, daily sanitation, cage construction and repair. Served as apprentice Zookeeper at the Santa Barbara and Los Angeles Zoos. Performed behavioral research studies of mammals and birds. Provided infant care of various exotic and domestic mammals and birds.

Animal Trainer
Raised and trained Bengal Tigers and Rhesus Macaques, Psittacines and other species of carnivores, herbivores and primates. Participated in educational animal presentations for public and private organizations with above animals and birds.

AFFILIATIONS CERTIFICATIONS:

Member of:
American Association of Zoological Parks and Aquariums (AAZPA)
Int'l Marine Animal Trainers Association, (IMATA)
Int'l Zoo Educators, (IZE)
American Association of Zookeepers, (AAZK)
Greater Los Angeles Zoo Association, (GLAZA)
San Diego Zoological Society
National Marine Educators Association, (NMEA)

High Fashion Designer—Chronological Resume

MARTIN PAUL JUSTIN
5920 St. Augustine Court
New York, NY 10023
(212) 921-0000

CAREER OBJECTIVE: To design men's and women's high fashion, ready to wear and sports apparel.

EDUCATION:

Graduate, Chambre Syndicale de la Haute Couture Parisienne
top 10-percent of graduating class - 1987-90
Paris, France

Bachelor of Arts in Fashion Design - 1986
Minor: Fashion Merchandising
Brigham Young University

Awards:
- Carol Crow Academic Scholarship - 1983-86
- May Billings Talent Award - 1985
- 1st Place, I.S.C. Design Competition - 1985

SKILLS:
- Couture techniques
- Draping and pattern drafting
- Textile design
- Fashion illustration
- Organizing fashion shows
- Marketing/sales
- Computer programming - CAD
- Fluent Spanish and French; semi-fluent in Italian

WORK EXPERIENCE:

FIRENZE
Designer/Pattern Maker - 1988-present
Design, illustration, first through production patterns; project supervisor.

CHRISTIAN LaCROIX DESIGN HOUSE
Internship - Winter 1988
Draped and constructed original LaCroix designs.

NANETTE OF NEW YORK
Retail Sales - 1986
Sold high fashion women's apparel.

DIANA SUZANNE PARKER
56 West End Avenue
New York, NY 01002
(212) 324-0001

JOB OBJECTIVE

Features Reporter for a newspaper that values tenacity, dependability and creativity.

PROFESSIONAL EXPERIENCE

MANHATTAN DAILY NEWS, New York, NY
Lifestyles Writer, 1986-present
General features include: current events, personality profiles, business and tourism. Entertainment articles range from film, theater and book reviews to celebrity interviews, previews and humor.

AMERICAN FILM, Hollywood, CA
Freelance Writer, Summer 1985
Wrote film and television articles. *American Film* is a national magazine of the film and television arts, published by The American Film Institute. Several articles were translated and re-published in Jaioliu, a film magazine from the People's Republic of China.

DAILY NEWS RECORD, Harrisburg, VA
Features Writer, 1980-84
Assigned to features and lifestyles. The *Daily News Record* is an AM daily with a circulation of 31,000.

GOOD TIMES, Santa Cruz, CA
Contributor/Columnist, 1975-80
Contributed book and film reviews, social commentary and general features. Wrote "Off the Cuff," a question and answer column covering any topic. *Good Times*, is a Santa Cruz bi-weekly entertainment magazine with a circulation of about 18,000.

SANTA BARBARA MAGAZINE
Contributor, 1973-75
Wrote features, personality profiles and the column, "Focus," a look at entrepreneurs and new businesses. A four-color city magazine with a circulation of 10,000.

EDUCATION

MA Degree, Journalism, University of California, Berkley, CA, 1980
BA Degree, English, University of California, Santa Barbara, CA, 1976

Finance Internship—Functional Resume
College Student, Business Economics Major

LOUISE S. GRANDY

6111 Frio, Goleta, CA 93117 (805) 888-4040

Objective: An Internship in Business and Finance.

PROFESSIONAL PROFILE

- Financed education with experience in sales, cash management and customer relations.
- Highly organized, enthusiastic with a positive attitude.
- Outstanding ability to communicate with all types of people.
- Member of Community Affairs; part of the Big Sister program.
- Secretary/Treasurer for the UCLA English Club.

PROFESSIONAL EXPERIENCE

Organization/Cash Management

- Set up/planned meeting agendas and prepared minutes for school activities.
- Balanced daily cash deposits with speed and efficiency for the college bookstore, grocery store and stationary retail store chain.
- Maintained opening and closing procedures, inventory/quality control, shipping/receiving, purchasing, pricing, returns and credits.

Sales Ability & Promotions

- Successfully sold Hallmark products and helped customers make satisfactory buying decisions at a busy retail store.
- Sold books and accessories at the college bookstore.
- Set up in-house displays that instantly boosted sales.

Customer & Employee Relations

- Developed a personal customer base while waiting tables at a busy family style restaurant.
  - Required ability to work well under pressure situations quickly and efficiently.
- Demonstrated strong phone skills, expediting challenges customers presented in a professional and concerned manner.
- Trained and supervised 6 employees, maintaining excellent staff relations.

EDUCATION

BA Degree, Business Economics, Spring 1989
University of California, Los Angeles

EMPLOYMENT HISTORY

Waitress/Cashier, Baker's Square Restaurant, LA, CA — 1987-present
Cashier/Sales, University of California Bookstore, LA, CA — 1986-87
Teacher's Aide, Los Angeles School District, LA, CA — Summer 1987

Finance Internship—Functional Resume
Economics Major with Related School Project Experience

TERRY RALPH ALEXIS

Current Address
666 College Place
Westwood Village, CA 90024
(213) 968-1538

Permanent Address
888 Circle Drive
Costa Mesa, CA 92626
(714) 555-1111

Objective: A summer Internship in the Finance Industry.

PROFESSIONAL PROFILE

- Gained valuable experience in financial analysis, sales and management while attending college to earn degree.
- Developed strong computerized research & problem solving skills.
- Dependable, conscientious and detail oriented.
- Member of the Investment Club at UCLA.

EDUCATION

BA Degree, Economics, Emphasis: Finance
University of California, Los Angeles, CA
Graduation· Spring 1989

RELATED EXPERIENCE

Related Courses
Gained valuable knowledge in Corporate Finance, Financial Accounting, Calculus, Micro/Macro Economic Theory, statistics, and Econometrics.

Research & Analysis Projects
- Assist professor/investment advisor with college projects.
  - Conduct in-depth computerized research to evaluate investment portfolios.
  - Research market conditions affecting current & future financial strategies.
- Learned to build financial model development and to follow the market closely using financial publications.
- Gained vital computer skills using the IBM PC with Lotus 1-2-3 software.

Management & Administration
- Developed marketing strategies for effective newspaper & media advertising.
- Train and supervise a staff of 20 employees, displaying strong leadership skills while maintaining a highly professional attitude.
- Successfully maintained inventory control, shipping and receiving demonstrated the ability to work well under pressure with attention to detail.

EMPLOYMENT HISTORY

Waiter, The Harbor Yacht Club, Seattle, WA — Summer 1987
Manager, Big Sam's Restaurant, Los Angeles, CA — Summer 1986

Finance Manager, International—Chronological Resume
Moving Up from Foreign Relations, Financial Adviser

DAVID ALAIN BRODY
67716 Loma Linda Road
Santa Barbara, CA 93103
(805) 569-0003

Objective: International Financial Management

PROFILE:

- Two years working experience in banking and int'l business.
- Business Translator for Veneconomia, a business journal;
- Computer skills: Lotus 1-2-3, dBase III and Word Perfect.
- Tri-lingual: Highly proficient in Spanish and French.

EDUCATION:

Master of International Management
American Graduate School, 1988
Thunderbird Campus, Glendale, AZ

Bachelor of Arts, Philosophy, 1983
University of California, Santa Barbara

EXPERIENCE:

1988-89 — **FINANCIAL ADVISOR**, Petroltubos, SA, Caracas, Venezuela

- Translated technical documents.
- Calculated business market value; projected/analyzed cash flow.
- Designed a program to automatically calculate sale prices.
- Prepared briefs analyzing the different areas of the company.
- Designed programs to organize depreciation and imports.

Summer-1988 — **MERCHANT BANKING INTERN**, Banque de Groof, Brussels, Belgium

- Translated, economic, and legal documents.
- Evaluated performance on pension fund management.
- Researched and wrote Venture Capital report.
- Calculated the return on funds managed according to the dividend discount model.

Spring-1988 — **INT'L TRADE INTERN**, Arizona Dept of Commerce, Phoenix, AZ

- Wrote a speech for an Arizona business conference on the "International Trade, The Falling Dollar and Third World Debt."
- Wrote a speech for Asian-American conference on "The Role of Asian-Americans in United States-Asia Trade."
- Designed economic/political country briefs.

1983-84 — **CORPORATE ENGLISH TEACHER**
Instituto de Loesher, Caracas, Venezuela

- Taught English lessons to corporate groups.

DANA SIGLER
225 Woodridge Road
Montecito, CA 93108
(805) 685-4231

FINANCIAL ACCOUNT EXECUTIVE

PROFESSIONAL OBJECTIVE: Seeking a progressive company with innovative products, salary and commission with unlimited earning potential.

PROFESSIONAL PROFILE: Success oriented with high energy and a positive attitude. outstanding talent for assessing client's needs...communicate effectively with all levels of management in a highly professional and diplomatic manner...problem solver and team player with ability to work independently...enthusiastic, creative and flexible.

QUALIFICATION SUMMARY: Six solid years professional experience of proven sales ability and management as "Top Producer" in the Sales Industry. Emphasize strong sales techniques, exceptional presentation and closing skills, and effective customer relations, resulting in production and profitability in this highly competitive market.

SALES EXPERIENCE WITH PROVEN TRACK RECORD:

1989-present **ACCOUNT EXECUTIVE**
Call America Business Inc, Santa Barbara, CA. Sell a wide range of long distance services to commercial accounts in Santa Barbara. Demonstrate effective cold calling, appointment setting and follow up. Deliver dynamic product presentations and write effective proposals. Identify clients' needs, problems and solutions through long distance analysis. Became #1 sales rep. in the first year through assertive sales ability, thorough product knowledge and consistent follow up.

1987-89 **COMMODITY BROKER (AP)**
West Coast Commodities Corporation, Santa Barbara, CA. Directly involved in buying and selling commodities, specializing in options. Maintain existing equity and client contact. Emphasis on telemarketing sales to raise equity for existing book. Develop and instruct sales training programs monitoring motivational meetings for sales staff.

Financial Analyst—Combination Resume
Recent College Graduate with Related Work Experience

ALAN JAY RIDER
PO Box 1123
Goleta, CA 93117
(805) 964-3333

OBJECTIVE
A Financial Analyst position

EDUCATION
BA Degree, Business Economics, 1991
University of California, Santa Barbara

Related Courses: Organization of Industry, Financial Accounting, Managerial Economics, Corporate Finance, Monetary Economics, Micro/Macroeconomics, Environmental Economics.

RELATED EXPERIENCE
SANTA BARBARA FEDERAL S&L, Santa Barbara, CA 1988-present

Accounting Intern (1990-present)
- Developed custom spreadsheet programs using Lotus 1-2-3 for finance and analysis of 100 branch offices in California.
- Analyze and research daily accrued interest reports for demand deposit accounts.
- Prepare and organize various statements for accounting staff.
- Assist accountants with outages and reconciliation projects.

Cash Reserve Specialist(1988-89)
- Reviewed customer applications and solved potential problems for 100 California branch offices.
- Prepared computerized payments to customer's cash reserve accounts.
- Answered customer account inquiries quickly and efficiently.
- Assisted branch personnel with proper cash reserve procedures.

PREVIOUS EMPLOYMENT HISTORY
Waiter, Marie Callenders, Santa Barbara, CA 1990-present
Systems Operator, Tri-Counties Regional Ctr, Santa Barbara, CA 1987-88
Document Control, Capello & Foley Law Firm, Santa Barbara, CA 1986-87

Financial Analyst, International—Functional Resume

RICHARD D. DAVIS
PO Box 123
Los Angeles, CA 90067
(213) 987-1234

Objective: A Financial Analyst position with an International Lender

PROFESSIONAL EXPERIENCE

Financial Management

- Founded with two other members, a software company which developed a system for institutions trading foreign exchange and related instruments.
  - Gathered information and made strategic decisions concerning target markets, advertising and company direction.
  - Achieved sales of $400K in the company's initial year.
  - Designed and implemented enhancements for proprietary system, working closely with traders and systems personnel.
  - Wrote promotional literature and client training manual.
  - Set up company accounting books and procedures.
- Managed the credit department of a corporate bank branch in Spain.
  - Analyzed loan proposals, and recommended decisions for approval.
  - Prepared accounting functions and monitored existing loan portfolio.
- Supervised a staff of 15 employees for a bank branch in Spain.
  - Met target levels resulting in profits of $100K per month.

Research Analysis & Evaluation

- Participated in the development of a financial analysis package to be used throughout the bank worldwide.
  - One of two junior officers chosen for the bank's internal consulting cell.
- Created a highly sophisticated system for tracking prospective clients.
- Selected to revise countrywide marketing strategies throughout Spain, working directly with the General Manager.
- Received "A" rating for performance in the academic bank training program.

EDUCATION

MBA Candidate, Emphasis: Finance & Int'l Business
The Anderson School of Management at UCLA

BS Degree, Economics, Emphasis: Finance May 1984
The Wharton School of the University of Pennsylvania

EMPLOYMENT HISTORY

Manager/Lending Officer, Bank of Commerce Espanola, Spain 1986-88
Junior Officer, Bank of Commerce International, London, England 1985-86
Management Trainee, Bank of Commerce International, New York, NY 1984-85
Co-Founder, Bundy Software, Inc, Los Angeles, CA 1980-84

BART A. ADLER

1020 Strawberry Road
Atlanta, GA 30306
(404) 872-1110

Objective: Financial Management Accounting

QUALIFICATIONS

Financial Management ..Financial Planning and Analysis ..Budget Analysis
Operation's Management ..PC Windows Applications

EMPLOYMENT HISTORY

Financial Management Accountant, Grant Thornton,, Atlanta, GA — 1989-present
Experienced Accountant, Arthur Andersen & Co., Atlanta, GA — 1987-89

Financial Management Accounting

- Analyzed and implemented successful financial business operations for Fortune 500 corporations and small businesses of Big 6 public accounting firms throughout the Southeast.

- Developed a Lotus based real estate financial reporting model for a client of a Big 6 accounting firm that improved reporting time and reduced the reporting process by over 40 percent.
  - Increased revenues by over $200K when model was sold to offices nationwide.

- Improved plant operations for a Fortune 500 manufacturing company by redesigning and coordinating processing cycles and product flow enhancing efficiency and space utilization.

- Conducted management consulting that improved procurement processing by implementing restructured forms, warehouse operations and planning inventory control.

EDUCATION

MBA, International Business, 1995
Emory University, Atlanta, GA

BS Degree: Accounting, 1987
University of Florida
Passed CPA Exam: 1988

PROFESSIONAL TRAINING

Fraud Auditing ..Management Internal Control Structure ..Financial Reporting
Physical Inventory Controls ..Implementing FASB's ..Capital Budgeting and Financing

JOHN C. BROOKS
9876 Rustic Road
Santa Barbara, CA 93110
(805) 569-1234

Objective: A Financial Management position.

PROFESSIONAL EXPERIENCE

Treasury Operations

- Monitored the accounting of short-term investment portfolios;
  - clarified corporate objectives and long term goals;
  - assessed financial resources and tolerance for risk.
- Prepared and filed SEC related reports.
  - annual reports...10K's...shareholder reports...10Q's.
- Established pension plans for businesses nationwide.

Management & Administration

- Supervised staff to insure accuracy of the pricing, billing and inventory control systems for a Fortune 500 corporation.
- Key member in the conversion and update of a more efficient computerized inventory and distribution system.
- Established/approved credit for product and service oriented corporations.
- Trained, supervised and reviewed financial operations personnel.

Investor Relations/Communications

- Successfully fulfill investor relations function;
  - key source of daily information for investors and financial analysts;
  - liaison between treasury department, transfer agents and trustees.
- Delivered effective presentations on financial disclosure issues to in-house functional managers, in conjunction with upcoming press releases.

EDUCATION

BS Degree Finance, - 1980
Pennsylvania State University

EMPLOYMENT HISTORY

Financial Accounts Manager, TMC Corporation, Santa Barbara, CA 1988-present
Treasury Operations Analyst, ABC Corporation, Los Angeles, CA 1983-88
Regional Credit Manager, Northern Inc, Long Beach, CA 1980-83

Financial Marketing Representative—Chronological Resume
Making a Lateral Change from Retail Sales Associate

JULIE MARIE BRIGNELL
5900 Mountain View Road
Seattle, WA 10602
(313) 560-9321

Objective: A Marketing position in the Banking Industry

PROFILE:

* 7 years experience in sales, management and customer relations.
* Highly organized, dedicated with a positive attitude.
* Thrive on working in a challenging environment.
* Excellent written, oral and interpersonal communication skills.
* Problem solver/team player with proven leadership qualities.
* Supervise employees in a professional and tactful manner.

EDUCATION:

BA Degree, Communication Studies, 1987
Western Washington University, Bellingham, WA

OFFICE SKILLS: Light typing...ten key by touch...cash register...daily banking deposits...billing...invoicing...purchasing...quality/inventory control...opening/closing procedures...shipping/receiving...data entry...excellent phone, customer & employee relation skills.

EXPERIENCE:

1987-present

SWEPT AWAY, Seattle, WA
Store Manager/Sales Associate

* Manage entire retail operation at this busy fashion boutique.
* Balance daily cash receipts and handle bank deposits.
* Set up window and in-house displays that boosted sales.
* Developed a large personal customer base and maintain a preferred customer list that includes customer follow up.
* Maintain opening/closing procedures, shipping/receiving, inventory/quality control, purchasing, pricing, returns and credits.
* Work closely with mfg. representatives to buy merchandise.
* Hire, train, supervise and schedule employees.

1982-87

ARABESQUE, Bellingham, WA
Sales Associate

* Sold clothing and accessories at this fashion boutique on a part-time basis while earning Associate of Arts degree.
* Assisted customers to help them make satisfactory buying decisions while developing a large personal customer base.
* Developed accuracy and speed balancing daily cash transactions.
* Expedited challenges customers presented in a professional manner.

HERBERT T. CRAFTS
8872 Steamboat Lane
Boulder, CO 80205
(303) 492-0009

OBJECTIVE

A Financial Sales/Marketing Management position

PROFESSIONAL EXPERIENCE

Sales/Management Experience

- Developed a unique retirement planning concept for employees of nonprofit organizations, corporations and self-employed individuals.
  - Identified, selected, trained and supported registered sales representatives.
  - Delivered weekly motivational sales and educational staff meetings.
  - Supported regional, divisional and registered representatives in the field.
- Achieved top 3% of companies $4 billion in assets through excellent sales ability, thorough product knowledge and superior customer service.

Financial Training Support

- Pioneered expansion for a major Wall Street firm from 43 to 180 sales offices nationwide.
- Identified, selected and educated mid-level and senior-level executives to provide retirement planning for employees of nonprofit organizations.
- Developed highly successful marketing strategies and workshops for promotions and sales.
  - Established modular training for 500 Registered Benefit Specialists.
  - Conducted motivational and education workshops.
  - Identified prospective clients; trained personnel to enroll clients.
  - Supervised and monitored programs on location nationwide.

EDUCATION

BBA, University of New York
Certified Financial Planner, 1974

PROFESSIONAL AFFILIATIONS

Board of Directors:
International Association. for Financial Planning
Certified Financial Planning Program, University of New York
Chamber of Commerce, Denver, CO
Sales & Marketing Executive Club, Denver, CO
President/Chairman, IAFP, Denver, CO

EMPLOYMENT HISTORY

Financial Advisor, Investors Management Corp, Denver, CO	1986-present
Sales Manager, The Investors Corporation, NY, NY	1972-86

Flight Instructor, Chief—Chronological Resume

LARRY A. GORDON
888 Arizona Street
Santa Barbara, CA 93103
(805) 682-1234

Objective: Airline Flight Instructor

PROFESSIONAL EXPERIENCE:

1988-91 **CHIEF PILOT/MANAGER OF MECHANICS**, Flight Services, Austin, TX. Built the foundation for this FAA approved air charter company. Established policy and procedure manuals and supervised maintenance and scheduling flights for six companies. Decision maker and problem solver working with FAA inspectors, corporate presidents and government officials, maintaining excellent client relations. Responsible for safe operation of equipment valued at $100K-2.5M.

- Researched and found several inconsistencies in the quality of an airplane newly purchased by the company. Responded with extreme tact and diplomacy to successfully resolve the situation and maintain effective client relations.

1985-88 **MANAGER/CHIEF FLIGHT INSTRUCTOR**, ACC Aerial Service, Austin, TX. Analyzed problem areas of company policy and procedures and successfully developed programs to improve the quality of this FAA approved school within first two months of employment. Maintained purchasing, supplies and recordkeeping to meet FAA standards.

- Increased the number of graduate students by 250%. All student pilots passed the FAA flight test on their first attempt, earning me the FAA Gold Seal designation.

1980-85 **MECHANIC/CORPORATE PILOT**, Worked for several aviation companies based in Midland, TX. Diplomatically worked closely with clients in the corporate industry. Successfully maintained aircraft maintenance. Pilot position involved constantly being 2-3-4 steps ahead of the present, overcoming problems in flight through sound, logical and analytical thinking.

1976-80 **CUSTOMER SERVICE/TECHNICAL FIELD REP.**, Aerostar Corp., Santa Maria, CA. Managed and taught entire program to corporate president pilots and mechanics. Trained pilots and mechanics for dealerships, on location, nationwide. Decision maker, problem solver and successful troubleshooter, working with aircraft owners and mechanics throughout the USA.

- Improved aircraft design; all changes suggested, was accepted by the aircraft manufacturer.

EDUCATION: AA Degree - Aviation Maintenance Technology, Northrop University
Airframe & Powerplant Mechanic's Program - Northrop University

General Contractor—Client/Project Resume

DAVID H. GLASSER
123 Rose Avenue
Santa Barbara, CA 93105
(805) 687-9908

Objective: General Contractor

PROFESSIONAL PROFILE

- 15 years experience with thorough knowledge and success in all phases of custom construction/project management.
- Outstanding ability to communicate with subcontractors.
- Gained valuable business and personal contacts in Santa Barbara through excellent client relations, hard work and word-of-mouth.
- Maintained a **100% accident free safety record.**

CLIENTS/PROJECTS

Sampson Estate - Performed extensive remodeling of finished carpentry work for the main house of a Spanish style Montecito estate.

Hoffman Estate - Performed extensive remodeling from rough to finished carpentry work for the main house and added a guest house on a Montecito estate. Developed excellent relationship with clients.

The Country Club - Carried out on-site supervision of carpenters and laborers. Performed extensive remodeling of the club house and kitchen. Built new office, tennis locker rooms and maintenance facility.

Brian Lewis Ranch - Supervised carpenters and laborers. Built a Spanish style 5000 square foot main house on a 300 acre ranch in Santa Barbara from initial to final phase.

Raymond Simon Ranch - Remodeled the kitchen, art studio and replaced existing redwood deck for an early 1900 ranch house built on 55 acres in Carpinteria. In charge of employee supervision, maintaining excellent relations among staff and clients.

Lana Parker Estate - Performed extensive remodeling of the main house of a Spanish style estate in Hope Ranch.

Dr. Rockland Beachhouse - Remodeled 46 windows, doors and patio lattice work on a three-story, 8000 square foot beachhouse in Montecito. Served as project manager for entire project, maintaining superior relations with staff and clients.

EMPLOYMENT HISTORY

Project Manager/Foreman, EM Clark & Sons, Inc, Santa Barbara, CA 1974-present

Geologist—Functional Resume
Recent College Graduate with School Project Experience

BERNIE ARTHUR MATTHEWS
118 Franciso Avenue
Ventura, CA 93003
(805) 966-7281

Objective: Entry level Professional Geologist position

EDUCATION:

BS Degree, Geological Sciences
University of California, Los Angeles
Graduation: June 1991

Geoscience Technology, Certified: 1987
Los Angeles City College, CA
Petroleum Geology emphasis

AS, Geological Sciences
Los Angeles City College, CA
Graduation: June 1986

HONORS:

- Top of class; six week summer field course, UCLA 1988
- Outstanding Geoscience Technology Major, LACC, 1986
- Selected for Honors Seminar, The Colorado Plateau, LACC, 1985

GEOLOGY SKILLS:

Petroleum geology, well logging, microfossil collection and analysis...electric log analysis, geophysics, methods in gravity, magnetics, resistivity, seismics, geologic illustration, geochemistry, ore mineralogy, structural geology.

Gained valuable field knowledge and experience. Mapped Paleozoic sedimentary, volcaniclastic rocks in Inyo and Alpine County and local formations of the Santa Ynez Mountains in Santa Barbara County, California. Mapped in Cuyama Badlands, Kern County, California.

Experienced on the IBM and Macintosh computer systems.

EMPLOYMENT HISTORY:

Carpenter, Blakely Construction, Goleta, CA	1987-present
Carpenter, Glen Construction, Goleta, CA	1983-87
Carpenter, McIntosh Construction, Mammoth Lakes, CA	1980-83

Graphic Artist Internship—Chronological Resume
College Student with Related Work Experience

ROBERT JASON STARKEY
4809 Riverview Road
Boulder CO 80303
(303) 449-4802

Objective: A Graphic Arts Internship position

EDUCATION:

BA Degree, Art Studio, 1991
University of Colorado at Boulder

Related Classes
Introduction to Graphic Design...
Drawing...Lithography...Painting

RELATED EXPERIENCE:

1989-present

CUSTOMER SERVICE/COPY PRODUCTION/GRAPHIC DESIGNER
Alternative Copy Shop, Boulder, CO

- Designed and illustrated two promotional posters.
- Produce and assemble a variety of projects for clients under tight deadlines.
- Operate Canon Laser Copier as graphics tools.
- Gained thorough knowledge of paste-up techniques with ability to work quickly and efficiently.
- Maintain a positive attitude working on multiple assignments under pressure.

1987-89

GRAPHIC PRODUCTION/ILLUSTRATOR
Daily Stars & Stripes, UC Boulder

- Worked with production team of a daily newspaper.
- Demonstrated effective teamwork with precision and versatility on a variety of graphics equipment.
- Gained knowledge of pica and columnar measuring systems, point sizes and type faces.
- Ability to read design layout.
- Illustrated line drawings to accompany articles.

Other Positions Held: Retail sales for a record store, camp counselor, food service.

KENNETH J. PASSMAN
4444 Westerly Road
Goleta, CA 93117
(805) 964-1111

Objective: Hospital Administrator

PROFESSIONAL PROFILE

- Senior level executive with successful leadership pattern since 1960.
- Achievements in retirement campus administration, management and operations; corporate and business development.
- Effective fiscal operations and fund development, staff and leadership development.
- Major marketing objectives achieved for national and local programs.

PROFESSIONAL EXPERIENCE

Strategic Planning

- Campus Administrator during $15M rebuilding program for 16-acre campus from 1982-90.
- Initiated the development of retirement facility - Modesto, CA, 1967-68
- Assisted in acquisition of major hospital for Eskaton.
- Established long range plans for Samarkand-Annual Updates.
- Developed three regional offices for Corporate Planning Association.

Operations

- Eight consecutive years of meeting corporate fiscal objectives while completing rebuilding program 1982-90. Operations budget is $6.5 million 1990.
- Strong resident relations contributing to a positive program, major gifts and resident satisfaction.
- Received awards five consecutive years for reducing Workmen's Compensation claims resulting in $30-40K a year in savings.
- Established excellent food service program, environmental services and marketing program.
- Established operational policies and procedures for campus - each department, performance standards for each employee position.
- President, Director and CEO of two proprietary operations:
  Corporate Planning Associates and Mastercarve Products, Inc.
- President and CEO for Christian Churches of Northern California-Nevada; Associate Executive for Christian Churches of Oklahoma.

Development Program

- Directed capital campaigns for local and regional church $300K to $2.5M.
- Board of Directors for Board of Finance of Christian Church (National).
- Capital campaign Director - Eskaton American River Hospital.
- Established Samarkand Long Range Development Program.
- Expanded Good Neighbor and Free Care Endowment Funds by $500K at Samarkand.

- More -

PROFESSIONAL EXPERIENCE (Continued)

Marketing Program

- Directed marketing program for Eskaton Corporation Data Processing, Facility Acquisition, Human Resource Services and Waste Management Systems...Local - Statewide - Nationally.
- Developed successful marketing program for Samarkand Retirement Campus leading to consistant occupancy level.

EDUCATION

Masters, Business Administration
Golden Gate University, Sacramento, California
1982-in progress

Masters Phillips University, Enid, Oklahoma
Graduate Seminary, 1958

Bachelor's Degree, Chapman College
Orange, California, 1954

AFFILIATIONS

Board of Directors: (Partial)
California Association of Homes for the Aging
Pacific School of Religion - Berkeley
Chapman College - Orange
Corporate Planning Associates, Inc.
Rotary Club, Santa Barbara
Transition House - Santa Barbara
Love Yourself Foundation - Santa Barbara
Visiting Nurses Association - Modesto
YMCA - Modesto
Oklahoma Association of Christian Churches

EMPLOYMENT HISTORY

Campus Administrator, Samarkand of Santa Barbara, CA 1982-90
Administrator, Marketing Director, Eskaton Hospital, Sacramento, CA 1976-82
CEO Corporate & Business Development, Sacramento, CA 1972-76
Director of Development and Community Relations
Eskaton, Sacramento, CA 1970-72

Hotel Manager Trainee—Functional Resume
Making a Lateral Change from Restaurant/Nightclub Manager

LESLIE E. SUMMERLAND
23679 A Street
Santa Barbara, CA 93103
(805) 682-6423

Objective: A Hotel Management Trainee position

PROFESSIONAL PROFILE

- Experienced in management, promotions and sales with superior customer relations in the restaurant/nightclub industry.
- Rapidly analyze/recognize company problems and solutions.
- Successfully market products, services and concepts.
- Extensive traveler; Europe, Asia, Middle East, Canada, USA.
- Completed extensive self-esteem seminars; American Airlines Travel Agency School.

PROFESSIONAL EXPERIENCE

Management & Organization

- Established two successful corporations.
  - Developed the conceptual idea for an entire restaurant and nightclub.
  designed menus...uniforms...kitchen...interior layout...architecture
- Conducted motivational meetings for all staff members.
- Created effective policy and procedures employee training manuals.
- Developed computerized systems for purchasing and cost/inventory control.
- Served as source of information concerning needs of all departments.
- Monitored labor cost factors and financial analysis for 5-year P/L margin.
- Hired, trained and supervised 40-60 employees.

Promotions & Sales

- Developed successful marketing campaigns to promote current and future events through radio, TV and newspaper advertising on a daily basis.
- Set up dozens of displays capturing excitement and promoting sales.
- Nightclub ranked #1 in Santa Barbara by The Santa Barbara Independent, a popular Santa Barbara entertainment newspaper.
- Co-founder for the Kenny Loggins Toys for Tots Toy Train Express, a successful fundraising campaign.

EDUCATION

BA Degree Political Science, 1985
University of California, Santa Barbara, CA

EMPLOYMENT HISTORY

General Manager, Jazz Pazzazz Dance Co, Santa Barbara, CA 1982-88
Sales Manager, Sandy Inc, Santa Barbara, CA 1974-82

SHARON L. LEBOW
PO Box 1234
Del Mar, CA 92014
(619) 481-1111

Objective: Hotel and Restaurant Management Instructor

PROFESSIONAL EXPERIENCE

Management & Administration

- In charge of daily operations of a busy nine-room bed and breakfast house. reservations...menu planning...food preparation...housekeeping...ground maintenance...payroll...accounts receivable...accounts payable.
- Purchased foods and supervised the high school kitchen facility that prepared all meals for elementary, junior/high schools and staff dining room.
- Planned and ordered 450 meals for a kitchen that served three meals a day, five days a week to children and teachers bused out of town.
- Catered 90-120 daily meals to a private program for the elderly.
- Hired, trained and supervised as many as 2-35 employees on a daily basis.

Organizational Skills

- Developed the concept of a successful restaurant serving 200-300 meals daily.
- Coordinated all planned events and membership sales for a racquet club.

Training & Administration

- Set up a mini-restaurant and restaurant training program for 70 students per semester for the Santa Barbara County School District.
  - Taught students how to plan menus and prepare food selections.
  - Maintained purchasing and processed accounting functions for facilities that served the faculty and staff for the entire school district.
- Catered special events on-site and on-location.
- Trained in all areas of dining room service i.e., tableside and wine service.

EDUCATION

California Teaching Credential, California State Poly University, SLO

EMPLOYMENT HISTORY

General Manager, Carriage House Bed & Breakfast, San Diego, CA 1988-present
Food Service Instructor, San Diego County School District 1986-88
Director/Instructor, San Diego County School District 1978-88
Food Service Manager, Orange County Unified School District 1975-78
Office Manager/Waitress, Hamburger Hamlet Restaurants, LA, CA 1972-75
Head Waitress, 57th Street Cafe & Deli, Santa Monica, CA 1969-72

Hotel and Restaurant Manager—Functional Resume

KRISTEN B. HARDY
3204 Kova Street
Santa Barbara, CA 93103
(805) 569-2201

Objective: A Management position in the Hospitality Field.

PROFESSIONAL EXPERIENCE

Hotel Management

- Started at the opening of a 5-star, 365 room, 24-acre oceanside resort hotel.
- Served as source of information concerning needs of the Activities Dept.
  - Coordinated all promotional events and hotel activities.
  - Established Aqua/Jazzercise activities offered to public & hotel guests.
  - Organized group conventions in-house and on-location for 10-500 people.
  - Initiated cost effective poolside barbecues for hotel members.
- Conducted motivational staff meetings on a weekly basis.
- Hired, trained, supervised 20 employees, maintaining a positive attitude under highly stressful situations.

Restaurant Management

- In charge of all operations for a busy jazz club restaurant.
- Established better restaurant policies and procedures resulting in more efficient productivity to deal with employees and clientele on a daily basis.
- Prepared daily bookkeeping and accounting procedures.
- Hired, trained and supervised as many as 60 employees.

Food & Beverage/Catering

- Supervised and delegated staff of 150 employees for banquets serving 20-1000 guests. Involved set up and serving guests for the following: conventions...luncheons...theme parties...weddings...special events.
- Developed successful marketing strategies for radio advertising campaigns.
- Established dynamic theme parties, prepared and displayed decorations.
- Performed tableside food preparation.
- Liaison between management and clients, expediting challenges customers presented in a quick and creative manner.
- Gained thorough knowledge through lifetime experience from a family catering service.

EDUCATION

AA Degree, Accounting, 1979
Santa Barbara City College

EMPLOYMENT HISTORY

Floor Manager, City Broiler, Santa Barbara, CA	1988-present
Banquet Captain, Fess Parker's Red Lion Resort, SB, CA	1987-88
Manager, The Famous Restaurant, Montecito, CA	1982-86

Illustrator—Artist Resume
Freelance Experience

PAMELA TAPIA
Illustrator...Line Art...Cartoons
3490 Sandy Lane
Santa Barbara, CA 93103
(805) 964-2663

PROFESSIONAL PROFILE:

- Artist specializing in realistic & cartoon black & white line art.
- Highly organized, dedicated with a positive attitude.
- Work quickly and efficiently under highly pressured situations while consistently meeting tight deadline schedules.

PUBLISHED WORK:

Tangerine Press - Illustrated the front cover and throughout the book titled "The College Student's Resume Guide." Written by Kim Marino.

Avery Press - Illustrated realistic cartoon drawings for the entire book titled "Computers & Small Fry." Written by Mario Pagononi.

Avery Press - Illustrated realistic line drawings for the chapter headings of the book titled "Shopper's Guide to Natural Food." Written by the Editors of the Far West Journal.

Avery Press - Illustrated technical & soft mood drawings for "Breastfeeding Today." Written by Candice Woessner, Judith Lauwers and Barbara Bernard.

Avery Press - Illustrated line drawing for the Canadian book "Having Babies." Written by Toula Hatherall.

Avery Press - Illustrated cartoon drawings throughout the book "Lamaze is For Chickens." Written by Mimi Green and Maxine Naab.

CLIENTS/ PROJECTS:

Ray's Liquor - Illustrated a drawing of the store front on a tee shirt for company promotions.

Ed's Bait & Tackle - Designed and illustrated tee shirts mass produced for in-house promotions and sales.

Visitor Press - Designed and illustrated two maps involving historical and tourist sites of Santa Barbara. Illustrated an in-house display that captured excitement and promoted sales.

Brown Pelican Restaurant - Designed and illustrated a promotional matchbook cover and the dinner menu for this fine dining restaurant.

Import/Export Manager—Chronological Resume
Recent College Graduate with Related Work Experience

PATRICIA WESTWICK
890 West Street
Santa Barbara, CA 93111
(805) 569-1234

OBJECTIVE

Import/Export Management position

EDUCATION

BA Degree, Economics/Business, 1990
Scripts College, Claremont, CA

Foreign Study Program, Summer 1988
University of Arizona, Guadalajara, Mexico

THESIS

Strategic Trade Policy: An Analysis of its Applicability in the United States

PROFESSIONAL EXPERIENCE

ALFIES IMPORTS, Santa Barbara, CA — 1988-present
Store Manager

- In charge of managing this antique furniture store.
- Sell Guatemalan and Mexican furniture to elite clientele while building a personal customer base through excellent client relations and thorough product knowledge.
- Create and maintain preferred customer lists; includes customer follow-up.
- Maintain inventory/quality control, merchandising, payroll disbursement, cash management, opening and closing procedures.

PERUVIAN CUISINE, Santa Barbara, CA — 1985-88
Head Hostess/Waitress

- In charge of running a smooth flow of restaurant operations for this upbeat, service-oriented Peruvian cuisine.
- Greet customers and wait tables in a professional and friendly manner.
- Solve potential problems for customers quickly and effectively.
- Coordinate staffing and entertainment.
- Set up banquets and serve 20-300 guests; prepare/display decorations.
- Create themes for company Fiesta parties as part of a 5-member team.
- Train and supervise new employees.
- Manage daily cash flow for the entire staff (including entertainment) as part of opening and closing procedures.

Insurance Sales Manager—Functional Resume

PATRICIA A. GRANT

PO Box 92380
Santa Barbara, CA 93190
(805) 569-0002

OBJECTIVE

An Insurance Sales Manager position

PROFESSIONAL PROFILE

- 20 years professional experience with office and sales management, employee supervision and customer relations.
- Excellent rapport with customers and fellow employees.
- Strong organizational skills with attention to detail.
- Work well in highly pressured, fast pace environments.
- Desire to achieve, accomplish & exceed objectives and goals.
- Licensed Property, Casualty, Life & Accident Insurance Agent.
- Former Board of Directors and Corresponding Secretary for: National Insurance Women's Association.

PROFESSIONAL EXPERIENCE

Sales Manager

- Developed and implemented an effective employee training manual.
- Established goals; evaluated staff performance and ability to achieve these goals.
- Hired, trained and motivated insurance agents in three locations.
- Exceeded all sales quotas for six consecutive years.

Office Supervisor/Manager

- Established all inter-office procedures to assure quality of work performed.
- Scheduled patients at a busy insurance office.
- Demonstrated quick, accurate and decisive results of customer problems/complaints.
- Prepared and maintained computerized insurance records, collections, weekly and monthly reports, bookkeeping and accounts receivable.

Insurance Claims Assistant

- Gained thorough knowledge of the following:
  property insurance...casualty insurance...life & accident insurance.
- Obtained notice of loss and determined the proper procedure for processing claims.
- Advised policy holder and claimants concerning these procedures.
- Interacted extensively with adjusters, providing them with necessary data.

EMPLOYMENT HISTORY

Sales Manager/Representative, State Farm Insurance, Goleta, CA 1985-89
Claims Assistant/Supervisor, Nationwide Insurance, Denver, CO 1979-85

DOROTHY TESSA WALKER
PO Box 3331
Encino, CA 91316
(818) 784-3109

OBJECTIVE

An Interior Design position.

PROFESSIONAL PROFILE

- Highly organized, dedicated with a positive attitude.
- Strength in assessing people's needs and gaining trust.
- Work well under pressure situations with attention to detail, consistently meeting tight deadline schedules.
- Outstanding ability to communicate with clients, subconstractors, employees and all levels of management.

EDUCATION

Certified Environmental and Interior Design
University of California Extension, 1987

BS Degree, Communications - 1978
University of California, Los Angeles

PROFESSIONAL EXPERIENCE

THE VALLEY REMNANT STORE, Los Angeles, CA — 1988-present
Drapery Department Manager
- Contract window coverings and upholsteries, acting as the liaison between subcontractors and customers at this busy retail fabric store.
  - Travel to location sites working closely with customers to interpret their needs for color scheme, space planning and style.
  - Negotiate contracts with workrooms in Santa Barbara and Ventura counties to find the best price of labor and quality of workmanship.
  - Solve potential problems and meet realistic demands at a fair price.
  - Locate custom order fabric to determine the best cost and quantity.
- Design window displays that quickly promoted sales.
- Install creative window coverings at customer location sites.
- Supervise and train a dynamic staff of six employees.
- Maintain inventory control, bookkeeping and cash management.
- Built a large personal base with thorough product knowledge, hard work and excellent customer service.

MALIBU PROPERTY MANAGEMENT, Malibu, CA — 1985-88
Assistant
- Coordinated fabrics and accessories for two Malibu Estate houses.
- Shopped for fabrics; performed seamstress duties on a daily basis.

SARA B. TAYLOR
1820 L Street
Lincoln, NE 68849
(402) 474-1110

Objective: An Interior Designer position.

DESIGN EXPERIENCE

Residential Interior Design Projects

- Successfully developed conceptual designs for several million dollar homes.
- Designed the interior of a 5000 square foot, Mediterranean style home.
  - Involved lighting, cabinet & kitchen design, ceiling and arch design.
- Designed interiors and finished surfaces for the exteriors of a 100-acre estate with a main house, guest house and stables.
- Developed the design concept through completion for a Beverly Hills home.
- Designed the interior of an estate on a 100 acre ranch outside, Omaha, NE.
- Successfully completed additional projects over the past eight years.

Communication Skills

- Developed presentation skills in drafting, rendering and material boards.
- Liaison between contractors, architects and clients, solving potential problems and meeting realistic demands at a fair price.
- Consulted with clients to interpret their needs and priorities for budget, color scheme, finished materials and space planning.

Project Management

- Oversaw and maintained the remodeling an estate on the Santa Fe Ranch.
- Manage and operate a successful design consulting firm.
- Locate qualified vendors and negotiate contracts with subcontractors.
- Hire, schedule and supervise subcontractors. Developed and enforce effective company policy, procedures and project safety regulations.
- Purchase, expedite materials/equipment; maintain efficient quality control.
- Assist with light bookkeeping, working closely with the accountant.
- Maintained daily contact and on-site supervision.

EDUCATION

Environmental and Interior Design
Professional Certificate Program, Graduated: 1989
University of Nebraska Extension, Lincoln, NE

EMPLOYMENT HISTORY

Interior Designer, Kristin B. Taylor Designs, Lincoln, NE 1988-90
Ranch Manager, Rancho Santa Fe, Norfolk, VA 1983-88
Project Manager/Designer, Sierra Designs, Beverly Hills, CA 1980-81

DAVID P. CASSERMAN
PO Box 1567
Santa Ynez, CA 93460
(805) 688-1234

Objective: A Landscape Architect Management position.

PROFESSIONAL EXPERIENCE

Landscaping Experience

- Design, install and maintain quality gardens for commercial projects and residential estates throughout the San Fernando and Simi Valley areas.
  - stonework...garden structures...decking...masonry...accent lighting... irrigation...large borders and annual color displays.
- Install and service drip and spray irrigation systems.
  - Gained thorough knowledge of irrigation control panels.
- Maintain and repair power equipment:
  - mowers...edgers...blowers...trenchers...sprayers.
- Thoroughly familiar with garden chemicals:
  - insecticides, herbicides and fertilizer programs.

Project Management

- Carried out daily on-site supervision.
  - Complete projects on-time while meeting strict budget requirements.
  - Located qualified vendors and negotiated contracts with subcontractors.
  - Hired, scheduled and supervised employees and subcontractors.
- Developed and enforced effective company policy, procedures and project safety regulations with power equipment, vehicles and chemicals.
- Familiar with worker's compensation rules and regulations and CPR.

LICENSES

Certified Advanced California Nurseryman, #2222
California Landscape Contractor #00000

EDUCATION

BA Degree, Botany; Graduated 1979
California State University, Northridge, CA

EMPLOYMENT HISTORY

Manager, David Landis Landscaping, Simi Valley, CA	1982-present
Nurseryman/Supervisor, East Bay Nursery, Simi Valley, CA	1979-82
Nurseyman, Northwoods Nursery, Chatsworth, CA	1976-79

Law Clerk—Combination Resume
Recent College Graduate with Related Internship Experience

MEGAN RYAN ESCOBAR

Campus Address
1704 Wilshire Blvd
Los Angeles, CA 90025
(213) 502-4455

Permanent Address
201 River Ridge Springs
Seattle, WA 10005
(201) 525-1223

Objective: A growth-oriented position leading to a career in Law.

EDUCATION

BA Degree, Political Science, December 1990
University of California, Los Angeles

LEGAL EXPERIENCE

CAREY T. LUNDSFORD, LAW CORPORATION, Los Angeles, CA — Summer 1990
Bilingual Law Clerk

- Interviewed Spanish speaking clients and served as translator for attorney.
- Prepared extensive bankruptcy cases with efficiency.
- Filed documents with the municipal and superior courts.
- Supervised office in absence of the attorney and staff.
- Demonstrated tact and diplomacy with clients and attorney under pressured situations; consistently met strict deadline schedules.

GOVERNMENT ACCOUNTABILITY PROJECT, Washington, DC — Summer 1989
Staff Associate Intern

- Partner on 4-person team whose advocacy for whistleblowers was a leading factor in stopping USDA's proposal to restructure government's approach to food safety oversight.
- Researched/analyzed over 1800 public comments on DI, and 240 comments on the Streamlined Inspection System to deregulate slaughter inspection.
- Conducted numerous telephone inquiries and library research to identify relevant military quality control standards for contractors.
  - Information used as reference to evaluate USDA's weaker QC criteria for the food industry.
- Served as media liaison to alert and recruit reporters to attend press conferences where investigative results were disclosed.
- Conducted library research to keep abreast of how journalists were covering clients' whistleblowing disclosures in each area.
- Served as client liaison to learn if/how information could be made public.
- Conducted exhaustive advance public relations outreach for GAP-sponsored awards ceremonies honoring specific whistleblowers.

EMPLOYMENT HISTORY

Teacher's Assistant, UCLA La Escuelita Program, Westwood, CA — 1988-89
Resident Assistant, UCLA Partnership Academic Institute, Westwood, CA — Summer 1988
Tutor, La Escuelita Tutoring Program, Franklin School, Los Angeles, CA — 1986-88

Law Clerk Internship—Functional Resume
College Student with Related Experience Working in Family Business

NICOLE E. DANSEN

Campus Address
25689 Rhino Street
Goleta, CA 93117
(805) 966-3049

Permanent Address
207 Oceanside Road
Corona Del Mar, CA 92625
(714) 644-5091

Objective: Law Clerk

EDUCATION

BA Degree, Law and Society, June 1991
University of California, Santa Barbara

EXPERIENCE

Related Courses

Law in Modern State...American Government and Politics...Law and Society... Critical Thinking...Sociology of Law...Criminal Justice... Constitutional Law.

Public Relations/Communications

- Greeted clientele and answered busy phones for a 10-attorney law firm expediting challenges customers presented in a highly professional manner.
  - Assisted attorneys quickly and efficiently maintaining tact and diplomacy.
- Demonstrated strong public relation skills while waitressing for two service-oriented sandwich shops.
  - Developed a personal customer base through excellent customer service, and thorough product knowledge.
  - Trained and supervised waitress personnel.
- Learned to work well with employees, clients and all levels of management.

Administrative Skills

- Operated computer for a law firm to convert manual procedures to computerized office system. Filed and sorted documents with accuracy and speed.
- Maintained opening/closing procedures as well as cash management at two restaurants.
- Learned to work on multiple projects under highly pressured situations and consistently meet strict deadline schedules.

EMPLOYMENT HISTORY

Office Assistant, Law Offices of Dansen & Pram, Irvine, CA — 1988-91
Waitress/Hostess, Cafe Del Mar, San Diego, CA — Summers 1987-88
Waitress, Matinee Bar and Grill, Irvine, CA — 1986-87

Legal Research Assistant—Functional Resume
Law Student with Related Volunteer and School Project Experience

DENISE L. CARPENTER

333 Austin Street
Santa Barbara, CA 93043
(805) 222-5678

OBJECTIVE

Research Assistant, Clerk or Writer/Editor for a Law Firm.

PROFESSIONAL PROFILE

- Developed excellent skills in legal writing and research.
- Outstanding ability to communicate with all types of people.
- Work well under pressure; thrive on challenging projects.
- Ranked in the Top 10 of first year students in law school.

EDUCATION

JD, Los Angeles College of Law
Graduation: December 1991

Law-Related Courses

Legal Writing & Research...Criminal Law...Criminal Procedure ...Contracts...Torts...Juvenile Law...Family Law...Wills & Trusts...Personal Property...Real Property...Civil Procedures ...Dispute Resolution...Bioethics

RELATED EXPERIENCE

Research Writing & Communication Skills

- Wrote/submitted a client history on behalf of a Cuban detainee at LA Federal Prison.
  - Contacted client's family to verify USA sponsorship.
  - Researched extensive criminal record.
  - Represented and counseled client at an INS deportation hearing.
- Researched and wrote a summary on the origins of Canons of Legal Ethics.
- Participant in a thorough research project to establish a curriculum for the Los Angeles College of Law Writing and Research class.

Project Coordination/Management

- Prepared income tax returns in conjunction with the IRS and the Volunteer Income Tax Assistance Program.
- Managed a major grocery store; hired, trained and supervised 2-120 employees.
- Oversaw the entire budget; Increased annual profits by 98 percent within the first year.
- Developed and coordinated an effective employee training manual and video.
  - Wrote, directed, casted and introduced the scanner system to 25,000 employees.

EMPLOYMENT HISTORY

Manager/Bookkeeper, Albertson's Market, Long Beach — 1978-present

Loan Officer—Chronological Resume
Making a Lateral Change from Trust Officer

DAWN E. GLICKMAN
56781 Soledad
Santa Barbara, CA 93103
(805) 569-1111

Objective: Loan Officer

PROFESSIONAL EXPERIENCE:

1989-present **TRUST REAL ESTATE OFFICER**
Santa Barbara Bank & Trust, Goleta, CA
Manage residential and commercial properties held in trust. Communicate with administrator and customers to provide excellent customer service. Establish business accounts. Hire, train and supervise departmental staff.

1986-89 **PROPERTY SUPERVISOR**
West-Tek Management Company, Santa Barbara, CA
Supervised the management of hotel, motel, commercial and multi-family properties. Recruited, hired and trained on-site management personnel. Oversaw special projects and rehab programs. Negotiated contracts. Prepared marketing plans and annual budgets including capital expenditures. Reviewed, approved and submitted to owner monthly operating statements and requirements.

1978-86 **SPECIAL PROJECTS COORDINATOR** (1984-86)
University of California, Santa Barbara, CA
Developed and coordinated educational, social and fund raising activities for the Alumni Association. Developed logistics, contract negotiation and staffing requirements.

ADMINISTRATIVE ASSISTANT (1978-84)
Maintain financial records for the major income-producing Alumni program. Prepare payroll, A/R, A/P. Monitor investment accounts and prepare operating budget. Hire, train and supervise clerical and summer student staff.

1972-78 **SENIOR ACCOUNT CLERK**
Post Properties & Investments, Santa Barbara, CA
Prepared entries to ledgers pertaining to firm's investments including newspaper publications and recreational parks. Balanced monthly journals, A/R, A/P, daily banking and reconcile monthly statements for 14 accounts.

PATRICIA J. STONE
1134 Peacock Lane
Santa Barbara, CA 93103
(805) 569-2222

OBJECTIVE
A Senior Loan Officer Position

PROFESSIONAL EXPERIENCE

BANK OF SANTA BARBARA, Santa Barbara, CA — 1969-present
Senior Loan Officer

Training, Management & Administration

- Trained/supervised loan and operation staff at branch offices throughout Santa Barbara.
  - Successfully set up and managed the Home Loan Center in Ventura for one year.
  - Supervised and cross-trained operations staff of 6-20 employees for six years.
  - Became main source of information for in-house loan officers in Santa Barbara.
  - Converted manual procedures to an effective in-house computerized office system.
  - Enforce policies & regulations, meeting daily demanding deadline schedules.
  - Develop and conduct effective policy and operation training seminars and presentations to the general public, real estate offices and in-house loan officers throughout Santa Barbara Tri-county areas.
- Prepare and monitor monthly reports and primary banking functions.
- Developed and designed original tracking reports now used to follow all loans.

Accounting & Cash Management

- Consistently funded monthly loans totalling over $1M, receiving numerous awards.
- Analyze problem areas and successfully develop and implement programs to improve operations and produce profits.
  - Analyze credit histories and cash flow projections for to determine loan requirements.
  - Effectively counsel, evaluate and inform customers of credit options for wise long and short term investments.
- Monitor cash requirements for the entire bank.

SPECIAL SKILLS

Cash handling, stop payments, returned checks, forgeries, fund posting, employee and depositor inquiries, process complex transactions, prepare financial records, supervise preparation of reviews, reconcile and verify monthly reports and investment portfolio accounting, statement preparation, posting/redemption of bonds, prepare/maintain detailed operating procedures, operate computers.

EDUCATION

BA Degree, Business Economics, 1969
University of California, Los Angeles

Loan Underwriter—Functional Resume
Moving Up from Customer Service Representative

MARGARITE U. HASKELL
PO Box 2223
Santa Barbara, CA 93105
(805) 682-3333

Objective: An Insurance Underwriter position

PROFESSIONAL PROFILE

- 20 years experience in loans and customer service in the finance and insurance industries.
- Success oriented with high energy and a positive attitude.
- Highly organized and ability to service several transactions simultaneously with attention to detail.
- Special talent for assessing client needs and gaining trust.
- Resourceful; skilled in analyzing and solving problems.
- Team player with proven leadership qualities; work well with all levels of management in a highly professional manner.
- Gained valuable business and personal contacts throughout the Santa Barbara community.

PROFESSIONAL EXPERIENCE

Insurance & Underwriting

- Calculated personal line policies and processed claims for a medium sized insurance company.
- Solved potential problems for customers while working closely with general agencies and hospitals nationwide.

Loan Processing & Banking

- Established and processed new real estate and consumer loan files from origination through funding and final audit.
- Interacted closely with branch and staff personnel, title companies, escrow companies and customers on a daily basis.
- Provided relief for branch operations personnel by opening savings accounts and performing teller transactions.

EDUCATION

Institute of Financial Education, 1989
Company training workshops & seminars

EMPLOYMENT HISTORY

Customer Service Rep., Goleta Valley Insurance Agency — 1987-present
Loan Processor, Home Federal Savings & Loan, Santa Barbara, CA — 1981-87
Loan Secretary, Mission Federal Savings, Santa Barbara, CA — 1975-81

Management Consultant—Functional Resume
Specializing in Human Resources/Change Management

NICOLE T. KIMBERLY

112 Peachtree Lane
Atlanta, GA 30307
(404) 872-0004

Objective: Management Consultant

EMPLOYMENT HISTORY

Management Consultant, ABC Consulting, Atlanta, GA — 1992-present
Senior Manager, American Express TRS, New York, NY — 1985-92
Program Manager, IBM Corporation, US Headquarters, NY — 1980-85

PROFESSIONAL EXPERIENCE

Human Resources Management

- Designed and implemented human resource programs for several Fortune 500 Corporations and small businesses that resulted in more effective and efficient management of companies assets.
  - Developed effective personnel policies and procedures, staffing needs analysis, incentive and recognition programs, resource planning tools, on-line communication and management development programs, value surveys.
  - Designed competency based interview tools, mentor programs, employee relations and benefit manuals, performance plans and customer developed measurements.
  - Introduced self-directed and structured workforce teams that resulted in high employee morale and empowerment.

Organizational Development

- Exceeded client goals and expectations for a Fortune 500 Corporation and Federal Agency nationwide by focusing on the integration of:
  human resources ..quality ..training and development ..tools and initiatives.
  - Identified and prioritized critical automation initiatives resulting in substantial productivity increases.
  - Led business process reengineering teams and assessed business strategies.
  - Redesigned incentive and recognition plans.
  - Aligned performance management goals that identified linkages between employee satisfaction drivers and customer driven measures.
  - Identified best practices that provided value to mission critical processes.
- Designed and implemented an Organizational Change process for a nationwide reorganization of a federal agency; workforce ..infrastructure ..centralized services.

EDUCATION

- **MBA, Business Administration**, 1977
  New York University, New York, NY
- **BA, Behavioral Sciences**, 1975
  John Jay College of Criminal Justice, NY

Marketing Internship—Functional Resume
College Student with Related School Activity Experience

CHARLES MICHAEL REYNOLDS
75 College Ave
Goleta, CA 93117
(805) 555-1111

Objective: A Marketing Internship

PROFESSIONAL PROFILE

- Highly organized, dedicated with a positive attitude.
- Resourceful; skilled in analyzing and solving problems.
- Good written, oral and interpersonal communications.
- Work well under pressure situations with the ability to meet demanding deadline schedules.

RELATED EXPERIENCE

UNIVERSITY OF CALIFORNIA, Los Angeles 1987-90
English Club President

Administration & Organization
- Delegate work and supervise staff members.
- Write proposals and appear before the Finance Board to renew annual budgets.
- Coordinate academic, cultural and social activities.
- Conduct bi-weekly meetings; coordinate guest speakers and field trips.
- Maintain finances and accounting procedures including auditing and annual budget forecasting for student organization.

Communications
- Compose announcements, newsletters and correspondence focused on organizational activities for the campus community.
- Assist members with research projects on a daily basis.
- Respond quickly and efficiently to inquiries, solving problems for members in a professional and concerned manner.
- Recognized by the University of California for effective public speaking.

EDUCATION

BA Degree, English Literature
University of California, Los Angeles
Graduation: 1992 GPA: 3.7

Marketing Representative, Foreign Relations—Chronological Resume
Recent College Graduate with Related Work and Internship Experience

OSCAR KIM TEWS
PO Box 321
Sunnyvale, CA 94087
(408) 733-1111

Objective: Foreign Relations Marketing Representative

PROFESSIONAL EXPERIENCE

FOREIGN RELATIONS MARKETING REPRESENTATIVE
LCS System Integration & Construct Ltd., Tokyo, Japan Summers 1988-90

- Wrote (in English) company overview presentations targeting the American businessman for the management of an organization based in Tokyo, Japan.
- Interviewed and assessed various established high-tech companies in Kyoto.
- Briefed and prepared extensive reports for high-level management to transfer/joint venture technology with US counterparts.
- Gained valuable hands-on knowledge and experience on structures of Japanese business organization.
- Repaired, maintained and packaged computer disk drives for a US based high technology research and development corporation.
- Led guided tours to American businessmen throughout Japanese facilities.

EDUCATION

BA Degree, Industrial Psychology, 1990
University of California at Los Angeles
Overall GPA: 3.98 Major: GPA 4.0

PROFESSIONAL PROFILE

- Speak, read and write Japanese; completed four quarters of college-level Japanese language.
- Ability to understand and speak Chinese.
- Traveled extensively throughout Japan, Taiwan and Hong Kong over the past 10 years.
- Skilled in Fortran, BASIC and WordStar languages and software.
- Founding member of the Japanese Roundtable Club; developed to help students enhance their language and social skills.
- Active in volleyball, softball, basketball, golf, tennis, baseball and swimming.

Marketing Representative, Nonprofit Organization—Chronological Resume
Making a Lateral Change from Publicity Coordinator

MOLLY RACHEL MCKINSEY
5720 Green Street
San Francisco, CA 94750
(415) 450-2378

Objective: To successfully market nonprofit organizations

EDUCATION

MBA, University of Santa Clara, Santa Clara, CA, December 1984
Emphasis: Marketing and Finance

BA, French Literature, UC Berkeley, Berkeley, CA, June 1980
Phi Beta Kappa

EXPERIENCE

AMERICAN LIBRARY, Geneva Switzerland 1987-90
Publicity Coordinator (volunteer position)

- Developed marketing program.
- Wrote magazine articles and radio announcements.
- Organized direct mail program.
- Designed and produced brochure for new members.
- Managed advertising campaign for annual booksale.
- Gave presentations to community groups.

WELLS FARGO BANK, San Francisco, CA 1985-87
Project Manager

- Managed implementation of the Wells Fargo/Crocker overdraft class action suit settlement, including 22 sub-projects and a $1,000,000 budget.
- Served as liaison between Consumer Marketing, Credit Card, Legal, Operations, Systems, and Public Relations departments.
- Coordinated development and production of customer communications.
- Awarded bonus and letter of commendation at completion of project.

Associate Product Manager

- Managed summer advertising campaign for checking accounts.
- Researched proposal for an upscale customer service program.
- Developed conversion plan for Crocker certificate of deposit accounts for the Wells Fargo/Crocker Bank merger.
- Edited and coordinated branch training materials.

- More

EXPERIENCE (Continued)

Assistant Product Manager
- Analyzed interest rates and presented pricing recommendations to senior management.
- Wrote monthly business reviews and marketing proposals.
- Researched and analyzed competitive products and institutions.
- Wrote telemarketing scripts and assisted with telemarketing training.
- Created and managed branch incentive campaign.

CLAIROL INC, Oakland, CA 1981-84
Sales Representative
- Responsible for selling Clairol haircare products directly to major drug store chains and mass merchandisers, e.g. Longs, Kmart.
- Achieved 15 percent annual increase for San Francisco-Sunnyvale sales territory.
- Designed and installed haircolor department layouts and displays.
- Presented new products, major promotions and business reviews.
- Provided personalized customer service and follow-up.

EMPORIUM-CAPWELL, Fremont, CA 1980-81
Department Sales Manager
- Trained, supervised and motivated sales staff of 15 employees.
- Analyzed sales trends and established sales goals.
- Negotiated procurement of best-selling items with central buying office.
- Redesigned layout of sales floors to emphasize faster growing businesses.

SPECIAL SKILLS

- Fluent in French (Diploma, University of Geneva, July 1988)
- Proficient on IBM and Macintosh PC's (Lotus 1-2-3, Microsoft Word)

Marriage, Family, and Child Counselor—Functional Resume

JOANNA HOUSTON
Marriage, Family & Child Counselor
3000 Southwest Park Road
Portland, OR 97219
(503) 293-0009

CLINICAL EXPERIENCE

JOANNA HOUSTON, MFCC, Portland, OR 1978-present

Marriage, Family & Child Counseling

- Provide crisis intervention, brief and long term counseling to:
  -individual children -adolescents -adults -couples -family groups
- Conduct group therapy sessions focused on assertiveness training, communication skills, self esteem and life transitions.
- Deal with clients of diverse backgrounds specializing in sandtray, dreamwork, art, journal exploration and authentic movement.

Grief: Life, Death & Transition Therapy

- Effectively counsel clients and offer emotional and spiritual support by maximizing participation in sharing grief experiences.
  - Educate clients on the basic tools necessary to accept and deal with loss and change.
  - Provide options to motivate sense of well being, positive growth and self-development.

EDUCATION

MA Degree, Counseling Psychology - 1978
Western College, Portland, OR
BA Degree, Psychology - 1966
Queens College, Charlotte, NC

SPECIAL TRAINING

- Oregon MFCC License #1000000 since 1980.
- In-depth seminar, **Life, Death & Transition**, Elisabeth Kübler-Ross.
- Attended 10-day, **Jungian Conferences**, Life meaning & individuation.
- Personal psychotherapy includes: Jungian Analysis, Gestalt Therapy, Couples Counseling, Sandtray Therapy, Authentic Movement Therapy, Intensive Journal Process. 1978-present
- Hospice Training for Volunteers. 1977

PROFESSIONAL AFFILIATIONS

- Member, Oregon Assoc. of Marriage & Family Therapists.
- Member, National Board for Certified Counselors.

STEPHANIE JANE WILBER
Marriage, Family & Child Counselor
20450 Laguna Niguel Way
Santa Barbara, CA 93103
(805) 963-2393

PROFESSIONAL EXPERIENCE

Marriage, Family & Child Counseling

- Provide crisis intervention, brief and long term counseling to:
  -individual adults -adolescents -couples -families -groups
- Assess, diagnose and treat clients in major life transitions.
- Conduct group therapy series focused on peer counselin, communication and self esteem.
- Educate, assess and counsel women who must decide between abortion, adoption or keeping the child.
- Faciliate all phases of open independent adoptions; supply community referral resources.
- Coordinate intakes, referrals, correspondence, case records.

Chemical Dependency Counseling & Assessment

- Develop and implement primary education on predictable course of recovery for chemical dependency patients focusing on the following:
  Overview of addiction, indicators of potential relapse, self esteem, addiction as a family disease, denial, co-dependency and congruent communication.
- Counsel couples, individuals, families, family groups and adult children of alcoholics during their participation in a 12-Step Program.
- Educate and counsel battered women, demonstrating the relationship between substance abuse and family violence.

EDUCATION

MA Degree - Counseling Psychology - 1984
Pacifica Graduate Institute, Santa Barbara, CA

SPECIAL TRAINING

- California MFCC License #MFC24707 since 1988.
- Assessment and Treatment of Alcoholism.
- Assessment and Treatment of Adult Children of Alcoholics.
- Diagnosis and treatment of child abuse.
- Attended 7-day workshops; Jay Haley, Virginia Satir, Carl Whitaker, Salvador Minuchin and Claudia Black.
- Gained knowledge through personal psychotherapy including: Couples Counseling and Gestalt Group Therapy.

EMPLOYMENT HISTORY

Adoption Counselor, Santa Barbara Adoption Center 1989-present
Substance Abuse Consultant, Shelter Services for Women, SB, CA 1986-89
Relaxation Trainer, Cottage Care Center, Santa Barbara, CA 1979-86
Staff Counselor, Community Counseling Center, Santa Barbara, CA 1972-79

Marriage, Family, and Child Counselor—Functional Resume
Recent College Graduate with Related Personal and Work Experience

LAUREL SUE KOSICH
264 Mountain Walk
Boise, ID 98750
(208) 999-2345

Objective: Marriage, Family & Child Counselor

PROFESSIONAL EXPERIENCE

Marriage, Family & Child Counseling

- Provided crisis intervention, brief and long term counseling to:
  -individual adults -adolescents -couples -families -groups
- Dealt with clients of diverse backgrounds in life transitions, suicide and eating disorders.
- Conducted group therapy series focused on maturation stages for early teens. Coordinated parent participation, guest speakers, field trips & written exercises.
- Served as primary crisis, individual and group counselor to emotionally disturbed teens living in a licensed group home.

Chemical Dependency Counseling & Assessment

- Counseled couples, individuals, families and adult children of alcoholics during their participation in a 12-step program.
- Primary educator on predictable course of early recovery for clients and student population.
- Instructed on indicators of potential relapse. Designed and implemented more effective treatment program, focusing on coping styles pertinent to the individual's social support system, workplace and family.

Student Personnel Services in Higher Education

- Provided individual career and developmental counseling to college students.
- Conducted eating disorder groups for the college level population.
- Multimodal case management, including video taping and presentation.
- Eating Disorders Task Force--case staffing for team of university and community professionals including psychiatrists, dietitian, individual & group therapist and eating disorder assessment & referral specialists.

SPECIAL TRAINING

- California MFCC intern license #IMF14356.
- 1-year certification program in **Alcohol & Drug** Counseling Skills - UC Santa Barbara.
- 1-year extensive **Family Therapy** training with California Center for Clinical Training and Open Systems Unlimited.
- Currently participating in 3-year **Gestalt** training program; Isabel Fredericson of the Cleveland Gestalt Institute.
- 6-month extensive training on Mental Research Institute's Model of **Brief Therapy**.
- Attended 5-day/weekend workshops - Carl Whitaker, Jay Haley and Ivan Boszormenyi-Nagy and Salvador Minuchin.

SPECIAL TRAINING (Continued)

- Full caseload at second nonprofit internship UC Santa Barbara with weekly individual and group supervision.
- Intensive training workshop in **Focusing Technique.**
- 4-month program; interpersonal communication skills and **Transactional Analysis** therapy model-Support Group Network.

EMPLOYMENT HISTORY

Counselor, UC Santa Barbara Counseling & Careers Center — 1988-present
Counselor, Santa Barbara Night Counseling Center — 1987-present
Counselor, Rivendell Group Home, Santa Barbara, CA — Fall-Winter 1988
Group Counselor, Santa Barbara Girls' Club — Winter 1987
Counselor, Ray E. Hosford Training Clinic, UCSB — 1986-87

PROFESSIONAL PROFILE

- Active member of Overeaters Anonymous.
- Active member of 12-Step Programs dealing with codependent relationships.
- Facilitator and member of Support Group Network.
- 3-year member in good standing; American Psychological Association.
- Member in good standing; California Association of Marriage and Family Therapists.
- Personal Psychotherapy for six years, including Family Therapy Gestalt Group Therapy, Cognitive/Behavioral, Strategic, Rogerian.

EDUCATION

- MA Degree - Counseling Psychology, UC Santa Barbara, June 1989
  Student Personnel Services in Higher Education
- Alcohol & Drug Counseling, Certificate, UC Santa Barbara, June 1989
- MA Degree - Counseling Psychology, UC Santa Barbara, June 1988
  Marriage, Family and Child Counseling
- BS Degree - Psychology, Cum Laude, University of Idaho, ID, 1986

Mechanic Supervisor, Diesel—Functional Resume
Moving Up from Senior Mechanic/Technical Adviser

TIMOTHY L. COOK
6134 45th Avenue
Santa Barbara, CA 93101
(805) 569-2111

Objective: Diesel Mechanic Supervisor

PROFESSIONAL PROFILE

- 13 years experience in diesel mechanics and supervision.
- Excellent manual dexterity with attention to detail.
- Problem solver/team player with proven leadership qualities.
- Established valuable business contacts within the diesel mechanics industry worldwide.

PROFESSIONAL EXPERIENCE

Diesel Mechanic Skills

- Completely renovated all public service vehicles sold throughout the USA and England; specialized in Classic English buses.
- Maintained routine safety checks, major overhaul repairs and purchased parts; -engine -mechanical body -electrical repairs.
- Represented company to solely service a fleet of tour buses for the Corning Glass Museum of New York; subcontracted for three summer seasons.
- Solely responsible for servicing a fleet of tour buses for Spirit of 76 in Washington DC; subcontracted for 4 months.

Client/Employee Relations

- Contacted clients at location sites to deliver vehicles and educate them on vehicle operation and basic maintenance.
- Represented company to advise and assess an estimated value of nine commercial vehicles for a client's potential resale.
- Developed excellent client rapport while servicing accounts at location sites throughout the USA and England.
- Through expertise in diesel mechanics, became main source of information for clients and entire staff; Solved problems face-to-face and through daily phone contact in a quick, professional and concerned manner.
- Trained and supervised 2-4 employees, maintaining excellent staff relations.

EDUCATION

Certified Heavy Equipment Vehicle
South Bristol Technology College
4-year apprenticeship Graduated: 1980

EMPLOYMENT HISTORY

Sr Mechanic/Technical Advisor, British Promotions, Norfolk, VA — 1985-91
Mechanic, Bristol Omnibus, Bristol, England — 1976-85

JESSE T. RUIZ
9924 Mission Street
San Francisco, CA 96328
(415) 552-0987

Objective: Media Account Executive

PROFESSIONAL PROFILE

- Special talent for assessing people's needs and gaining trust.
- Communicate effectively with all levels of management.
- Team player with ability to work well independently.
- Gained valuable business and personal contacts in the broadcasting industry throughout the Bay area.

PROFESSIONAL EXPERIENCE

Professional Salesmanship

- Sold radio advertising to local businesses throughout the Bay area.
- Sold advertising space to major multi-national corporations throughout the entire Atlantic Seaboard for a business publication.
  Digital Corp...AT&T...Bell Atlantic...Dean Witter...Kodak...Pepsi.
  - Identified corporate and product advertising needs, problems, solutions.
  - Demonstrated effective cold calling techniques through assertive sales ability, thorough product knowledge and consistent follow up.
  - Delivered presentations and wrote proposals, recommending and advising maximum impact and effectiveness to CEO's and other decision makers.
- Developed successful marketing strategies for promotions and sales.

Broadcasting Experience

- Established highly successful radio shows; received awards for community service and for music and public affairs talk shows.
  - Hosted a wide variety of general interest programs aired weekly on local radio.
  - Interviewed concert promoters, musicians/artists and political candidates.
- Produced weekly specialty music shows aired on local radio since 1975.
- Currently hosting a local radio music show.

EDUCATION

BA Degree, Chicano Studies, 1980
University of California, Santa Cruz
Emphasis: Broadcast Communications

EMPLOYMENT HISTORY

Account Executive, PC Business (Magazine), San Francisco, CA	1987-present
Radio Announcer, KCSC-FM, Santa Cruz, CA	1975-present
Broadcast-Research Consultant, Freelance, San Francisco, CA	1984-87
Announcer, KTSF-FM, San Francisco, CA	1979-81

Medical Assistant, Front Office—Chronological Resume
Making a Lateral Change from Hospital Admitting Representative

SUSAN ARLENE McDUFFY
PO Box 5902
Santa Barbara, CA 93190
(805) 569-9876

OBJECTIVE

A Front Office Assistant for a private physician

OFFICE SKILLS

Insurance billing...ten key adding machine...data entry... medical terminology...accounts payable & receivable...excellent phone skills...filing. Typing speed: 65+ wpm.

PROFESSIONAL EXPERIENCE

SANTA BARBARA CITY HOSPITAL — 1985-present
Admitting Representative

- Admit in-patients, out-patients and emergency room patients.
- Schedule future surgeries.
- Verify benefits and receive prior authorizations for Medi-Cal and Medicare patients.
- Work closely with insurance companies, doctors' offices and county agencies throughout Santa Barbara county.

KELCOM MEDICAL SOFTWARE CONSULTANTS, Santa Barbara, CA — 1985-88
Administrative Assistant

- Performed word processing typing and editing with accuracy and speed.
- Coordinated marketing strategies for in-house advertising, promotions and sales.
- Demonstrated strong phones skills, maintaining excellent customer relations.
- Hired, trained, supervised and scheduled staff members.

SANTA BARBARA COUNTY, (Medical Records Department) — 1981-83
Medical Clerk/Computer Trainer

- Trained employees in data entry procedures on a new IBM computerized system.
  - Traveled daily to clinics, working closely with programmers, subcontractors, management and staff throughout the Santa Barbara county area.
- Typed and filed medical records; answered phones.

EDUCATION

Front Office Assistant Graduate
Kellogg Business Institute
Santa Barbara, CA 1989

DIANE AMANDA WHITE
60 Valley Creek Road
Montecito, CA 93108
(805) 962-5044

MEDICAL SALES REPRESENTATIVE

PROFESSIONAL OBJECTIVE: Seeking a progressive company in the medical field offering salary and commission sales with unlimited earning potential.

PROFILE: Success oriented with high energy and a positive mental attitude...strong sense of responsibility and self motivation...good written and oral communication skills...attention to detail...great problem solver and team player with the ability to work independently...creative... flexible and efficient.

EDUCATION: **BA Degree - Psychology/Sociology** 1973
University of Oregon, Portland, OR

PROFESSIONAL EXPERIENCE:

1976-present **SR TERRITORY MANAGER/SALES REPRESENTATIVE**
Stuart Laboratories, Santa Barbara, CA. Sell tube feeding equipment, feeding pumps and devises and infant and adult nutritional products to hospitals, nursing homes, physicians and public health clinics throughout the Santa Barbara to San Luis Obispo territory. Successful sale of product line required full use of the proven abilities to assess physician and patient needs and present appropriate products through the consultants approach. Sample and demonstrate products.

- Developed highest market share of pediatric nutritionals in the region.
- Maintained strong commitment to professionalism while concurrently functioning as Territorial Manager and Member of Pharmaceutical and Hospital Panels.

1974-76 **MARKETING COORDINATOR**
The Browne Corporation, Portland, OR. Provided product usage training for a line of urological and gynological instruments sold through trade show exhibition and telecommunications. Client prospect base included hospitals and physicians nationally. Monitored the smooth day-to-day servicing of all accounts. Liaison between corporate and field representative, maintaining excellent client and employee relations.

KATHERINE ANN WILLIS
4590 Mountain Creek Road
Oceanside, CA 90266
(619) 630-4582

OBJECTIVE

A Nursing position in an OB/GYN clinic environment

PROFESSIONAL EXPERIENCE

FETAL MONITORING SERVICES, San Diego, CA 1990-present
Antepartum Consultant

- Perform 25-50 non-stress tests per month for the County of San Diego and provide testing for several private physicians.

GENERAL HOSPITAL, San Diego, CA 1977-present
Obstetrical & Out-Patient Nurse

- Provided total patient care and support and during the antepartum, labor and delivery process for eight years.
  - Counsel and educate patients in labor, post partum and newborn care.
  - Assessed and triaged incoming labor patients.
  - Assisted doctor with delivery and provide immediate newborn care.
  - Managed obstetrical emergency intervention.
- Provide total to postpartum and long-term antepartum patients on the mother infant unit.
- Provided complete care for short-term surgery patients... Admitting...circulating...recovering...discharge planning.

Administration & Management

- Charge nurse for the labor and delivery unit; 120-160 births per month.
  - Supervised and scheduled a staff of 18 nurses.
  - Interviewed, hired and oriented new personnel.
- Oversaw the Antepartum testing unit.
  - Assisted in developing effective antepartum policies and procedures.
  - Performed NSTs, OCTs, BSTs and assisted with fetal versions and amniocentesis.

EDUCATION

BS Degree, Nursing, 1974
Humboldt State University

LICENSE/CERTIFICATES/AFFILIATIONS

- California State Nursing License #678910
- Public Health Certificate, #1234
- Treasurer/Co-Founder, San Diego County Chapter of NAACOG; Awarded Nurse of the Year for 1990.

NELCY KNUTSON, R.N.
6245 Olympic Blvd
Los Angeles, CA 90046
(213) 344-9999

Objective: Occupational Health Nurse

PROFESSIONAL EXPERIENCE

Occupational Health Nurse

- Established and maintained health care programs for two manufacturing corporations each employing over 1500 employees for a one-nurse office.
  - Provided and performed emergency first aid, pre-employment physical examinations and Worker's Compensation cases on a daily basis.
  - Prepared and maintained all medical records and OSHA reports.
- Conducted in-house CPR and first aid classes for all employees.
- Developed safety programs and participated in Safety Committee meetings.
- Provided continued medical treatment, working closely with clinics and hospitals throughout the community.
- Performed services for the Rehabilitation Program and routine follow-up.
- Interacted with all levels of company management personnel in a highly professional and diplomatic manner.
- Purchased and maintained inventory/quality control of all clinical equipment and supplies.

Acute Emergency Assessment & Intervention

- Superior performance in critical care unit; general..medical..surgical..coronary care..post trauma..neurological..gerontological..open heart surgeries.
- Expert in management of pain control and hyperalimietation (TPN).
- Assessed patient's physiological, emotional and social needs.
  - Ability to quickly determine and perform the best care possible.
- Thoroughly skilled in family dynamics to effectively counsel patients and offer emotional/spiritual support to the terminally ill and their families.

EDUCATION

BS Degree, Psychology/Registered Nurse
University of Minas Gerais, Brazil
Critical Care Nursing Certificate
West Valley College, Saratoga, CA
MBO Certificate, Business Administration
University of California, San Diego
Intensive Care/Rehabilitation
Santa Clara Valley Medical Center, SC, CA

EMPLOYMENT HISTORY

Occupational Health Nurse, Hiebert MFG Inc, Carson, CA 1989-91
Intensive Care Nurse, VA Hospital, Los Angeles, CA 1978-89
Staff Nurse, Carroll's SNF Lexington, San Diego, CA 1977-78

LAURA ANN NEW
335 Rocky Creek Road
Boise, ID, 83712
(208) 342-9990

Lieutenant Colonel
Idaho Air National Guard
125th USAF Clinic, Riverton, ID

OBJECTIVE: **A Civilian Nursing position in a US Military Health Care Facility.**

LICENSE/ EDUCATION:

BS Degree - Nursing, 1973 - Summa Cum Laude
Idaho State University, Boise, ID

Registered Nurse, State of Idaho (A123456)
State of Idaho Standard Lifetime Services Credential

MILITARY TRAINING:

- Nursing Service Management for Air Reserve Forces, 1985
- Air Command and Staff College, 1982
- Regular attendance, Association of Military Surgeons of the US
- Regular attendance, annual active duty, USAF hospitals in the Western United States.

EXPERIENCE:

1986-present

CLINICAL NURSE (RN), County of Boise, Health Care Services, Boise, ID. Provide health care services at this very busy clinic of 18,000 patients (annually) in numerous clinics throughout the facility: Family Planning, Tuberculosis screening and referral, Well Baby Clinics (CHDP), Immunizations, Pregnancy Testing, counseling and referral, Primary Care, total Obstetrical Outpatient care, Blood Pressure screening. Operate clinical laboratory, ordering and maintaining supplies, compiling statistics, supervision of service aides, traige, crisis intervention including psychiatric, social/medical referral, pre/post HIV counseling.

1974-76

MIGRANT NURSE (PHN), Boise County Department of Education Migrant Education Program, Boise, ID. Traveled extensively throughout the valley area to provide health care services, physical exams, referral and follow-up care to children qualifying under Migrant Services and AFDC funding. Developed working knowledge of Spanish.

AFFILIATIONS:

- Association of Medical Surgeons of the United States
- Air National Guard Association
- ANG Nurses Association

BROOKE E. CHILCOTT, RN
6912 Cordova Court
Montecito, CA 93108
(805) 569-9992

Objective: A Utilization Review Nurse position.

PROFESSIONAL EXPERIENCE

Administration & Management

- Manage the Comprehensive Perinatal Services Program for Carpinteria and Franklin clinics.
- Supervise the assessment of designated patients for prenatal care:
  - physical...nutrition...psycho-social...and health education.
  - Monitor patient care and review documentation to determine accuracy and compliance with California State guidelines.
- Coordinate care for 350 Hispanic and low income Prenatal and Postpartum patients.
- In charge of ordering and interpreting lab tests, triaging and appropriate follow-up within Santa Barbara County protocols.

Acute/Residential Nursing Care

- Performed plasmaphoresis for oncology patients at a 500-bed government hospital.
- Participated in the Oncology Department rounds to ensure appropriate care.
- Charge nurse for a 30-bed unit Chemical Dependency and Acute Medical/ Surgical patients. Monitored care of short-stay surgical patients.
  - Liaison between patient, family and therapy staff and physicians.
  - Worked with PSRO, Medicare and SSI to provide documentation within their guidelines.
- Provided care to developmentally disabled patients in a 200-bed resident facility.
  - Developed individual health care program for residents.
  - Reviewed medical history for resident's admission.

Counselor/Educator

- Counseled and educated HIV testing individuals.
- Provided post pregnancy test counseling to women.
- Educated patients in Diabetes, PIH, AFP screening, PTL, RH sensitization.

EDUCATION

AA Degree, Nursing, Santa Barbara City College, 1975

LICENSE/ORGANIZATIONS

California State Nursing License #A0000
Member, US-Mexico Border Health Association/WHO

EMPLOYMENT HISTORY

OB Clinic Manager, County of Santa Barbara	1983-90
Plasmaphoresis Nurse, Royal Hobart Hospital, London, Eng.	1978-83
Staff Nurse, Devereaux School, Santa Barbara, CA	1975-76

Nursing Director—Functional Resume
Moving Up from Nurse/Acting Director

DANA E. CLARKMAN
5510 Madison Court
Santa Barbara, CA 93103
(805) 569-1000

Objective: A Director of Nursing position

PROFESSIONAL PROFILE

- 17 years experience in the health care industry.
- Deal with sensitive situations in a professional and concerned manner.
- Highly organized, dedicated with a positive mental attitude.
- Outstanding written, oral and bilingual communication skills.
- Co-authored an article with Joan Probert, RN, published in the *Journal of Christian Nursing*, Winter 1985.
- Member, Nat'l Hospice Nurses Assn and Nurses Christian Fellowship.
- Gained valuable business and personal contacts throughout the Santa Barbara health care community.

PROFESSIONAL EXPERIENCE

Management & Supervision

- Supervised entire hospital evening nursing staff and became main source for troubleshooting among nursing professionals at St. Francis Hospital.
  - Responsible for overall nursing staff performance and total care of 100 bed facility.
  - Assured that family members were very well informed and involved.
- Supervised home health aides and private duty nurses for hospice home care. Successfully filled in as Director of Nurses in Directors absence.
- Charge nurse on a 40 bed surgical floor for six months.
  - Relief charge nurse of 32 bed floor in a 400 bed hospital for two years.
- Received extensive health care management training.

Hospice Home Care

- Expert in pain control and symptom management for five years.
  - Assessed patient's pain with ability to quickly determine best analgesic and method of delivery.
  - Thoroughly skilled in family dynamics to effectively counsel patients and offer emotional/spiritual support to terminally ill adults and their families.
  - Coordinate overall home care program with other community resources and services throughout Santa Barbara County.

- More -

PROFESSIONAL EXPERIENCE (Continued)

<u>Acute Emergency Assessment & Intervention</u>

- Superior performance in intensive care unit for eight years: general..medical..surgical..coronary care..post trauma..neurological
  - Eight year member of the Code Blue Team, responding to cardiac arrest situations throughout the hospital.
  - Served as the only evening shift IV Therapist for three months at a 400 bed facility.
  - Assisted in the Emergency Room as needed.

<u>Foreign/Domestic Community Relations</u>

- Volunteered as a Red Cross Nurse for five years.
- Educated parents as a PEP volunteer. (Post-Partum Education for Parents)
  - Served on the steering committee.
  - Developed a Baby Basics Class for expectant parents.
- Provided health care assistance in a remote clinic in Mexico as a World Health Volunteer.
  - Studied at the Jaime Balmes University in Saltillo, Mexico. Resided with a Mexican family.
- Volunteered through the American Heart Association. (Project Re-Entry)
  - Visited Stroke patients in their homes.
  - Coordinated outpatient therapy, arranged for supportive equipment and offered emotional support.

EDUCATION

AA Degree, Nursing, <u>Sacramento City College</u>, 1972
President, Chapter of the Student Nurses Association

EMPLOYMENT HISTORY

Hospice Nurse/Acting Director, <u>Hospice of Santa Barbara Inc</u> 1984-90
Relief Supervisor/Staff Nurse, <u>St. Francis Hospital</u> 1976-84
Evening Clinic Nurse, <u>Outpatient Clinic</u>, Sacramento, CA 1/76-7/76
IV Therapist/Charge & Staff Nurse, <u>Mercy General Hospital</u> 1972-75

Operations Management—Functional Resume
Financial Institution

BRADI J. MORELAND

221 Lenox Road
Atlanta, GA 30306
(404) 872-1124

Objective: Financial Operations Management

QUALIFICATIONS

Operations Management ..Client Relations ..Organizational Development
Problem Solving ..Liaison ..Research and Adjustments ..New Division Start-Up
Training and Implementation ..Database/Forms Generation Software
Banking/Remittance Processing ..Word Processing ..Spreadsheet

PROFESSIONAL EXPERIENCE

Operations Manager, Nationwide Bank, Atlanta, GA 1989-present

Operations Management

Managed the daily operations of Client Services and Item Processing divisions.

- In charge of processing multimillion dollar deposits under strict deadlines for 14 independent financial institutions throughout the Southeast.
- Prepared annual budgets, billing statements and employee evaluations.
- Interview, hired, trained, supervised and scheduled a staff of 14 employees.

- Restructured the Item Processing division of corporate headquarters by installing an automated series of procedures that improved daily operations of a 19 bank site.
  - Rewrote policies and procedures manual and technical programs.
  - Created forms to track data for production and tracked statistical input for billing.
- Coordinated Quality Management Forums for five location sites.
- Active member of the traveling crisis management team to standardize successful production practices companywide.

Client Relations

- Served as resident expert and primary client contact of problem solving for three financial services institutions.
- Provided clients with daily or weekly customized reports.
- Worked with clients to improve account processing.
- Accompanied sales representative on location to provide technical expertise.
- Gained clients' confidence through computer and new account conversion processes.
- Cross-sold financial products and services to existing clients.

EDUCATION

BS Degree: Business Administration
Broward Community College, Fort Lauderdale, FL

Operations Manager—Functional Resume
Travel Industry

CHARLES OTTOBAUN

220 Ivy Lane
Atlanta, GA 30303
(404) 872-2300

Objective: **An Operations Management position**

QUALIFICATIONS

Negotiating ..Marketing ..Advertising ..Sales
Operations Management ..Computer Implementation
Training ..Customer Service ..Excellent Oral/Written
Communication ..Seasoned Traveler Worldwide

PROFESSIONAL EXPERIENCE

OPERATIONS MANAGER 1985-95
Travel International, Atlanta, GA

Operations Management

- Managed daily operations for a wholesale travel industry leader.
  - Set up and maintained a highly sophisticated computerized reservations system.
  - Conducted computer training workshops; provided on-going support to users.
  - Recruited, trained and supervised a staff of travel consultants, operations personnel, technical and creative support.
  - Integrated a team concept approach to management that promoted a positive work environment, increased productivity and employee morale.
  - Processed accounts payable and payroll and met strict deadline schedules.
  - Defined and analyzed corporate problems and found cost effective solutions.
  - *Received recognition for timely and efficient evacuation of clients in China during the Tianenmen Square crisis in June 1989.*
  - Resolved problem situations for clients with professionalism, diplomacy and tact.

Marketing and Sales

- Advised operations, reservations and sales personnel on up-to-date products, promotions and incentive information.
  - Located and utilized quality outside resources at the best possible price.
    printers ..separators ..mailing and faxing services ..newspaper/trade publications
- Directed production/distribution of 6-64 page travel brochures and sales collateral.
- Initiated, organized and escorted familiarization trips for 40-60+ travel agents, employees and airline personnel annually.
- Coordinated, set-up booths and delivered sales presentations at trade shows nationwide.
- Evaluated marketing trends to sustain a competitive edge resulting in substantial profitability.

EDUCATION

- **Certificiate: Travel and Tourism**, 1978
  Travel Institute of Georgia, Atlanta, GA

Peace Officer—Chronological Resume
Changing Careers from Mobile Crisis Intervention Specialist

ANGELA S. PENELOPE
PO Box 3333
Santa Barbara, CA 93169
(805) 966-1111

Objective: Full-time position as a Peace Officer

PROFESSIONAL HIGHLIGHTS

- Licensed Psychiatric Technician #LG 00000 since 1985.
- Certified in CPR, first aid, management of assaultive behavior.
- Ability to speak and understand sign language and Spanish.
- Team player with the ability to work independently.
- Attended communication and anger management workshops.
- Feel confident working in stressful, often unpredictable, potentially dangerous situations.

PROFESSIONAL EXPERIENCE

MOBILE CRISIS INTERVENTION SPECIALIST 1986-present
The Mobile Unit, LCSW, Inc, Santa Barbara, CA

- Mobile crisis team member.
  - Perform mental status exams. Determine suicide/homicide potential.
  - Help patients negotiate acute crises, forestall hospitalization, prevent recurrences.
  - Arrange inpatient psychiatric hospitalization as voluntary patient, or under W&I 5150 law as deemed necessary.

MENTAL HEALTH TECHNICIAN II 1984-86
Santa Barbara County, Psychiatric Health Facility

- Functioned in a psychiatric nursing capacity in acute care.

COUNSELING/TEACHING ASSISTANT 1982-84
Juvenile Services Center, (Detention Facility), San Luis Obispo, CA

- Assisted in all academic areas of the classroom.
  - Lead communication groups and conducted monthly first aid classes.

EMERGENCY MEDICAL TECHNICIAN 1980-82
Bay Ambulance, Morro Bay, CA

- Provided basic emergency medical services.
  - Taught CPR to law enforcement officers, firefighters, hospital personnel private citizens.

EDUCATION

BA Degree, Psychology, 1985
University of California, Santa Barbara

AA Degree, Psychiatric Technology
Ventura College, Ventura, CA, 1981

Personnel Administrator—Functional Resume
Making a Lateral Career Change

CARROLL S. ZEBRICK
9876 Rolling Hills Road
Montecito, CA 93108
(805) 966-3456

OBJECTIVE

Personnel Administrator

EDUCATION

BS Degree, Business Administration
University of Wyoming, Laramie, WYO

PROFESSIONAL EXPERIENCE

Personnel/Human Resources

- Oversaw Human Relations Departments for staffs of 35 to 120 employees.
  - Established effective policy and procedure personnel manuals.
  - Standardized all procedures to assure uniformity of operations.
  - Maximized employee morale and productivity.

Management & Administration

- Successful Administrator/General Manager for multi-million dollar corporations including corporate headquarters and five retail divisions in two states.
  - Established effective budgets and fiscal policies and procedures.
  - Administered and maintained warehouse and distribution facilities.
- Acted as management & planning consultant for numerous corporate clients in the areas of manufacturing, franchising and property development.

Business Development & Marketing

- Developed and implemented cost-effective programs to improve operations.
  - Restructured divisions resulting in increased product sales and profits.
  - Tripled gross receipts through six corporate acquisitions and mergers.
- Established a complete warehousing system, providing better service to dealers resulting in more efficient product management.
  - Increased sales from 45 to 285 percent.
- Successfully developed effective marketing strategies.
  - Moved large & small businesses operating at a loss to substantial profits.

EMPLOYMENT HISTORY

Administrator, Arrowhead Water Corporation, Santa Barbara — 1984-present
Management & Planning Consultant, Orange, CA — 1981-84
General Manager, Orange Water Company, Orange, CA — 1978-81

Personnel Adviser—Functional Resume
Making a Lateral Change from Administrator

DOROTHY MARGARET ALISON
7892 Forest Lane
Santa Barbara, CA 93105
(805) 966-9022

OBJECTIVE

A Student Personnel Advisor position in higher education

EDUCATION

- MA, Student Personnel Service & Counseling, 1975-79
  Trenton State College, New Jersey
- MS, Administration, 1972-74
  Fordham University, New York
- BS, Elementary Education, 1962-66
  St. Bonaventure University, New York
- Certification, St. Luke's Hospital School of Radiologic Technology, MA
- Spanish in the Workplace, Word Perfect
  Santa Barbara City College, 1990

PROFESSIONAL EXPERIENCE

Facilitator/Administrator

- Developed marketing strategies for the first Three-In-One Concepts programs throughout the Northeastern United States.
  - Became the main sponsor and source of information for...
  - training...seminars...workshops...private consultations...referrals.
- Conducted individual stress management consultation with clients.
- Presented Three-In-One Concepts professional development programs and special interest workshops to groups of 2-25 people.
  - Designed creative educational graphic materials.
  - Coordinated the entire setup: selected conference site, negotiated contractor fees, liaison between attendees and Three-In-One Concepts.
- Maintained public relations, appointment scheduling, bookkeeping, purchasing, inventory control and office management.

Chairperson - Higher Education

- Chairperson for the Radiography Education Dept. of a community college.
- Interviewed and recommended individuals for faculty and clerical staff.
  - Developed and assigned schedules for faculty and student personnel.
  - Submitted budgetary requirements meeting strict deadline schedules.
  - Conducted monthly department staff meetings and student orientation meetings.
- Coordinated educational assignments with 20 hospital affiliations thoroughout the state.
- Served as troubleshooter liaison between hospitals and the college.
- Planned/organized review classes for the National Registry Examination.
  - Responsible for a significant college success rate increase.

- More -

PROFESSIONAL EXPERIENCE (Continued)

Teaching Faculty - Higher Education

- Taught radiography education courses in classroom, laboratory and hospital environments for groups of 4-35 community college students.
  - Human anatomy & pathology...radiographic positioning...medical ethics.
  - Designed specific courses including visual support materials.
  - Evaluated and graded students through observation and written testing.
- Advised and referred students concerning education, curriculum transfer, career options and personal issues.
- Assisted students with course registration procedures.
- Participated in monthly departmental, divisional and college wide meetings.

PUBLICATIONS

"The Ultimate Belief System," Int'l Association of Specialized Kinesiologists, Apr-89; "One Brain," HOLISTIC LIVING, Nov/Dec-86, Volume III, No. 6

SPECIAL TRAINING/CREDENTIALS

* Ericksonian Hypnosis Training, Eastern NLP Institute, 1988
* Three In One Concepts Facilitator, Burbank, CA, 1984-85
* Holistic Health Education, 1983
  Kripalu Center for Holistic Health, MA
* Licensed Radiologic Technologist LRT (R), 1965
  New York State Department of Health
* Licensed Radiologic Technologist LRT (R), 1973
  New Jersey Dept of Environment Protection
* Registered Radiologic Technologist ARRT (R)
  American Registry of Radiologic Technologists

EMPLOYMENT HISTORY

Administrator, Concept to Reality, SB, CA — 1984-present
Chairperson/Associate Professor, Middlesex College, NJ — 1973-84
Instructor, Hostos Community College, NY — 1970-73

Personnel Counselor—Functional Resume
Recent College Graduate with Volunteer Related Experience

JULIE P. BRIGHTON

Current Address	**Home Address**
522 Lopez Road	PO Box 10775
Tarzana, CA 90405	Bellingham, WA 85271
(881) 999-6666	(202) 667-3333

Objective: A growth position in Personnel Relations

PROFESSIONAL PROFILE

- Outstanding ability to communicate with all types of people.
- Work well in highly competitive and challenging environments.
- Problem solver/team player with proven leadership qualities.
- 3-year member of the UCLA Leadership program.
- Studied English in eight countries of Great Britain, Europe and Israel.

PROFESSIONAL EXPERIENCE

Counseling & Supervision

- Counseled and supervised 50 freshman girls at UC Los Angeles.
- In charge of high school campers at two summer camps.
  - Demonstrated leadership skills during a 3-day backpacking trip and 6-day bike trek.
  - Counseled extensive one-on-one sessions with campers.
  - Led recreational activities and seminars.
- Scheduled appointments and counseled members in nutritional weight loss, weight gain diet plans for a busy health spa in Los Angeles, CA.

Human Relations/Organization

- Planned educational and recreational dorm activities for 50 freshman girls.
- Student Officer/Representative for University of California in Los Angeles.
  - Planned annual budget and coordinated activities including a major fund raising event and managed an eight team member committee.

EDUCATION

BA, Interpersonal Communications/English
University of California, Los Angeles, CA
Graduation: May 1988

EMPLOYMENT HISTORY

Counselor, Redwood Forest Lodge, Redwood, CA	Summer 1988
Camp Counselor, Mammoth Summer Camp, Mammoth Lake, CA	Summer 1987
Dorm Representative, UC Los Angeles, CA	1986-87

Personnel Supervisor—Functional Resume
Moving Up from Administrative Assistant

POLLY ANN PLACER
PO Box 3331
Los Altos Hills, CA 94022
(415) 941-0000

Objective: Personnel Supervisor

EDUCATION

BA Degree, Personnel Administration, 1988
University of California, Santa Barbara

PROFESSIONAL EXPERIENCE

HEWLETT PACKARD, (DMK Division) Sunnyvale, CA 1988-present
Personnel Administrative Assistant

Organization

- Established a purchase ordering system, resulting in faster productivity and a more efficient streamline operation; worked closely with buyers.
- Repaired and maintained photocopy machines for the whole division.
- Scheduled weekly meetings on the HP computer for the personnel dept.
- Gained vital computer, organizational and communication skills.

Administrative

- In charge of ordering and preparing bookkeeping of office supplies for the Direct Marketing Division of approximately 500 employees including... Personnel...Accounting...Sales...Telemarketing...Info systems etc.
- Maintained inventory control quickly and efficiently.
- Prepared expenditure reports for each office with attention to detail.
- Proficient on the Hewlett Packard, IBM and Macintosh computers.
- Learned to work on multiple projects in highly pressured situations, maintain a positive attitude and consistently meet deadline schedules.

Employee/Customer Relations

- Greeted clients and vendors, expediting challenges presented in a quick and friendly manner.
  - Operated a 150 multi-line computerized phone system.
- Learned to communicate effectively with fellow employees, clients and all levels of professionals in a highly diplomatic manner.

JESSE A. GONZALEZ
3459 Bear Creek Road
Anchorage, AK 99503
(907) 561-0002

OBJECTIVE: Manager of Latin America Operations for a major Petroleum Exploration Company.

PROFESSIONAL PROFILE:

- Possess thorough knowledge and understanding of the US/Latin American approach to business in the oil industry.
- Wrote and coordinated technical and administrative manuals and seminars, providing better systems and procedures.
- Gained valuable personal and business contacts throughout the oil industry of Latin America and the US market.
- Born and raised in Latin America; educated in the USA.

QUALIFICATION SUMMARY: Over 20 years experience in all phases of petroleum management and operations. Strong emphasis on contract negotiations between the United States and State-owned companies in Latin America. Maintain strong diplomatic relations, resulting in effective production and profitability in this highly competitive market.

PROFESSIONAL EXPERIENCE:

1979-present **GENERAL MANAGER**
XYZ Oil, Latin America, Inc, Anchorage, AK
Established a successful network of operations throughout Latin America selling oil tools and services to State-owned oil companies.

- Increased sales volume from $168K to $35M and staffing to 49 employees within 10 years.
- Developed a close rapport with the top executives and operating engineers of State-owned oil companies throughout the continent.

1976-79 **MANAGER OF LATIN AMERICAN OPERATIONS**
AK Production Services, AK Oil Tools Division, Anchorage, AK
Analyzed problem areas of company policy and procedures. Developed and implemented programs that improved operations and produced profits.

- More -

PROFESSIONAL EXPERIENCE: (Continued)

- Oversaw the operations of a $42.5M annual sales budget in 12 countries throughout Latin America.
- Set-up a distribution network, providing quick and efficient market penetration.
  - Increased sales revenue from $26.5M to $42.5M in 3-years.
  - Directly increased annual net profit margins by 10 percent.
- Wrote and coordinated technical publications and employee training manuals, seminars and workshops.
- Hired, trained, supervised and motivated 65 employees.

1965-73 **MANAGER OF EXPLORATION & DRILLING OPERATIONS**
AC Latin Oil, Lagunillas, Las Morochas, Maracaibo, Venezuela
Gained valuable knowledge of oil company operations in Latin America through promotions of the following positions:
Production Engineer...Special Projects Manager...Manager of Exploration and Drilling.

EDUCATION: **MBA Degree, International Marketing & Finance**
Rutgers Graduate School of Business
Rutgers University, Newark, New Jersey, 1974

MS, Industrial & Management Engineering
New Jersey Institute of Technology
Newark, New Jersey, 1972

BS, Geology & Petroleum Engineering
Universidad Central del Ecuador
Quito, Ecuador, 1965

AFFILIATIONS: Member, American Institute of Petroleum Engineers
Member, American Management Association

Pharmaceutical Sales Representative—Combination Resume
Housewife/Mom Re-Entering the Workforce

KARLA J. CAMPBELL
1256 Rocky Lane
Boulder, CO 85721
(303) 872-4444

OBJECTIVE

Sales/Marketing Representative for a pharmaceutical company

EDUCATION

BA Degree, Communication Studies, 1975
University of Colorado, Boulder, CO

Semester at Sea Program, Summer 1970
University of Pittsburgh
Around the world studies (12 countries)

RELATED PROFESSIONAL EXPERIENCE

BOULDER COTTAGE HOSPITAL, Boulder, CO 1980-85
Pharmacy Technician

- In charge of work flow for 16 technicians in the pharmacy department of a busy 6-floor, 400+ bed hospital.
- Key member in converting manual procedures to a highly sophisticated computerized pharmacy system.
  - Developed effective training methods for staff members.
  - Organized/conducted training sessions for technicians and pharmacists.
- Prepared/distributed unit dose & intravenous drugs for all nursing units.
- Interpreted and clarified physicians' orders with attention to detail.
- Served as liaison between pharmacists, physicians and nurses to insure accuracy and safety of pharmaceutical procedures for patients.
- Worked on multiple projects simultaneously under highly pressured situations and consistently met strict deadline schedules.

FT COLLINS PLAZA DRUG, Ft Collins, CO 1975-80
Pharmacy Technician/Cashier/Sales

- Answered customer inquiries and developed a large personal customer base, demonstrating thorough product knowledge and excellent customer service.
- Typed prescriptions into the computer. Thoroughly familiar with medical terminology.
- Prepared claims for Medi-Cal and Health Net insurance customers.
- Maintained purchasing, inventory/quality control, cash management, filing and phone skills with ability to work well under pressure situations in a professional and concerned manner.

PREVIOUS EXPERIENCE

Home Management, Research, Study, Boulder, CO 1980-91
Administrative Assistant, University of Pittsburgh 1970-75
Sales Associate, Paradise Drug, Paradise, CA 1968-70

Photographer, Commercial—Artist Resume
Recent College Graduate with Freelance Experience

ANGELA NORWOOD PHOTOGRAPHY
5160 Denny Avenue #22
North Hollywood, CA 91601
(818) 762-2814

COMMERCIAL PHOTOGRAPHER

EDUCATION: **BA, Commercial Illustration**, February 1989
Brooks Institute of Photography, Santa Barbara, CA
GPA: 3.85 Honor Roll/President's Honor Roll 7 times
Won "Pentax Tokina Photographic Scholarship" for $1,000
Won "Illustration Department Award" for outstanding achievement

PHOTOGRAPHIC SKILLS:

- Experience with 35mm, 2-1/4, 4x5 and 8x10 cameras.
- Professionally capable of lighting with Balcar, Comet, Norman and Speedotron strobes.
- Extensive knowledge of printing and processing color, black & white, kodalith and flat art copy films

CLIENTS/ PROJECTS:

Western Studios - Photographed production stills of Uncle Ben's Rice food commercial for company portfolio. Winter 1989

Half Baked Gourmet - Photographed and illustrated a food container with complete gourmet dinner for an advertisement and promotional display. Fall 1988

Alabama New Potatoes - Photographed and illustrated a sack of potatoes with company logo for farmer in Mobile, AL. July 1988

Photographer/Coordinator - Developed conceptual idea for a behind the scenes look at the filmmaking of The Long EZ; a two projector audio/ visual slide show at Brooks Institute. Produced, directed, photographed and programmed the entire project. Summer 1988

Internship, Henry Bjoin, Los Angeles, CA. Assisted photographer in filming commercial food products for Coca Cola, Cantadina, Kerr Pie Filling and Carnation. Gained extensive experience working in a professional commercial studio. Fall 1988

EMPLOYMENT: **Facility Coordinator**, Brooks Institute of Photography. Studio Manager Illustration Dept. Checked in/out equipment, scheduled studio space, assisted students using equipment and equipment repair. 1987-89

Photographer, Editorial—Artist Resume
Recent College Graduate with Freelance and Employment Experience

JIM ANTONIO
7770 Landre Lane
Santa Barbara, CA 93101
(805) 555-1123

EDITORIAL PHOTOGRAPHER

EDUCATION: **BA Degree, Illustration Photography,** 1988
Brooks Institute of Photography, Santa Barbara

PHOTOGRAPHY SKILLS: Gained a broad range of knowledge and skills in special techniques and still life, concept development, location/studio and set building. Strongly emphasize editorial and fashion photography.

- Experience with 35mm, 2-1/4, 4x5 and 8/10 cameras.
- Professionally capable of lighting with Balcar, Tungsten, Norman, Speedatron strobes and audio visual equipment to produce slide shows.
- Extensive knowledge of printing, black & white, kodalith, duping, and flat art copy films.

CLIENTS/ PROJECTS: **Alexis Productions** - Selected to photograph "Fall Vision," the annual fashion show for merchants in the Montecito and Santa Barbara area. 1986-87

Santa Barbara Independent - Photographed a variety of editorial work for the style section of this popular weekly news and entertainment newspaper. Summer 1988

DeMarcos Modeling Agency - Photographed fashion models for test shooting. Selected models, chose clothing, accessories and set scenes for a theme or to create the environment. 1986-88

EMPLOYMENT:

Spring 1988 HENDRY'S STUDIOS, Santa Barbara, CA
Internship
- Assisted the illustration photographer in all phases of commercial photography for this busy studio.
- Sharpened my technical skills and creative ability while working well under tight deadline schedules.

1986-88 BROOKS INSTITUTE OF PHOTOGRAPHY, Santa Barbara, CA
Technical Assistant
- Assisted students in the producing slide shows in the Audio Visual Dept.

Political Writer—Chronological Resume
Recent Graduate with Related Internship Experience

BLAIR LONDON
PO Box 12345
Santa Barbara, CA 93190
(805) 682-0799

OBJECTIVE: Political writer position

EDUCATION: **BA Degree, English,** May 1990
Bates College, Lewiston, Maine

EXPERIENCE:

1986-88 THE WHITE HOUSE, Presidential Advance Office, Washington D.C.
Presidential Trip Coordinator/Writer (1987-90)
- Created, coordinated and implemented all Presidential events: in-house...in-town...domestic...international.
- Coordinated logistics of Presidential events.
- Composed Event Concept Memo to the Chief of Staff.
- Wrote President's personal detailed schedule and Staff schedule for Presidential events.
- Liaison between White House Advance Office, White House Staff, Host Committee and all other entities involved in Presidential events and travel.

Press Schedule Writer (Spring 1986-87)
- Wrote and coordinated White House Press Corps schedule for the following International Presidential Travel:
  - 1986 Tokyo Economic Summit.
  - 1987 Official Visit to Ottawa, Canada.
  - 1987 Venice Economic Summit.
- Traveled in support of White House Press Advance to the following locations: Tokyo, Japan...Ottawa, Canada...Rome & Venice, Italy...Bonn & West Berlin, West Germany.

1982-86 ABC COMPANY, Santa Barbara, California
Executive Assistant to the President
- Composed, edited & typed personal/professional correspondence.
- Scheduled meetings, appointments; coordinated travel arrangements.
- Monitored local City Council & Re-Development Agency Hearings.
- Attended legal and architectural planning sessions.

Portfolio Manager—Functional Resume

CYNTHIA MEGAN KINNEL
369 Pacific Coast Highway
Malibu, CA 90265
(213) 971-4443

OBJECTIVE

A challenging career in Portfolio Management.

PROFESSIONAL PROFILE

- Valuable business contacts in the bond market worldwide.
- Extensive knowledge of financial instruments.
- Thrive on new opportunities for accomplishment and success.
- Sharp analytic, problem solving and presentation skills.
- Work well under highly pressured situations.
- Special talent for understanding client needs.

PROFESSIONAL EXPERIENCE

LOS ANGELES FIXED INCOME MANAGEMENT, Beverly Hills, CA 1980-90
Principal & Portfolio Manager/Trader

Portfolio Management
- Manage $5 billion of total-rate-of-return fixed income portfolios.
  - long duration...short duration...taxable...tax-exempt...sterling...individuals...nuclear decommissioning...immunization funds.
- Implement a highly disciplined investment process, flexible under all market conditions.
- In charge of active trading room and corresponding settlement operations.

Trading
- Maintain critical mode of evaluating and analyzing fixed income investment instruments and strategies.
- Analyze and trade various fixed income securities: governments...municipals...foreigns...corporates...mortgages.
- Evaluate yield curves, currencies, option adjusted spreads, duration and convexity.

Research Analysis & Evaluation
- Established an efficient credit research system.
- Organize client goals, objectives and restrictions.
- Monitor client characteristics.

EDUCATION

BA Degree, Business Economics, 1982
University of California, Los Angeles

Product Development Manager—Functional Resume
Financial Software Corporation

ROGER S. SAMPSON

5431 Virginia Avenue
Atlanta, GA 30306
(404) 815-1117

Objective: Product Development Manager

EMPLOYMENT HISTORY

Product Development Manager, MBI Technology., Atlanta, GA — 1988-present
Project Manager, Financial Credit Services., Atlanta, GA — 1980-88

PROFESSIONAL EXPERIENCE

Product Development Management

Managed the product development department for a $2.5B financial services corporation.

- Served as business solutions specialist, software development/modifications expert for operations personnel ..sales/marketing group ..technical staff ..national client base.
  - Conducted monthly status and motivational staff meetings.
- Hired, trained, supervised and scheduled product development staff.
- Prepared budgets, financial reports, executive management reports and employee evaluations and reviews.

Project Management

Managed a $1.6 million project and created the strategic plan for a financial services industry leader that currently serves as a model for all corporate and large scale development efforts.

- Planned, designed and implemented a unique comprehensive commercial accounts receivable system within strict timeline restraints.
- Organized and developed a 53 member team of computer programmers, systems analysts, marketing/sales staff, operation's personnel and outside consultants.
- Established a quality team system of communications between executive management, department directors and project team members.
- Developed a national client base working closely with national account managers and customer service representatives.
- Recognized for outstanding leadership efforts four times and received a formal award upon project completion.
- Developed and managed strategic initiatives that maximized client offerings and minimized all operating expenses.
  - Migrated accounts receivable systems in-house for two divisions.
  - Converted 12 new clients in one year including Goodyear and Tandy Corporation which became two of the business's most profitable clients.

EDUCATION

BS Degree: Computer Science, 1980
University of Georgia, Athens, GA

Product Development Manager—Functional Resume
Travel Industry

REBECCA LANDSBURY

1090 Florist Lane
Atlanta, GA 30303
(404) 815-0000

Objective: A Product Development Management position

QUALIFICATIONS

Product Development and Management ..Negotiating ..Marketing ..Advertising Research ..Sales ..Operations Management ..Computer Implementation Training ..Customer Service ..Excellent Oral/Written Communication ..Seasoned Traveler Worldwide

PROFESSIONAL EXPERIENCE

PRODUCT MANAGER 1985-95
Bermuda Tour Corporation, Atlanta, GA

Product Development

- Developed successful and innovative travel programs for wholesale tour operators to destinations throughout the world.
  Mexico ..Caribbean ..Asia ..China ..South Pacific ..Central and South America
  - Managed negotiations and contracting with hotels, resorts, airlines, tour companies and car rental agencies worldwide.
  - Devised and implemented independent and escorted air/land tour products.
  - Expanded a product line by 400 percent within first six months of employment.
- Analyzed pricing and tour inclusions of major competitors resulting in product expansion and improvement of existing line.

Product Management

- Established and implemented operational procedures for wholesale tour products.
  air control ..tour and escort management ..documentation control ..internal and external quality control ..costing and pricing
- Developed/implemented a centralized report system which reduced work hours by 40%.
- Researched and wrote a functional 60-page tour escort manual.

Marketing and Sales

- Developed marketing strategies with hotels, resorts, airlines, tour companies and car rentals. media kits ..marketing proposals ..newsletters ..postcards ..fliers ..documents.
  - Created/implemented newspaper, radio and trade publication advertising.
  - Developed seasonal and on-going promotions and incentive programs.

EDUCATION

- **BS Degree: Business Administration**, 1978
  University of Georgia, Athens, GA

Pro-Football Player—Chronological Resume
Moving Up from College Football Player

WADE ARTHUR WALLACE

Current Address
3211 Equestrian Court
Santa Barbara, CA 93103
(805) 569-1111

Agent
Greg Steele, President
Santa Barbara Sports Management

Objective: Pro-Football Player

PROFILE:

Birthdate:	December 21, 1966
Height/Weight:	6′ 4″, 235 Lbs
Position:	Tight End
40 yard dash:	4.69
Special Teams:	Kickoff, Kickoff Return, Punt Return, Punt

EDUCATION: **BA Degree, Physical Education**, 1990
University of California, Santa Barbara

PRO-FOOTBALL TRYOUTS:

May 1989
- WINNIPEG BLUE BOMBERS, CFL, Tryout
- DALLAS COWBOYS, NFL, Tryout
- UC IRVINE, NFL, Combine

FOOTBALL EXPERIENCE:

1987-89 UNIVERSITY OF CALIFORNIA SANTA BARBARA GAUCHOS
Robertson Gym, Santa Barbara, CA 93106
(805) 961-4153/961-3291

Record:	14 wins, 6 losses
Coach:	Mike Warren,
Stats:	72 receptions, 812 yards, 6 TD's, 11.3 yards per catch
1987 Jr:	24 receptions, 311 yards, 1 TD
1988 Sr:	48 receptions, 501 yards, 5 TD's

1985-87 CABRILLO COLLEGE JC SEAHAWKS, Santa Cruz, CA

Record:	15-5
Coach:	Don Montgomery/Joe Marvin
Stats:	38 receptions, 433 yards, 5TD's, 12.7 yards per catch

1981-85 SANTA CRUZ HIGH SCHOOL CARDINALS, Santa Cruz, CA

Record:	6-4 (senior year)
Coach:	Ron Mehuron
Stats:	33 receptions, 581 yards, 6 TD's, 17.6 yards per catch

CHARLES SAMUEL CHRISTOPHER
PO Box 333
Goleta, CA 93117
(805) 964-6666

Objective: A Programmer Analyst position.

COMPUTER SKILLS

Languages: "C", Pascal, Fortran, BASIC, COBOL, Prolog, Assembly, C++, dBASE
Hardware: IBM, Macintosh, VAX, NOVA
Software: MS DOS, DBASE III, Ctree, AOS, UNIX

PROFESSIONAL EXPERIENCE

CSR SOFTWARE INC, Santa Barbara, CA 1988-present
(A book publication software development manufacturer)
Computer Programmer Analyst

Programmer Analyst
- Maintain publication software programs for the Systems Development Dept.
- Developed software application and analyzed systems.
- Redesigned system resulting in a faster more efficient program.

Software Support Specialist
- Liaison between 1500 customers and 25 computer programmers.
  - Troubleshoot data management and other publication software systems.
  - Certify and test new publication software packages.
- Demonstrated strong analytical and written skills with ability to communicate with clients, employees and management in a professional manner.
- Scheduled, supervised and trained programming staff in the manager's absence.

Software Development Certification
- Developed several effective testing procedures on the IBM mainframe computer for 20 book publications.
- Wrote extensive testing reports; reported directly to the Department Manager.

EDUCATION

BA Degree, Computer Science, 1988
University of California, Santa Barbara
Graduated with honors

Michael T. Kelley

472 Peachtree Lane
Atlanta, GA 30307
(404) 872-5674

Objective: Project Manager

Employment History

Business Consultant, ARC Consulting, Atlanta, GA — 1990-present
Project Manager, IBM Corporation, New York, NY — 1985-90
Project Manager, American Express, New York, NY — 1983-85

Professional Experience

Project Management

- Oversaw the Corporate College Recruiting Program for IBM's 33 manufacturing and development locations and 12 area offices for engineering including: programming ..finance ..accounting and marketing professionals.
- Led several employee relation task forces that increased employee morale and provided management awareness.
- Designed and conducted several career development workshops for IBM and American Express that identified skill gaps.
- Created and delivered an innovative, interactive diversity awareness training module for managers and employee relations professionals.
  - speak with poise and confidence to audiences of 5-500 people.

New Business Start-up, Diversification

- Developed marketing plan for a private college increasing enrollment by 400%.
- Advised clients on details of how to start up new domestic services venture that increased market share by 500 percent.

Education

- **MA, Higher Education, 1980**
  New York University, New York, NY
- **BA, Psychology, 1978**
  John Jay College of Criminal Justice, NY

Project Manager—Functional Resume
Publications Industry

NICOLE E. GROUP

3321 Bridgetown Lane
Rosewood, VT 00120
(222) 904-0000

Objective: Project Manager

QUALIFICATIONS

Project Management ..Advertising Production ..Sales/Marketing ..Special Events
Project Coordination ..Negotiations ..Complex Problem Solving ..Color Reproduction
Magazine/Newspaper Makeup ..Strong Organizational Skills

PROFESSIONAL EXPERIENCE

PROJECT MANAGER 1978-present
Rosewood Publications, Rosewood, VT

Project Management

- Managed, coordinated and implemented over 30 special projects annually for a major daily newspaper with a circulation of over 850,000.
  Weekly TV Book ..Color Comics ..Daily 4-Color Newspaper Advertising
  - Obtained quality printers and successfully negotiated for best possible price.
  - Collaborated with Sales, Editorial, Creative Services, Scitex and Publication Departments to set up project specifications, procedures and scheduled deadlines.
  - Evaluated quality of materials and made recommendations to maximize revenues.
  - Analyzed proofs for quality color, style and accuracy of content.

Vendor and Client Relations

- Educated clients on specifications to maximize quality and insure efficient production.
- Developed and maintained excellent customer relations by creatively solving problems through increased advertising visibility to enhance results.

Sales, Marketing and Advertising Production

- Planned and oversaw new product from inception to printing of design and layout to insure appropriate color availability and advertising adjacency to editorial matter.
- Redesigned format of TV book which allowed more useable advertising space and increased advertising income by $4K per week.
- Motivated sales staff to meet quotas of $192K for semi-annual home magazine.
- Saved $250K annually by recommending alternative make-up of weekly TV magazine.
- Reviewed printers invoices and saved $3.5K in charges.
- Sold contract account advertising.

EDUCATION

AA Degree: Graphic Arts, 1978
Rosewood Community College, Rosewood, VT

MAGGIE CRENSHAW
PO Box 345
Santa Barbara, CA 93190
(805) 963-2222

Objective: Concert Promoter

PROFESSIONAL EXPERIENCE

Promotions/Management

- Showcase Director and President of the Songwriters Guild from 1986-88.
  - Interviewed and coordinated showcases for songwriter publishers and producers from Los Angeles looking for new material for major artists.
  - Set up monthly seminars, benefits and workshops for songwriters showcases.
  - Researched and located prices, dates and location for bookings.
  - Promoted events through radio, television and newspaper advertising, working closely with the media management staff.
- Musical Director for the production of *Godspell* in Hawaii in 1981.
  - Set up rehearsals, taught actors/actresses their musical parts and played keyboards for the production.
- Organized showcases to promote original music at "At My Place" in LA.
  - Booked club, hired outstanding backup musicians, taught them songs to showcase original material. Rehearsed with musicians individually and together as a band.
  - Sent out 70-100 invitations to record producers and publishers throughout Los Angeles to listen to new material.
- Coordinated special benefit for Child Help, an organization for abused children.

Songwriting Talents

- Wrote/recorded hundreds of songs in jazz, soul, rock/blues & contemporary pop.
- Wrote/sang "If My Love Is Blind" in the movie *Spellbinder,* an MGM release.
- Received numerous awards for "Best Song" with several offers to publish material through the Songwriters Guild in Santa Barbara, CA.
- Won 1st place for best vocal and songwriter out of 300 contestants in the production of Hawaii HomeGrown 4.

Musical talents

- Sing and play piano, electronic keyboards (synthesizer) in studio work, clubs, concerts and benefits nationwide. Successfully completed two demo albums.
  - Performed on an album and video for TV and radio for "Hawaii for Africa" and "Hawaii HomeGrown 4". Performed and interviewed for cable TV network.
  - Appeared as special guest for George Winston, Windham Hill Label.
  - Opened concerts for Dave Brubeck, Jesse Colin Young, Richie Havens.
  - Performed and choreographed dancing and singing at dozens of conventions throughout the Hawaiian Islands.
  - Performed with Cecelio & Kapono popular performers in Hawaii.

Promoter, Special Events—Functional Resume
Making a Lateral Career Change from Special Projects Coordinator

MELISSA D. PEARL
Special Events Promoter...Projects Coordinator
920 Calle Fiesta
Santa Barbara, CA 93111
(805) 569-9999

Objective: Special Events Promoter

PROFESSIONAL EXPERIENCE

Retail Sales & Client Relations

- Established a retail discount clothing store; increased annual sales volume to $1.5M.
- Reviewed wide range of designs, selected best combination of style, quality price, and on-going availability to purchase new clothing.
- Delegated preferred customer mailing lists, including customer follow-up.
- Oversaw and organized a successful visual merchandising team.

Promotions & Event Coordinator

- Planned, directed and coordinated innovative ideas for company parties, fund raising, weddings and other promotional events.
  -grand openings -fashion shows -seasonal events -employee functions
- Organized large retail clothing events for the fashion industry in 14 locations throughout the entire state of California.
  - Oversaw 10-30 employees for events that held as many as 2000 customers.
- Promoted fund raising events for organizations and businesses in southern and northern California through art exhibitions, aerobic marathons, theater and fashion shows.

Management & Finance Skills

- Established an effective computerized inventory control system.
- Set up a small business bookkeeping system for a retail store.
  - Consulted with accountants to insure proper recording.
  - Oversaw and processed payroll for 10-30 employees.
  - Designed forms for a better cash flow security system.
- Prepared monthly reports, financial budget and cash flow projections.
- Forecasted annual sales goals.
- Created an employee and customer discount credit system.
- Evaluated management staff for quarterly reviews.
- Conducted strategic and motivational meetings for all staff.
- Hired, trained, supervised and scheduled a dynamic management team.

EMPLOYMENT HISTORY

Special Projects Coordinator, Outlet Inc. No Retail Club, Ventura, CA	1985-89
Retail Store Manager, Esprit De Corp, San Francisco, CA	1983-85
Fashion Model, Allen & Hart Agency, San Francisco, CA	1982-84
Aerobic Instructor, Santa Barbara Athletic Club, SB, CA	1980-82
Sales Associate, Robinson's Department Store, Santa Barbara, CA	1979-80

Property Manager—Functional Resume
Property Owner with Related Personal Experience

BRIAN JESSE MORALES
39090 Water Drive
Santa Barbara, CA 93108
(805) 982-9000

Objective: A position with a Property Management firm.

PROFESSIONAL EXPERIENCE

Management & Supervision

- Six years experience as a highly successful owner/manager of two apartment buildings and three residential rental properties.
- Analyzed problem areas and developed systems to improve operations.
- Supervised maintenance and landscape personnel.
- Scheduled and monitored subcontractors to refurbish apartments within a strict budget.
- Increased security and improved landscaping.
- Reduced vacancy rates and overdue rents.
- Consistently administered annual rent increases.

Tenant, Vendor and Public Relations

- Located qualified vendors and accepted bid proposals.
- Interviewed prospective tenants, ran credit checks and drew up competitive rental contracts.
- Handled tenant complaints, requests and arranged maintenance services.
- Designed effective rental advertisements and arranged for open houses.
- Familiar with landlord/tenant legal rights.
- Developed superior professional rapport with tenants, vendors and subcontractors.

EDUCATION

Bachelor of Arts Degree, Biology, 1977
University of California, Santa Barbara

EMPLOYMENT HISTORY

Property Manager, Ray Montgomery Realty, Santa Barbara, CA	1984-present
Director of Int'l Sales, Signal Technology, Inc., Goleta, CA	1980-90
Sales Representative, Monroe/Litton Industries, Goleta, CA	1977-80

Property Manager, Real Estate—Functional Resume
Making a Lateral Career Change from Auto Leasing Manager

CRAIG J. LAWRENCE
PO Box 999
Santa Barbara, CA 93190
(805) 966-5432

Objective: Commercial Real Estate/Property Manager

PROFESSIONAL EXPERIENCE

Property/Business Management

- Managed and purchased three commercial real estate properties for corporate expansion, completing projects on-time and within budget.
  - Located qualified vendors and negotiated contracts.
  - Hired, scheduled and supervised vendors.
  - Acquired zoning variance and building permits.
- Established a better computerized payroll system.
- Developed an efficient transportation networking system for the government.
- Created time and motion studies for the trucking industry.
- Hired, trained and supervised 2-20 employees including: sales staff...drivers...mechanics...office staff...accountant.

Professional Salesmanship

- Sold equipment to Central California corporate and individual businesses.
  - Established leasing agreements, terms and equipment to meet customer specifications. Identified clients' needs, problems and solutions.
  - Demonstrated cold calling, telemarketing techniques and lead follow up.
- Established a loyal customer base and increased sales from $800K in 1983 to $2.5M in 1989 with thorough product knowledge, assertive salesmanship and consistent follow up.
- Conducted monthly motivation sales meetings for corporate officers.
- Successfully won Government contract bids for transportation services and purchased assets from vendors to meet government standards.

EDUCATION

BS Degree, Business Administration
Cal Poly, San Luis Obispo, 1984
Emphasis: Finance & Property Management

EMPLOYMENT HISTORY

Operation's Manager, Ajax Truck Leasing, Los Angeles, CA 1983-1991
Sales Manager, ABC Delivery Service, Los Angeles, CA 1984-89
Sales Representative/Manager, Valley Equipment Rental, Los Angeles, CA 1984-88

LESLIE J. CALLAHAN
5900 Lansing Street
Santa Barbara, CA 93105
(805) 966-9876

OBJECTIVE

A Marketing position for an advertising agency.

PROFESSIONAL EXPERIENCE

Seminar Coordinator & In-house Promotions

- Set up and oversaw marketing seminars involving extensive travel to major cities nationwide. Located guest speakers, handled client needs, etc.
- Developed and organized educational staff programs and presentations.
- Created and implemented social staff functions.
- Acting liaison between chief executive officer and all staff members.
- Coordinated and implemented marketing strategies with advertising agency.
- Illustrated and wrote correspondence for CEO.
- Composed thank you, policy change and apology letters to clients.

Marketing, Advertising & Outside Promotions

- Developed highly successful marketing strategies for promotions and sales.
  - Designed advertising and slogans for a monthly talk show and bi-monthly news program as a host and co-producer of a popular television station.
  - Promoted various shows resulting in an audience increase of 35 percent.
  - Established contact with local companies adding 20K members to potential audience.
  - Created designs for video advertisements and contributed to the production of concerts as the university Promoter.
- Wrote and presented two-weekly newscasts as a DJ and Newscaster.

Product Development & Organization

- Developed new products (tapes) to fill clients needs and requests.
  - Recommended and advised use to CEO and other decision-makers.
  - Promoted the use and goals of new and current products available.
  - Edited and reviewed products for maximum impact and effectiveness.
  - Recorded in-house sessions for reproduction.
  - Duplicate, label, order, budget and monitor new product.
- Established and maintained an effective bookkeeping system for clients request and payments for audio cassettes.
- As program director, successfully established a department for the university television network; recruited, trained and motivated staff members.

EMPLOYMENT HISTORY

PR Coordinator, Henry Mason Co, Santa Barbara, CA	1/88-present
DJ, Newscaster, WUNH 91.3 FM, Ventura, CA	1985-87
Program Director, STVN Television Network), Goleta, CA	1985-86
Host, Co-Producer, STVN, Goleta, CA	1984-86

Public Relations Representative—Chronological Resume
Recent College Graduate with Related Internship Experience

KATHRYN A. JACQUARD
444 College Avenue
Goleta, CA 93117
(805) 555-1234

Objective: A position leading to Public Relations career

PROFESSIONAL PROFILE: Success oriented with high energy and a positive attitude... strong sense of responsibility and self motivation...good written and oral communication skills...great problem solver and team player with the ability to work independently...creative, flexible and efficient.

EDUCATION: **BA Degree - Public Relations** - 1991
University of California, Los Angeles, CA

Study of the Arts, Paris, France - 1987
American Institute for Foreign Studies

PROFESSIONAL EXPERIENCE:

Summer 1989 **PUBLIC AFFAIRS INTERN**, General Hospital, Los Angeles, CA

- Wrote and edited press releases for local media and articles for in-house weekly newsletters and quarterly magazines.
- Developed successful advertising campaigns to promote major fund raising events; worked closely with TV, newspaper and radio news media.
- Created and designed effective brochures and flyers utilizing the desktop publishing system.

Fall 1988 **PUBLIC RELATIONS INTERN**, CBS Television, Los Angeles, CA

- Wrote and published effective newspaper advertising copy, press releases and letters to the business community.
- Developed marketing strategies to promote television services and sponsor community events throughout Santa Barbara.
- Learned research skills, writing techniques and the ability to communicate effectively with professionals of all levels.

1986-87 **SALES ASSISTANT**, Bullock's Department Store, Los Angeles, CA

- Persuasion and promotional skills used in product sales.
- Innovation to create new displays.
- Disciplined time management in a 50 hour work week.
- Active listening and professionalism employed in customer service and employee relations.

Public Relations Representative—Combination Resume
College Student with Related Internship Experience

JANICE CALDWELL

Campus Address
6643 Sueno #A
Goleta, CA 93117
(805) 562-8411

Permanent Address
207 Evening Canyon Road
Corona Del Mar, CA 92625
(714) 644-8018

Objective: An Internship leading to a career in Public Relations.

EDUCATION

BA Degree, Law and Society, June 1991
University of California, Santa Barbara

PUBLIC INTEREST EXPERIENCE

CALIFORNIA PUBLIC INTEREST RESEARCH GROUP — Santa Barbara, CA
Research Intern (Fall 1990)

- Researched and reviewed current periodicals and books pertaining to environmental energy policy and other public interest issues.
- Identified, reviewed, recommended and located new publications and articles for the resource center.
- Served as precinct leader for environmental electoral initiative campaign.
- Contacted local community through phone and door-to-door solicitation.
- Delegated, trained and supervised responsibilies to volunteer staff.
- Gained vital leadership, organization and interpersonal communication skills.

PUBLIC CITIZEN'S CRITICAL MASS ENERGY PROJECT — Washington DC
Researcher, Writer, Editor, Coordinator (Summer 1990)

- Researched/edited reports, press releases/editorials related to energy policy issues.
- Wrote a letter to Congress as part of an active lobbying campaign.
- Co-authored two published reports on pertinent energy issues.
- Worked directly with the media and national citizen groups. Learned how to communicate effectively with all levels of professionals.
- Helped organize and promote a national seminar and two press conferences.
- Consistently met demanding deadlines under highly pressured situations.

PREVIOUS EMPLOYMENT HISTORY

Wordprocessor, Freelance, Santa Barbara, CA — 1988-present
Community Service, Nat'l Charity League, Newport, CA — 1980-87
Office Assistant, Law Offices of Kasdan, Irvine, CA — 1985-86

Public Relations Representative, Broadcasting—Chronological Resume
Recent College Graduate with Related Internship Experience

LAURA K. DAMIAN

Current Address
45 Triego Avenue
Goleta, CA 93117
(805) 555-1111

Permanent Address
222 Circle Lane
Oceanside, CA 92667
(619) 222-1111

OBJECTIVE: **A Public Relations position in the Broadcast Industry.**

PROFILE:

- Financed education with experience in sales and management.
- Highly organized, dedicated with a positive attitude.
- Excellent written, oral and interpersonal communication skills.
- Problem solver/team player with proven leadership qualities.
- Traveled throughout Europe, Asia, India, Japan, Russia, USA.

EDUCATION: **BA Degree, Communications**
University of California, Los Angeles
Graduation: June 1989 GPA: 3.5

EXPERIENCE:

1988-89 **News Assistant Intern,** ABC Television, Los Angeles, CA

- Assisted the entire news broadcast management and staff.
- Wrote documentaries and news coverage.
- Teleprompt for the news staff during broadcasting.
- Coordinated advertising and processed extensive mass mailings on a weekly basis; consistently met demanding deadlines.
- Contacted public service throughout the Santa Barbara Tri-County area to provide information for news staff.
- Position requires the ability to handle multiple assignments under pressured situations quickly and efficiently.

Fall 1987 **Rush Counselor,** UC Los Angeles, CA

- Counseled 20 girls in the UCLA Sorority Rush Program.
- Set up/conducted stress management and problem solving meetings.
- Demonstrated strong leadership skills with the ability to maintain a positive attitude in highly pressured situations.

ACTIVITIES:

- Alumni Relations Committee member
- Rush Counselor
- Alumni Representative
- Philanthropy Volunteer

Public Relations Representative, Government—Functional Resume
Recent Graduate with School Project and Work Experience

ANDREW T. GILBERT
231 Forest Creek
Helena, Montana 59601
(406) 442-1112

SECURITY CLEARANCE

Objective: A position in Government Public Relations

EDUCATION

BA Degree, Political Science, 1990
University of California, Santa Barbara
Emphasis: International Relations

RELATED EXPERIENCE

Public Policy Writing & Research

- Researched and reviewed current and historical periodicals and books on domestic defense policy and constitutional theory issues.
- Wrote reports and speeches for numerous issues including defense procurement, interest groups and public policy elected officials.
- Consistently met demanding deadline schedules under pressure situations.

Public Speaking

- Set up and coordinated speeches for a public speaking group.
  - Reviewed speech outlines, scheduled topics and wrote transitions.
- Demonstrated poise and confidence while conducting presentations on international relations and public policy to large groups of students and faculty.
- Gained vital leadership, organization and interpersonal communication skills.

Security Clearance Position (Secret)

- In charge of eight buildings for a governmental defense contractor.
- Opened/closed facility through a computerized system securing confidential and secret information.
- Trained and supervised 10 security employees.
- Dealt with confidential and sensitive situations quickly and calmly.
- Thoroughly familiar with investigative and seizure policy and procedures for department of defense contractors.
- Currently hold an active security clearance (over two years).

EMPLOYMENT HISTORY

Security Corporal, ABC Research Inc, Santa Barbara, CA	1988-90
Bartender, The Galley Restaurant, Santa Barbara, CA	1987-90
Bartender, Glacier National Park, Montana	Summer 1989

Public Works Director—Chronological Resume
Moving Up from Principal Civil Engineer

DALE R. MASTERS
9032 Camaro Drive
Ventura, CA 93003
(805) 644-3333

Objective: Director of Public Works.

EDUCATION: BS Degree, Engineering Design
Brigham Young University, 1972

Registered Civil Engineer #1234
State of California Board of Professional Engineers

PROFESSIONAL EXPERIENCE:

1988-present JONAH, HART, & SPENCER, INC., Ventura, CA
Principal Engineer III

- Supervise design and prepare grading storm drain, sewer, and street improvement plans of land development projects.
- Coordinate extensive design and construction plans with utility companies; city, county, and state agencies.
- Supervise preparation of parcel and tract maps.
- Perform and review various street, retaining wall, hydrology and hydraulic calculations.

Deputy City Engineer (City of Santa Barbara)

- Supervise public works inspection.
- Prepare and administer issue street, grading, and storm drain permits.
- Inspect improvements for private development projects.
- Determine compliance of private development projects with city standards and conditions.
- Provide direction for developers and private engineers for processing improvement plans and maps.
- Prepare engineering conditions for tentative maps.
- Member of city's environmental review committee and development review committee.

1984-87 CAMPBELL & ASSOCIATES, INC., Camarillo, CA
Project Engineer

- Managed land development projects from concept review through all phases of design, approval, and construction.
- Performed extensive field coordination with survey crews, contractors, inspection, and utilities during construction phase of development projects.

Purchasing Manager—Functional Resume
Electronics Industry

DESIREE S. MUELLER
1120 Spruce Lane
Atlanta, GA 30306
(404) 872-1111

Objective: Purchasing Manager

EMPLOYMENT HISTORY

Senior Buyer, Georgia Pacific, Atlanta, GA 1985-present
Production Buyer, USA Industries, Atlanta, GA 1980-85
Assistant Electro-Mechanical Buyer, World Electronics, Atlanta, GA 1977-80
Assistant Buyer, Standard Electronics Co., Atlanta, GA 1976-77

PROFESSIONAL EXPERIENCE

Purchasing Agent/Senior Buyer

- Purchased electronic and electro-mechanical parts, MRO items, communication products, government contract items, food service equipment, office equipment and supplies for large and small manufacturers.
- Implemented buy-card system-accumulate order/cost history of purchased parts.
- Assisted in implementing an automated stock records systems.
- Compiled and loaded data for a computerized inventory control system which generated Bills of Material, stock lists and other inventory-related documents.
- Determined buy requirements for project buys.
- Negotiated and implemented annual orders for key components...integrated circuits, resistors, capacitors, connecters and special wirewrap boards.
- Negotiated/implemented annual purchase agreements at local and national level.
- Performed value analysis for product improvement.
- Located, evaluated and utilized new vendors.
- Reviewed receiving data and invoices for payment.

Purchasing Manager

- Supervised company purchasing activities for three manufacturers and established a purchasing policies and procedures manual.
- Trained and supervised purchasing clerical staff, buyer and expeditor.
- Coordinated the purchasing of electronic and mechanical parts, MRO items, outside fabrication and raw materials.
- Expanded the vendor base to insure a steady flow of parts at competitive pricing.

EDUCATION

BS Degree: Computer Science, 1977
University of Georgia, Athens, GA

PAULA L. GERALD
2954 Ignacio Lane
Montecito, CA 93108
(805) 569-0001

Objective: Real Estate Associate

PROFESSIONAL PROFILE

- Special talent for assessing people's needs and priorities.
- Outstanding ability to communicate with all types of people.
- Gained valuable contacts throughout the Santa Barbara community.

PROFESSIONAL EXPERIENCE

MERRILL LYNCH FINE HOMES, Montecito, California — May 1988-present
Real Estate Sales Associate

Real Estate Experience

- Exclusively sell fine homes throughout the Santa Barbara County.
  - Demonstrate strong visual insight and stage homes to obtain the best price for the seller and buyer.
  - Research computerized comparative analysis for appraisals.
- Attend City Council meetings to keep up with community projects...
  -condominiums -planned unit developments -new zoning ordinances

Client Relations

- Demonstrate poise and competence as a professional business representative in any social or business situation; work closely with elite clientele.
- Advise clients in a professional and concerned manner, securing their trust and confidence.
- Established a large personal customer base through thorough product knowledge, excellent sales ability and superior customer service; maintain continuous client follow-up lists.

Sales & Promotions

- Evaluate territories to develop successful marketing strategies.
  - Distribute promotional newsletters to potential clients.
  - Arrange and conduct open houses on a weekly basis.
  - Identify inventory every week through the local newspaper.
  - Active bi-weekly caravan member to obtain the Hot Sheet for new listings.
  - Attend weekly sales meetings and seminars to keep up with the current marketplace and latest, innovative sales techniques.

EDUCATION

California Real Estate Salesman's License, 1988

Real Estate Associate—Functional Resume
Changing Careers with Related Work and Personal Experience

PEGGY HOLDEN
111 Butter Lane
Santa Barbara, CA 93111
(805) 599-2345

REAL ESTATE ASSOCIATE

PROFESSIONAL PROFILE

- Outstanding talent for assessing people's needs.
- Proven ability to gain clients' confidence and trust.
- Gained valuable business and personal contacts throughout the Los Angeles and Ventura Tri-County areas.

RELATED EXPERIENCE

<u>Real Estate Experience</u>

- Assisted in the design, construction & sale of a Los Angeles condominium.
- Established an effective marketing strategy to promote the sale of property.
  - Designed flyers and newspaper advertising; distributed flyers.
  - Arranged and conducted open house.
- Familiar with blueprints and architectural plans; understand conceptual design.

<u>Sales, Promotions & Organization</u>

- Organized and coordinated an entire summer tennis program for children at a private tennis club in Montecito.
- Promoted services through effective telemarketing techniques, thorough product knowledge and exceptional client relations.
- Compiled computer data to keep track of profits & losses of monthly sales.

<u>Client Relations</u>

- Interface with clients and members to interpret their needs and priorities.
- Develop innovative, non-competitive teaching techniques for adults and children, focusing on individual strengths.
- Advise clients and members in a professional manner, securing trust and confidence.

LICENSE

California Real Estate Salesman's License, 1989

EMPLOYMENT HISTORY

Tennis Instructor, <u>A Tennis Club</u>, Montecito, CA	1987-present
Teacher's Assistant, <u>Los Angeles School District</u>	1985-87
Pre-School Teacher, <u>Children's Pre-School</u>, LA, CA	1983-85

Receptionist—Chronological Resume

DEBORAH ANNE BARETTO
PO Box 567
Santa Barbara, CA 93190
(805) 966-2222

Objective: Receptionist

PROFESSIONAL PROFILE:

- 6 years' experience in customer relations with office skills in the Medical and Aviation professions.
- Highly organized with attention to detail.
- Dependable, dedicated with a positive attitude.
- Outstanding ability to communicate with people.
- Excellent written and oral communication skills.
- Work well under pressure situations maintaining a concerned and professional manner.
- Eager to learn with ability to learn quickly.

OFFICE SKILLS: Light typing...filing...excellent phone skills...medical insurance and billing...scheduling appointments...data entry/IBM PC...posting monthly statements and accounts receivable.

EXPERIENCE:

SANTA BARBARA AVIATION, Goleta, CA 1989-present
Receptionist/Flight Dispatcher

- Greeted customers, answered phones and filed documents at this busy airport.
- Scheduled appointments for entire flight school, aircraft rentals and private corporate aircraft, working closely with corporate VIP's on a daily basis; scheduled fuel and catering orders.
- Required ability to work well with all types of people professionally and tactfully.

SANTA YNEZ CLINIC PHARMACY, Santa Ynez, CA 1986-89
Pharmacy Technician/Cashier/Sales

- Assisted four pharmacists at this busy clinic pharmacy.
  - Prepared claims for Medi-Cal and Worker's Compensation insurance customers.
  - Prepared accounts receivable and posted monthly statements.
  - Typed prescriptions into the IBM computer. Familiar with medical terminology.
  - Maintained excellent phones skills, expediting challenges presented in a quick and efficient manner.
  - Position required excellent customer relations, cash management, filing and phone skills with the ability work well under pressure situations in a professional and concerned manner.

RUTH ROUSSEAU

569 San Simeon Road
Ventura, CA 93003
(805) 656-3250

Objective: A Receptionist position

PROFESSIONAL PROFILE

- 10-years experience as receptionist, general office with superior customer relation skills.
- Excellent written/oral & interpersonal communication skills
- Highly organized, dedicated with a positive attitude.
- Ability to work on multiple assignments under pressure and consistently meet deadline schedules.

OFFICE SKILLS

IBM PC...DisplayWrite IV word processing...computerized billing...ten key adding machine...data entry...excellent phone skills...filing. Typing speed: 45 wpm

PROFESSIONAL EXPERIENCE

Communication Skills

- Key member in the installation of a customized ROLM phone system for IBM Corporation.
  - Worked with sales reps, management and technicians to establish Phone Mail system; responsible for all Phone Mail functions.
- Quick and efficient on the ROLM answering multiphone line system for 100 extensions.
  - Screen phone calls, expediting challenges customers presented in a highly professional manner.
- Responsible for answering customer and staff inquiries regarding to department rules, regulations and procedures.
- Scheduled appointments and travel arrangements for management staff.

Office & Organizational Skills

- Typed correspondence and memos on the word processor.
- Scheduled appointments for management staff.
- Maintained inventory control and purchased departmental supplies.
- Updated and maintained library manuals and policy/procedure manuals on a timely basis.
- Ordered IBM manuals for in-house staff members and customers.
- Processed orders and computerized billing.

EMPLOYMENT HISTORY

Secretary/Receptionist, IBM Corporation, Santa Barbara, CA — 1984-1990
Account Clerk, County of Santa Barbara, (Auditor-Controller) — 1981-84
Research Assistant, Professor William Madsen, UCSB, CA — 1980-81

Regional Sales Manager, Wine—Functional Resume
Moving Up from Store Sales Manager

PAMELA CATHERINE PARKS
PO Box 123
Sebastopol, CA 94098
(415) 244-2005

Objective: Regional Wine Sales Manager position

PROFESSIONAL PROFILE

- 10+ years experience in sales, management, public relations and promotions in the wine industry.
- Demonstrate exceptional presentation and customer relations, resulting in profitability in highly competitive markets.
- Highly organized, dedicated with a positive mental attitude.
- Outstanding ability to communicate with all types of people.
- Supervise employees with professionalism, diplomacy and tact.
- Gained valuable personal/business contacts throughout the local wine community.

PROFESSIONAL EXPERIENCE

MANAGER/EVENTS COORDINATOR
Sonoma Winery, Sonoma, CA — 1979-present

Administration & Management

- Manage the wine tasting room, conduct tastings and tours for the second largest winery in Santa Barbara County with international distribution.
  - "Most knowledgeable sales staff for tours and tastings", LA Times.
- Developed effective educational staff training programs with guest speakers for 17 wineries throughout Santa Barbara County.
- Hire, train and supervise employees, maintaining excellent staff relations.
  - Organized monthly motivational and educational staff meetings.
  - Maintain accurate records on a daily basis, meeting deadline schedules.

Customer Relations & Sales

- Market new products and successfully developed new territories.
  - Coordinate winemaker dinners and major special events for promotions and sales.
  - Set up displays that captured excitement and promoting sales.
  - Conduct winetastings in the retail room, private parties, restaurants and wine festivals nationwide.
  - Compose and type correspondence to customers regarding new releases and general information.

EDUCATION

BA Degree, Communications, 1979
University of California at Berkeley

JODY S. DAVIDSON

3321 Pharr Road
Atlanta, GA 30308
(404) 255-1209

Objective: Research Analyst

EMPLOYMENT HISTORY

DREXEL, BURNHAM LAMBERT, INC., Atlanta, GA 1988-present
Research Analyst, Institutional & Retail Sales

PROFESSIONAL ACHIEVEMENTS

Portfolio Trading and Sales Management

- Managed assets for 500+ accounts of select individual investors Institutional Sales and Retail Sales at Drexel Burnham Lambert and Oppenheimer.
  - Traded a high volume of equity and fixed income securities, specializing in index options and stock options.
  - Generated total annual retail and institutional commissions in excess of $4MM.
  - Coordinated accounts bond placements with corporate/municipal bond traders.
  - Negotiated/obtained large IPO allocations, working with local syndicate managers.
  - Bought and sold precious metals and other commodities.
- Strengthened business success while updating clients on market developments and informing them on current investment opportunities.
  - Coordinated and organized bi-annual educational seminars for investors.
  - Advised clients on asset allocation possibilities, consistently achieving objectives.
  - Educated new clients on the total investment process.

Financial Operations Management

- Managed all operations matters and resolved all problems for 500+ retail accounts at Drexel Burnham Lambert and Oppenheimer.
  - Produced annual profit and loss statements for 100+ accounts, maintaining strict tax deadline schedules.
  - Administered an employee profit sharing plan with assets in excess of $500M, ensuring asset liquidity.
  - Oversaw two university trust accounts with assets each of $100M, consistently meeting all trust agreement guidelines.
- Identified client needs, problems and solutions, serving as liaison between clients and senior vice president, demonstrating special talent for gaining client trust and confidence.

EDUCATION

MBA Degree: Ecconomics and Finance, 1994
Emory University, Atlanta, GA

BBA Degree: Finance, 1988
Kennesaw College, Dean's List

Research Historian—Functional Resume
Recent Graduate with Related Volunteer, School Project and Work Experience

SUSAN E. PERLMAN
39 Wilcox Lane
Ft Collins, CO 80521
(303) 671-4798

Objective: Research Historian

EDUCATION

MA Degree, History, 1990
New Mexico State University, Las Cruces, NM
Master's Thesis: "Livestock Policy of the Zuni"
Indian Tribe: 1900-1942

Paralegal Certificate, 1983
Denver Paralegal Institute, Denver, CO

BS Degree, Environmental Interpretation, 1979
Colorado State University, Fort Collins, CO

PAPERS PRESENTED

"New Deal at Zuni: The Range Management Program,"
Historical Society of New Mexico, Annual Conference, April, 1990

"Zuni Indian Livestock Policy During the Early Twentieth Century,"
Historical Society of New Mexico, Annual Conference, 1989.

"Apache Scouts and the United States Army,"
Phi Alpha Theta Regional Conference, 1988.

PROFESSIONAL EXPERIENCE

Research: Historical & Technical

- Prepared reports on natural resource utilization on Indian lands in New Mexico and Arizona.
  - Researched government documents, regulations, serials, archives, secondary sources.
  - Compiled, abstracted, and analyzed raw data.
  - Performed title searches in county and federal records.
- Coordinated court exhibits and data tables prepare for submission of land claims report.
- Conducted historical research projects as a graduate research assistant.
- Performed legal research and administration of law library.
- Conducted technical research in the following fields: forestry...agriculture...animal husbandry...and hydrology.

- More -

PROFESSIONAL EXPERIENCE (Continued)

Writing: Historical & Technical

- Wrote reports on Native American land and water utilization and rights for litigation use.
- Assembled annotated bibliographies for economic and resource study.
- Drafted pleadings for real estate, litigation, and estate administration.
- Composed and maintained correspondence with clients.Communication Experience
- Conducted extensive oral interviews; interviewees included Native American prison inmates, Native American livestock producers, alumnae for university centennial, legal and social services clients.
- Served as liaison between Native American self-help group and prison administration.
- Initiated development of cooperative programs with government agencies and community organizations.
- Worked closely with local, state, federal agencies and community groups.
- Established US Forest Service Visitor Center; responsible for development of exhibits.

Technical Experience

- Operate computers for database, writing, research, file management, and abstracting.
- Skilled interpreter of photographs and topographic maps.
- Maintained timber inventory and timber sale layout.
- Supervised timber field crews.

EMPLOYMENT HISTORY

Historian, Historical Research Associates, Missoula, Montana — 1989-present
Sponsor, Native American Council,
Southern New Mexico Correctional Facility, Las Cruces, NM — 1988-89
Research Assist, Institute of North American West, Albuquerque, NM — 1988
History Research/Teaching Assistant, New Mexico State University — 1987-89
Medicaid Elig Tech, Larimer Cty-Social Serv, Ft Collins, CO — 1984-86
Legal Sec/Paralegal, Remington Plaza Law Offices, Ft Collins, CO — 1984
Paralegal Intern, Environmental Defense fund, Boulder, CO — 1983
Forestry Tech, US Forest Service, Ft Collins, CO — 1979-81

Restaurant General Manager—Functional Resume

ROBERT C. CARUSO
501 Sandstone Avenue
Hollywood, CA 90067
(213) 969-2345

Objective: General Manager in the Food Service Industry

PROFESSIONAL EXPERIENCE

General Management

- Successfully started up a new business with three locations.
  - Setup floor plans, employee stations and master schedules for restaurant/bars.
  - Developed and implemented restaurant and bar training manuals.
  - Established better policies and procedures resulting in more efficient productivity to deal with employees and clientele on a daily basis.
  - Developed effective computerized accounting procedures.
  - Interviewed, hired, trained and supervised all personnel (100 employees).
- Located and booked entertainment; setup annual contracts with local hotels resulting in bottom line savings of $10K per year.
- Set up and maintained on-time work schedules, food preparation, menu selection and cost control and quality & inventory control, payroll budget, purchasing, accounting procedures, weekly sales forecast.

Client Relations

- Oversaw efficient, courteous and friendly service, consistently providing a pleasant atmosphere for our customers.
- Established excellent rapport with clientele, expediting challenges customers presented in a quick and creative manner.

Head Bartender/Regional Trainer

- Taught professional bartending to bartenders throughout Southern California for TGI Fridays, a fast-paced restaurant and bar.
  - Became main source of information and troubleshooter for entire region.
  - Developed highly successful incentive & training programs; involved creativity & high energy atmosphere, focusing on flair and showmanship.
- Worked with waiters/waitresses to maintain working order of establishment emphasizing high quality of professionalism and excellence.

Sales, Marketing & Promotions

- Created company-wide incentive programs increasing monthly sales by $5K.
- Developed, effective advertising techniques organizing special events to generate new business for seasonal promotions and sales.
- Created holiday bar drinks and decorations for promotions and sales.
- Achieved five awards for #1 regional sales and training in California.

EMPLOYMENT HISTORY

General Manager, BB O'Briens, Santa Monica, CA — 1988-present
Head Bartender/Reg'l Trainer, TGI Fridays, Los Angeles, CA — 1984-88

Restaurant Manager Trainee—Combination Resume
Moving Up from Head Waiter

DARREN N. ROSCOE

PO Box 456
Santa Barbara, CA 93190
(805) 968-0001

Objective: Restaurant Management Trainee

PROFESSIONAL PROFILE

- Highly organized, dedicated with a positive attitude.
- Effective problem solver with attention to detail.
- Special talent for assessing company needs and priorities.
- Outstanding ability to communicate well with clients, fellow employees and all levels of management.
- Traveled extensively throughout Asia, Australia, Micronesia, North and South America.
- Gained valuable business and personal contacts through my corporate membership at the Santa Barbara Athletic Club

EDUCATION

Hotel & Restaurant Management Program
Santa Barbara City College, 1988

CURRENT RELATED EXPERIENCE

THE PALACE CAFE, Santa Barbara, CA 1986-present
Head Waiter

Management & Organization Skills

- In charge restaurant operations for a very upbeat, service-oriented fine dining Cajun cuisine.
- Represent restaurant at banquets and special events serving 20-500 guests for major companies throughout Santa Barbara county.
  - Involves in set up and serving guests; prepare and display decorations.
- Train and supervise 7-8 dynamic employees with professionalism, diplomacy and tact.
- Work well under pressure situations and meet strict deadline schedules.

Professional Salesmanship

- Developed incentive programs through media advertising increasing sales and visibility.
  - Consistently achieve "Top Sales Producer" during company promotions.
- Set goals to achieve customer satisfaction on a daily basis.
- Built a large personal customer base through excellent sales ability, thorough product knowledge and superior customer service.

PREVIOUS EMPLOYMENT HISTORY

Waiter, Enterprise Fish Company, Santa Barbara, CA 1985-86
Busboy, Arnold's Diner, Manhattan Beach, CA 1984-85

PAULINA CANTWELL
2905 Whittley Drive
Washington, DC 13201
(202) 234-1809

RETAIL SALES MANAGER

PROFESSIONAL OBJECTIVE: An innovative and progressive company in the Fashion Industry

PROFESSIONAL PROFILE: Success oriented with high energy and a positive mental attitude...strong sense of responsibility and self motivation...good written and oral communication skills...great problem solver and team leader/player abilities...highly creative and flexible.

QUALIFICATION SUMMARY: Five years professional experience of proven leadership and salesability in the retail Fashion Industry. Emphasize strong sales techniques, excellent employee and customer relations, resulting in production and profitability in this highly competitive market. Responsible for over $1M annual sales and merchandise.

PROFESSIONAL EXPERIENCE:

1984-90 **SALES MANAGER**, Rumours, Washington, DC. Started as a sales clerk for this busy medium sized fashion boutique. Responsible for entire retail sales operation, maintaining $100K monthly inventory for two locations. Hired, trained and supervised a dynamic staff of 20 personnel, maintaining excellent employee relations. Conducted motivational sales meetings for all staff.

Developed successful advertising campaigns for promotions and sales involving fashion shows, direct mailouts and trunk shows. Generated and maintained new business, successfully developing a large personal customer base and created and maintained a "Preferred Customer List" that included customer follow up. Position involved buying ($65K monthly), inventory and quality control, merchandising, shipping and receiving, accounts payable, payroll, banking and cash management.

** Consistently increased sales over quota.
** Successfully reorganized department and rewrote employee training manual and new, effective policy and procedures.
** Converted manual accounting procedures to in-house computerized accounting system.

Retail Sales Manager—Chronological Resume
Recent College Graduate with Sales Work Experience

SUSAN M. SALLENOFF
1251 26th Avenue
Bellingham, WA 22220
(202) 777-1234

SALES MANAGER/REPRESENTATIVE

PROFESSIONAL OBJECTIVE: Seeking a reputable company offering salary based on individual contributions to goals.

PROFESSIONAL PROFILE: Success oriented and competitive with high energy and a positive mental attitude...strong sense of responsibility and self motivation...good written and oral communication skills...great problem solver and team player with proven leadership qualities... enthusiastic...creative...flexible and efficient work habits.

SALES EXPERIENCE:

1982-present **SALES ASSOCIATE**, Sears Department Store, Santa Barbara, CA.

- Consistent award winner and top percent over goal of maintenance agreements for the entire store.
- Successfully generate and maintain new business with thorough product knowledge in the Appliance, Men's Clothing and Shoe departments meeting deadlines on a daily basis.
- Help customers make satisfactory buying decisions while developing a large personal customer base, involving maintenance agreement sales and customer follow up.
- Demonstrated effective problem solving skills, expediting challenges customers present in a quick and creative manner.

1988-present **MARKETING REPRESENTATIVE**
Market Source Corporation, Cranbury, NJ.

- Set up booths to promote products of major charge card, food, corporations nationwide.
- Work closely with the University of California and real estate agencies throughout the Tri-County.
- Consistently meet company quota of promotions and sales.

EDUCATION: **BA Degree - Physical Education/Health**, 1988
Westmont College, Santa Barbara, CA

LUCY L. FIDDERMAN

PO Box 10005
Santa Barbara, CA 93150
(805) 569-0000

Objective: A Retail Sales Management position

PROFESSIONAL PROFILE

- 15 years experience with inside/outside sales and management.
- Highly organized, dedicated with a positive attitude.
- Special talent for developing excellent rapport with clients.
- Team player with outstanding ability to communicate with all levels of professionals.
- Problem solver with attention to detail.

PROFESSIONAL EXPERIENCE

Professional Sales Ability

- Developed highly successful marketing strategies for promotions and sales.
- Established new territory and met quota on a quarterly and annual basis.
  - Identified clients' needs, problems and solutions.
  - Introduced products to buyers at trade shows throughout the western United States.
  - Demonstrated effective cold calling techniques.
  - Delivered product demonstrations to business groups and individuals.
  - Developed a large personal customer base through excellent sales ability, thorough product knowledge and superior customer service.
  - Created and maintained a preferred customer list with lead follow up.
- Became the #1 company in the retail sales field for the State of California.

Management & Administration

- Established, managed and operated two manufacturing companies and a chain of art and fashion retail stores.
  - Hired, trained and supervised staff of 10-33 employees.
  - Conducted weekly motivational sales meetings for all sales staff.
  - Prepared bookkeeping and annual sales forecasting.
  - Maintained inventory, quality control, shipping and receiving, banking and cash management. Selected and purchased merchandise.

EDUCATION

Bachelor of Arts Degree, San Francisco State University

EMPLOYMENT HISTORY

Consultant, LF & Company, Santa Barbara, CA — 1986-present
Sales Representative/Manager, Brice Fashions, San Francisco, CA — 1980-86
Sales Manager, Lucy's Boutique, San Francisco, CA — 1973-80

Retail Sales Manager—Functional Resume

RICHARD L. RHODES
678 Del Rio Way
Goleta, CA 93117
(805) 964-2222

OBJECTIVE

Retail Sales Manager

PROFESSIONAL PROFILE

- Experienced in management, sales and customer relations.
- Highly organized, dedicated with a positive attitude.
- Special talent for assessing company needs and priorities.
- Resourceful; skilled in analyzing and solving problems.
- Work well under pressure; maintain a professional manner.

PROFESSIONAL EXPERIENCE

Retail Management Capabilities

- Proven success and thorough knowledge in all aspects of retail management.
- Maintain efficient inventory and quality control.
- Attend seasonal buyer shows.
- Familiar with cash management, purchasing and merchandising.
- Supervise and train all types of personnel in a highly professional manner.
- Correspond effectively with vendors.
- Satisfy all types of customers.
- Develop effective advertising strategies for promotions and sales.

Special Achievements

- Set up a better inventory control system.
- Increased sales in major department stores and built a large customer base through excellent sales ability, hard work and superior customer service.
- Cut profit losses in half.
- Improved employee morale.

EDUCATION

Santa Barbara City College, Santa Barbara, CA
Retail Management...Marketing...Business Math

EMPLOYMENT HISTORY

Sales Manager, The Emporium, Santa Barbara, CA	1987-present
Sales Associate, The Clothing Mart, Santa Barbara, CA	1985-87
Head Cashier, Orchard Supply Hardware, San Diego, CA	1983-85

MICHAEL KENNETH DANIELS
9 East Olive Avenue
Santa Barbara, CA 93103
(805) 569-1111

Objective: University Rowing Coach position

COACHING EXPERIENCE:

1987-91 **FRESHMAN/NOVICE MEN'S ROWING COACH**
University of California, Santa Barbara, CA
Responsible for on and off campus and mail recruitment, fundraising efforts, public relations, equipment maintenance, travel/ accommodations, scheduling, supervision and training. Became the the most successful team in the history of UCSB.

HEAD COACH/COORDINATOR
Santa Barbara Rowing Club, Santa Barbara, CA
Developed and operated the Santa Barbara Junior Rowing Program for all high school and junior high school men and women. Responsible for all public relations, advertising, recruitment, budgeting, equipment repairs, purchasing and fundraising. Achieved national recognition within two years.

1984-86 **FRESHMAN/NOVICE MEN'S ROWING COACH**
San Diego State University, San Diego, CA
Responsible for all recruitment, fundraising, public relations, supervision and various administrative aspects of the program. Program was highly successful in all respects.

1983-84 Summers **VOLUNTEER COACH**
West Side Rowing Club, Buffalo, NY
While training for the US National Championships, served as volunteer coach for novice and recreational rowers.

1982-83 **ASSISTANT COACH (Freshman/Novice Programs)**
San Diego State University, San Diego, CA
Assisted with all aspects of coaching, administration and training of young college athletes.

EDUCATION: **Graduate Studies, Athletic Administration**
University of California, Santa Barbara, 1988

BA Degree, Athletic Administration
San Diego State University, San Diego, CA 1982

JOSEPH S. HAMPSHIRE
PO Box 12334
Santa Barbara, CA 93190
(805) 569-1111

Objective: National Sales Director

PROFESSIONAL PROFILE

- Consistently build organizations with major sales and profit increases in hospital capital goods, disposables and services.
- Proven record in successful product identification, development and introduction.
- Skilled in managing diverse multiple functions to achieve corporate objectives.
- Highly adaptive strategic thinker equally able to direct entrepreneurial as well as more mature organizations.

PROFESSIONAL EXPERIENCE

MEDICAL SOFTWARE CORPORATION, Santa Barbara, CA 1986-present
Director of Sales & Marketing
Managed all aspects of business operation for this start-up medical software company including strategic and business plans and venture capital fund raising activities.

- Developed strategic and short-term operating plans.
- Secured bridge financing of $800K.
- Reduced operating expenses from $140K monthly to $70K/mo.
- Restructured license agreements and negotiated contract closure with two major university centers representing $450K.
- Developed and implemented staff requirements plan for recruiting Marketing, Client Services and key management eliminating less critical/productive personnel.

MEDICAL EQUIPMENT CORPORATION, Ventura, CA 1971-86
Marketing/Sales Manager
Managed all domestic marketing, sales, service and clinical education activities for this $100M cardiovascular and anesthesia device and equipment manufacturer. Revenue in excess of $80M. Operation budget in excess of $25M. Total staff exceeding 250 personnel, including three national sales organizations, marketing administration, national field service and clinical education organization in six regional centers.

- Achieved sustained 5 year revenue growth in excess of 25 percent annually with pretax earnings above 20 percent.
- Introduced 10 major new monitoring products and 5 cardiac assist products.
- Established company as the dominant manufacturer of intraaortic balloon pumping with market share exceeding 80 percent and as the leading supplier of patient monitoring equipment for hospital surgical suites.
- Built company sales, service, marketing and education departments into industry model as reported by independent industry analysts.
- Established key clinical relationships for advanced product R&D and premarket clinical acceptance testing in all market product areas.

BRYAN WHENT
201 Lenox Road
Atlanta, GA 30306
(404) 815-3412

Objective: Sales Management

PROFESSIONAL EXPERIENCE

SALES MANAGER 1989-present
World Hair Care Products, Inc., Atlanta, GA

Sales Management & Organizational Development

- Managed, organized, coordinated and maintained over 200 accounts for a multimillion dollar distributor, recognized as a leader in the hair care industry.
  - Developed promotional campaigns to increase sales of customer products lines.
  - Recovered and secured commercial and individual accounts in a South Georgia territory that increased profit margins by 30 percent per month.
  - Expanded quarterly account base by 40 percent, exceeding all quotas through cold calling techniques.
  - Established a loyal customer base through excellent customer service, thorough product knowledge and regular follow up procedures.
  - Delivered powerful sales presentations to groups of 5-50 people and increased sales revenues by an average of 28 percent each month.
  - In charge of the North Metro Atlanta territory including Marietta, Kennesaw, Roswell and Buckhead, the oldest and largest accounts in the distributorship.
  - Coordinated and conducted monthly financial, marketing and motivational meetings to educate customers and solidify their business success.
  - Worked closely with customers to write and design effective newspaper and radio advertising and promote their product lines.
  - Delivered product demonstrations at annual international trade shows nationwide.

Operation's Management

- Set up and installed a highly sophisticated custom computerized inventory and financial software program for several hair care accounts.
- Reorganized territories for the multimillion dollar hair care distributorship that resulted in better customer service and increase in sales potential corporate-wide.
- Managed, trained, supervised and scheduled a staff of 2-8 employees for the new location of a very service-oriented national sports retail chain in Atlanta.
  - Promoted an in-house team concept that increased employee morale.
  - Selected and purchased quality merchandise at the best possible price.
  - Helped customers make buying decisions and developed a dependable customer base through dedication, product knowledge, hard work and word-of-mouth.

EDUCATION

- **BA Degree: Communication and English**, 1989
  University of Georgia, Athens, GA GPA: 4.0

BRANDEN STARK
1120 Trailridge Road
Atlanta, GA 30306
(404) 815-0039

Objective: Sales Management

PROFESSIONAL EXPERIENCE

Sales Manager, USA Freight Lines, Atlanta, GA 1988-present

Professional Sales Ability

- Developed highly successful marketing strategies and maintained *120 active food and beverage accounts* including 5-star hotel, resort and restaurant chains in South Carolina and Southern Georgia for one of Southeast's premium food and supplies corporations.
- Expanded account base by 30 percent through leads and cold calling techniques and total volume by 52 percent; identified clients' needs, problems and solutions.
- Established new territory and exceeded quota on a quarterly and annual basis.
- Set up and implemented successful product distribution centers throughout the Southeast.
- Introduced products to buyers at trade shows throughout the Southeast.
- Delivered strong and powerful product demonstrations to business groups and individuals.
- Conducted seminars and workshops at three locations throughout the Southeast on: *Quality Improvement ..Customer Service ..Reducing Claims ..Driver's Safety*
- Taught and certified 20 managers and supervisors in Statistical Management.

Management & Administration

- Supervised 3-52 drivers, dock workers and customer service personnel at three locations for the Southeast's #1 multi-million dollar transportation corporation.
- Received Quality Without Question Awards, eight times for outstanding customer service and operational achievements. Promoted three times in less than two years.
  - Ranked #1 in 1994 by maximizing operation efficiency/customer service.
  - Reduced service errors on the inbound shift from 11 per day to one error by-monthly.
  - Became the first employee to reduce destination delay from 1.07 to 0.57.
  - Decreased Freight No Paperwork (FNP) errors from 3 weekly to 0.
  - Reduced service errors on outbound shift from 5 weekly to 1 per week.
  - Increased pickup and delivery productivity by 11 percent in 1994.
- Increased load average from 20,000 pounds to 25,000 pounds per trailer in 1995.
- Served as expert to identify problems/solutions for sales, service, claims and production.
  - Provided a study of the outbound workforce of 135 employees at the Atlanta terminal that resulted in reducing turnover ratio by 19 percent.
  - Prepared weekly statistical analysis of customer claims and service errors.
  - Compiled, analyzed data, identified problems, reduced liability of all vehicle accidents.

EDUCATION

BA Degree: Political Science, 1987
College of Charleston, Charleston, SC

Sales Manager, Fine Arts Gallery—Functional Resume

ZORAH A. HURD
6390 Central Park East
New York, NY 10021
(212) 431-0002

Objective: Sales Management position for a Fine Arts Gallery

PROFESSIONAL PROFILE

- 25 years experience in all phases of fashion and editorial design and management in retail, advertising industries.
- Excellent written, oral, interpersonal communication skills.
- Problem solver/team player with proven leadership qualities.
- Invited to display artwork at private and public shows nationwide. Won several awards.

EDUCATION

Editorial/Fashion Illustration, Parsons School of Design, NY

PROFESSIONAL EXPERIENCE

Design and Illustration

- Designed/illustrated original artwork on greeting cards and 3-dimensional ornamental designs for accredited Scandinavian department store and several design firms.
- Designed artwork for engravers of Steuben Glass Fine Arts Crystal.
- Traveled to major fashion shows throughout New York City to design and illustrate the fashion booklet for Associated Merchandising Corporation.
- Coordinated fashion/accessories for photographer in the fashion catalog.
- Displayed original acrylic paintings at art shows/galleries nationwide.

Management and Administration

- Managed and supervised employees at a busy antique shop in Corning, NY.
- Hired, trained and supervised a staff of four employees.
- Buyer of antique, vintage clothing and mid-century designs.
- Maintained inventory/quality control, merchandising, shipping/receiving, accounts payable and receivable, payroll, banking and cash management.

Promotions & Customer Relations

- Designed interior and window displays that promoted sales.
- Developed successful advertising campaigns.
- Illustrated fashion and accessories of fine women's clothing store for advertising, promotions and sales.
- Established a large personal customer base. Maintained a preferred customer list.

EMPLOYMENT HISTORY

Sales Manager/Buyer, The Sow's Ear, Corning, New York — 1975-present
Greeting Card Designer, Bergdorf Goodman, New York City, NY — Freelance
Engraving Designer, Steuben Glass, New York City, NY — Freelance

Secretary—Chronological Resume
Moving Up from Clerk Typist/Office Assistant

SANDI L. LYONS
PO Box 333
Santa Barbara, CA 93105
(805) 687-0009

Objective: A Secretary position

PROFESSIONAL PROFILE:

- Highly organized, dedicated with a positive mental attitude.
- Exceptionally reliable, conscientious and thorough.
- Thrive on challenging tasks in a busy office.
- Studied BASIC computer language, office management, Microsoft Word and Word Perfect word processing, ten-key by touch and computerized accounting in Lotus 1-2-3.

EDUCATION:

Secretary/Word Processor, 1991
Santa Barbara Business College, Santa Barbara
Graduated in the top 5% of my class.

Office Machine Skills Class, 1990
Santa Barbara City College, Santa Barbara

EXPERIENCE:

1986-91 NEW YORK LIFE AMERICA, Santa Barbara, CA
Clerk Typist
- Prepared calculating sheet from clients file.
- Typed data entry into computer, assembled updated material.
- Answered agents questions concerning clients file, quickly and efficiently.
- Improved filing system.

1980-85 EQUITY LOANS INC., Santa Barbara, CA
General Office Clerk
- Financed education with this part-time position.
- Typed, filed and copied documents, memos and correspondence.
- Accurately posted ledgers and delivered bank deposits.
- Developed excellent phones skills; dealt with customers in a professional manner.

Securities Analyst Manager—Chronological Resume
Moving Up from Securities Analyst

RICHARD I. DONAHUE
PO Box 118
Newport Beach, CA 90041
(714) 255-1111

Objective: A Securities Analyst/Management position

EDUCATION

BS Degree, Social Psychology, 1986
University of Florida, Gainesville, FL

Liberal Arts, Emphasis: French, 1986
University of Florida, Gainesville, FL
Successfully completed a course in Commercial French. This certificate was awarded by the French government for proficiency in commercial French.

PROFESSIONAL EXPERIENCE

MSI SECURITIES, Newport Beach, California 1986-present

Securities Analyst

- Manage over 60 million dollars in tax free debt securities.
- Research the bond market daily to find highest yield available.
- Use Lotus to structure clients' maturity schedule within a 1-5 year range.
- Educate clients concerning Mercer investment philosophy.
- Establish relationships with brokerage houses across the nation.

Account Executive (1988-89)

- Responsible for over 300 client accounts.
- Provided client services with quarterly financial reviews, practice management advise, structuring the specific pension plan to meet client's retirement needs.
- Plan annual funding of pension plans, fee review, employee relations, consolidation of debt, profitability monitors.

Coordinator (1986-87)

- Performed as the conduit between new clients and the entire firm.
- Conducted preliminary analysis of new client's financial material.
- Worked directly with Senior Consultant to create a financial structure to lead client to economic freedom.

Shipping and Receiving/Warehouse Supervisor—Functional Resume
Moving Up from Spare Parts Coordinator

JEFFERY A. BARROW
PO Box 618
Santa Barbara, CA 93121
(805) 687-3334

Objective: Shipping & Receiving/Warehouse Supervisor

PROFESSIONAL EXPERIENCE

Customer/Employee Relations

- Train and assist employees in a shipping and receiving department for a manufacturer of printed circuit board machinery.
- Provide excellent customer service resulting in:
  - Increase daily orders shipped and minimize open orders backlog.
- Research the status of customer orders for repair, return and field servicing; examine warranty claims; followed up on vendor orders.
- Interface with departments to ensure delivery schedule and help resolve account billing.

Shipping & Receiving

- Process and expedite customer orders, following through to shipping date.
- Liaison between field service technicians and warehouse.
  - Maintain computerized records of sales orders, product prices and inventory levels.
- Determine stock levels for spare parts.
- Evaluate pricing, time and labor cost.
- Set and consistently met monthly goals resulting in a more efficient flow of operations of a spare parts and service department.

EDUCATION

Computer Technology & Management Courses
Santa Barbara City College, Santa Barbara, CA

EMPLOYMENT HISTORY

Spare Parts Coordinator, Tri-Counties Shipping, Santa Barbara, CA	1988-91
Shipping/Receiving Clerk, Tri-State Metals, Santa Barbara, CA	1985-88
Freight Handler, McClean's Trucking, Goleta, CA	1979-85

Social Service Manager—Chronological Resume
Moving Up from Shelter Coordinator/Client's Advocate

LESLIE ANNE LEONE
1265 Cedar Place
Los Angeles, CA 90024
(213) 344-2359

Objective: A Social Service Management position

EDUCATION:

BA Degree, Sociology, December 1988
University of California, Santa Barbara

EXPERIENCE:

1988-present

BATTERED WOMEN'S SHELTER, Los Angeles, CA
Shelter Coordinator (7/89-present)
Hire, train, schedule and supervise shelter personnel. Ensure proper maintenance of client records and statistical documentation as required for funding purposes. Interface with community agencies to increase awareness of agency services and to promote services for battered women. Demonstrate poise and confidence with extensive public speaking as shelter representative and educator of domestic violence. Administer funds maintaining strict budget requirements. Serve as liaison between Shelter and Board of Directors by providing monthly written and oral reports. Write grant proposals and assist in fund-raisers.

Client Advocate/Volunteer Coordinator (12/88-7/89)
Responded to crisis calls. Determined women's eligibility for shelter residency. Assessed needs of women and children; provided appropriate advocacy, referrals and counseling to women and children. Represented agency through public speaking for the community educational program. Recruited volunteers and organized Volunteer Training Program. Created and implemented fundraiser.

1987-88

ALLIANCE CHARITIES, Santa Barbara, CA
Social Work Intern
Explained available resources, programs and registration procedures. Made referrals and performed advocacy for homeless and low-income individuals and families. Developed and conducted art and play therapy group for children. Collaborated with other interns in complete organization of fundraiser for Relief House.

Social Worker—Combination Resume
Moving Up from Eligibility Worker

JENNIFER M. EMPEY
9000 Juniper Street
La Crescenta, CA 91214
(818) 248-1116

OBJECTIVE

A Social Worker position.

PROFESSIONAL EXPERIENCE

COUNTY OF LOS ANGELES, (Department of Social Services) — 1989-present

Eligibility Worker

- Interview and inform welfare clients of rights and responsibilities.
- Research documentation and approve or deny applications for clients of the County of Los Angeles Bureau of Assistant Payment Department.
  - Issue county and federal grants on a monthly basis.
- Worked on multiple projects under pressured situations and consistently meet strict deadline schedules.
- Maintain a highly professional and concerned manner under sometimes sensitive situations.

RELIEF HOUSE, Los Angeles, CA — Summers 1987-88

House Relief Staff Internship

- Managed a home for homeless, single, pregnant women and mothers with newborns.
- Co-facilitated group discussions used for conflict resolutions between residents.
- Provided information concerning pregnancy and made appropriate referrals.

EDUCATION

BA Degree, Sociology, December 1989
University of California, Los Angeles

American Field Service, Education Abroad
Liberia, West Africa, Summer 1985

EMPLOYMENT HISTORY

Assistant Bookkeeper, Security Pacific Asian Bank, LA, CA — 1985-88
Head Counselor, Friendship Day Camp, Los Angeles, CA — 1983-85
Sales Associate, Bachrach Men's Clothing, Glendale, CA — 1980-83

Solar Energy Resource Consultant—Functional Resume

STEFEN ROBERT ORFALON
8900 Dry Gulch Road
Santa Barbara, CA 93109
(805) 966-1111

Objective: Solar Energy Resource Consultant

QUALIFICATION SUMMARY

- 15 years experience in alternative energy resources.
- Sole Owner of co-generation/solar installation and design subcontract business.
- Skilled at construction site management and supervision of work force.
- Sound intuitive/practical engineering skills providing flexible in site plan application; strong problem solving ability.

EDUCATION

AS Degree, Mechanical Drafting, 1968
Long Beach City College, Long Beach

Ocean Engineering/Civil Engineering
University of California, Long Beach

PROFESSIONAL EXPERIENCE

SRO SOLAR ENTERPRISES, Santa Barbara, CA 1982-present
Alternative Energy Resource Consultant

Co-generation & Solar Projects

- Built 16 co-generator units for IPS Group of San Diego.
  - Construction of acoustic environmental chambers; anechoic chambers, sonic fatigue and climate control chambers.
- Subcontracted to Bill Easter Plumbing Company as Foreman/Supervisor.
  - Installed six co-generation plants throughout the entire State of California including the largest co-generation plant in Santa Barbara County.
- Subcontracted to area's solar heating companies.
  - Foreman/Supervisor for commercial installations including the two largest commercial solar heating systems in Santa Barbara County.

Clients; Solar Water Heating Installation

- Subcontracted to install solar water heating systems for the following businesses.
  - Art Grossmans & Sons...Energy Matrix...Santa Barbara Solar Systems... Solar Energy Company...Pool Supply & Patio Center...El Camino Solar Systems...Mac's Solar.

PREVIOUS EMPLOYMENT HISTORY

Installer, Max's Solar Heating, Santa Barbara, CA 1977-81

Stockbroker—Chronological Resume
Moving Up from Account Executive

CHRISTINE MELINDA SCOTT
PO Box 89301
Santa Barbara, CA 93190
(805) 569-1020

OBJECTIVE: **A Stockbroker position.**

WORK EXPERIENCE:

DEAN WITTER REYNOLDS, Los Angeles, CA — 1988-present
Account Executive
Received Series 7 and Insurance License in 1988. Established over 100 new account relationships. Raised over $1.5M in new equity. Developed Retirement Planning Team concept for branch office, focusing on institutional and individual qualified plan assets. Extensive financial research and analysis based on balance sheets, annual reports, and cash flow figures. Specialize in marketing of mutual funds, equity products, unit trusts and life insurance.

SANWA BANK, Los Angeles, CA — 1987-88
Assistant to Vice President of Marketing
Assisted with daily management of over 65 cold callers for Account Executives. Led recruiting, hiring, firing, and training. Managed personnel and office operations. Negotiated contracts for office space, and computer purchases, establishing a new branch office. Promoted to managerial assignment. Supervised spreadsheet analysis and data entry of all marketing research.

JOHNSON, TAMBARELLO, STEIN, Beverly Hills, CA — 1985-87
Broker's Assistant
Assisted with prospecting and follow up on clients. Researched Financial and Marketing analysis. Experience with various Macintosh and IBM programs.

EDUCATION:
BA Degree, International Relations
University of Southern California
Emphasis: International Economics
Graduation: 1987

HONORS:
University Scholarship, University of Southern California
USC, Academic and Financial National Elks Scholarship
Elected Treasurer, International Business Association

Student Affairs Officer—Functional Resume
Recent Graduate with School Activity Experience and Personal Insight

CHRISTOPHER B. FRANCES

<u>Current Address</u>
22 Churchill Drive
Santa Barbara, CA 93110
(805) 555-1111

<u>Permanent Address</u>
225 Westwood Drive
Los Angeles, CA 90043
(213) 555-2345

Objective: Student Affairs Officer.

EDUCATION

BA Degree, Law and Society, June 1990
<u>University of California</u>, Los Angeles

RELATED EXPERIENCE

<u>Educational Opportunity Program (EOP)</u>

- A Student Affairs Officer from UCLA recruited me from Valley College to this program.
- Gained valuable knowledge and personal insight at UCLA through the experience of transferring to a 4-year university from a community college.
- Became keenly aware of situations students face and look forward to the opportunity of passing this knowledge on to them. Such as...
  - counseling resources available to guide me through this program.
  - peer/faculty support network available to minority students who qualify to be admitted to UCLA; tutorial services made available.

<u>Organization & Promotions</u>

- Organized an effective alcohol and risk reduction program.
  - resulted in reduced financial liability for incidents involving the Greek community.
- Coordinator for GRACE, an awareness committee to increase minority involvement in the Greek community.
- Developed a support network organization of American Indian college students.
- As Alumni Committee Member, contacted members to promote fund raising events.
- As Rush Committee Member, created promotional themes for fraternity annual events.

<u>Public Speaking Skills</u>

- Represented fraternity to promote fund raising events for the American Cancer Society and Diabetic Association.
- Conducted meetings and presented ideas on the formation and structure of the Organization of North American Indian College Students.
- Prepared several speeches and conducted presentations and seminars.
- Learned to speak confidently and fluently in front of large groups.

EMPLOYMENT HISTORY

Resident Coordinator, <u>University of California</u>, LA, CA — 1988-89
Sales Assistant, <u>Standard Brands</u>, Los Angeles, CA — Summers 1985-87
Corporate Security Guard, <u>Trans-America</u>, Los Angeles, CA — Summer 1984

JEREMY ROGER SILLS
PO Box 1234
Bellingham, WA 98225
(206) 244-0000

Objective: Superintendent for the County Road Department.

PROFESSIONAL PROFILE

- 20+ years experience in construction and project management.
- Highly organized, dedicated with a positive attitude.
- Special talent for assessing company needs and priorities.
- Gained valuable business and personal contacts statewide.
- Maintain a **100% accident free safety record.**

PROFESSIONAL EXPERIENCE

Safety Officer
- Established safety policy & procedures for Whatcom County County employees.
- Conduct bi-monthly safety seminars, workshops and tailgate meetings for the County of Whatcom County Road Department employees.
- Member of the APWA & MSA in Whatcom County, WA.

Project Management/Vendor Relations
- Supervised special construction site projects for the State of Washington. Bridges...roads...beach access...off-the-road recreational vehicle parks.
- Inspect daily multiple construction sites for Whatcom County.
  - Completed projects on-time while meeting strict budget requirements.
  - Located qualified vendors and negotiated contracts with subcontractors.
  - Hired, scheduled and supervised subcontractors; Developed and enforced effective company policy, procedures and project safety regulations.
  - Purchased, expedited materials/equipment; maintained quality control.
  - Carried out daily on-site supervision, maintaining excellent communication skills and safety standards.

Clients/Projects
Whatcom Canyon sewer and overlay projects...City Dam project...Treacher Dam project...Highway Interstate 5, Seattle/Whatcom County...Highway Interstate 210, Seattle County...Whatcom Bus Lane project...the Whatcom County Valley.

EMPLOYMENT HISTORY

Safety Officer/Assistant Superintendent, County of Seattle, (Road Dept) 1984-present
Construction Supervisor, State of Washington, (Parks & Recreation) 1978-84
Foreman, Whatcom Contruction, Bellingham, CA 1976-78

TINA A. BOLTON
420 Sandcastle Way
Provo, UT 84604
(801) 377-5620

SYSTEMS PROGRAMMER

PROFESSIONAL PROFILE:

- Highly organized, dedicated with a positive attitude.
- Strong analytical skills with attention to detail.
- Communicate well with clients and management in a highly professional and diplomatic manner.

COMPUTER SKILLS:

- **Programming Languages** - "C", Assembly, COBOL, BASIC
- **Software**, - MS DOS, AOS/VS, DBMS, AOS, DBASE III, System II, UNIX, INFOS and Ctree.
- **Hardware/Mainframe**, - Data General Eclipse, C350, MV15000 and NOVA.
- **Hardware Micros** - IBM PC, IBM AT, 386 Based Computer, Apple II and Macintosh.
- **Hardware/Mini** - Jacquard J100, DG30 Desktop Generation.

PROFESSIONAL EXPERIENCE:

1981-91 REGISTRATION CONTROL SYSTEMS, Ventura, CA
Systems Programmer

- Wrote and maintained operating systems on Data General NOVA computers in Assembly language.
- Traveled to major tradeshows for service calls worldwide.
- Performed program definition/analysis, flowcharting, coding and testing.
- Developed detailed user documentation and conducted training program.
- Designed and wrote a cross assembler for the NOVA Eclipse Series.
- Wrote custom software in "C" language for sales lead collection, assorted report generations and database conversion programs.

CERTIFICATES:

AOS/VS Systems Programming, Registration Control Systems
Data General AOS Systems Manager, Registration Control Systems
Programming Jacquard Mini Computers, Jacquard Systems

EDUCATION: **BS Degree, Computer Science**, 1980
Brigham Young University, Provo, UT

Systems Programmer—Combination Resume
Recent Graduate with Related Work Experience

ANNIE LINDSEY
34518 Beverly Glen
Los Angeles, CA 90024
(213) 567-1238

Objective: A Systems Programmer position

COMPUTER SKILLS

Languages: "C" Pascal, Fortran, Prolog, 8088 Assembly
Software/Hardware: UNIX, MS-DOS, IBM, Macintosh, VAX

EDUCATION

BS Degree, Mathematical Science, 1990
University of California, Los Angeles

CURRENT PROFESSIONAL EXPERIENCE

DARCY CORPORATION, Los Angeles, CA — 1989-present
(A pension software development manufacturer)
Software Support Specialist

- Liaison between 400 customers and seven computer programmers.
  - Consult customers and troubleshoot data management and pension software systems.
  - Certify and test new software packages.
- Required strong analytical and written skills with ability to communicate well with clients, fellow employees and all levels of management.

Software Development Certification

- Developed several effective testing procedures on the IBM computer for three pension plans in Expert systems.
- Wrote extensive testing reports; reported directly to the Vice President.
- Received thorough training in pensions participant eligibility.
- After 3-month internship progressed to full-time Software Certification.

ACTIVITIES

Member, Society of Women Engineers

PREVIOUS EMPLOYMENT HISTORY

Mathematics Lab Assistant, UC Los Angeles, (Math Dept) — 1987-88
Billing Assistant, UC Los Angeles, (Billing Office) — 1986-87

SUSAN J. DWORSKI
124 Kova Lane
Santa Barbara, CA 93109
(805) 962-2222

Objective: Bilingual Elementary School Teacher

EDUCATION:

University of California at Santa Barbara
Bachelor of Arts, Psychology
Graduated with honors, June, 1983

Special Courses
Social and Cognitive Development, Language Development, Psychological Issues of the Chicano Child, Independent Research, Bilingual Development and Migrant Children, Masters Course in Special Education.

FOREIGN STUDY:

Secundaria del Colegio Guadalupano
Romita, Guanajuato, Mexico, 1972

TEACHING CREDENTIAL:

California Multiple Subject Credential Bilingual/ Cross Cultural Emphasis English - Spanish
University of California at Santa Barbara

TEACHING EXPERIENCE:

1985-91 **Bilingual Elementary Teacher**
Adams School, Santa Barbara, California
Taught 1st grade and 4th-6th grade after school Spanish classes.

1985-88 **Bilingual Migrant Teacher**
Migrant Summer School Program, Santa Barbara, California
Taught K-1, 1st grade, 2nd-3rd grade and 3rd grade classes.

1984-84 **Student Teacher**
Carpinteria School District, Carpinteria, California
Taught 3rd grade classes at the Aliso School. Responsible for teaching Reading (English and Spanish), Math, ESL, Physical Education and Science.

ROBERT H. TERRACE
2289 Richmond Drive
Encino, CA 91211
(818) 360-1111

Objective: A Teaching position

EDUCATION

Master's Degree: Reading, 1969
Bachelor's Degree: History, 1966
California State University, Northridge, CA

TEACHING CREDENTIALS

California State Reading Credential, (K-12) (Life)
California Secondary Credential, (History/Political Science), (Life)
California Children's Center Teaching Permit, (Life)

PROFESSIONAL EXPERIENCE

TEACHER (High School) 1970-present
Los Angeles Unified School District

Lennon High School, Los Angeles, CA

- Teach courses in World History, American History, Economics, Government, Reading Improvement, Books for Pleasure.
- Created *Wall Street*, a gaming situation devised to develop awareness of the numerous economic avenues available.
  - provided skills to operate within a market system and an understanding of the micro and macro economic world and their inter-relationship.
  - Awakening awareness of world inter-dependency.
- Developed *Comparative Government* instructional program.
  - compare legislative, executive and judicial aspects of major governmental systems "i.e., democracy, socialism, communism, dictatorship."
  - U.S.A: analysis, comparison and evaluation with other systems.
- School Representative:
  - Core Literature Program within a New State Framework (1988).
  - Communications Advisor to *English/Language Arts Team* (1987).
- Served as Reading Department Chairperson from 1985-90.
- Served as school Reading Coordinator from 1987-90.
- Supervised school-wide reading tests of vocabulary and comprehension.
- Developed reading stratagems in Content Areas of math, social studies, science.

COMMUNITY INVOLVEMENT/MEMBERSHIPS

Coach, American Youth Soccer, 1983-present
Manager, Granada Hills Little League, 1983-present

ROBIN T. COUPLES
4432 Amanda Drive
Granada Hills, CA 91202
(818) 360-1111

Objective: A Teaching position

EDUCATION

Master's Degree: Mathematics, 1969
Bachelor's Degree: History, 1966
California State University, Northridge, CA

TEACHING CREDENTIALS

California State Mathematics/Reading Credential, (K-12) (Life)
California Secondary Credential, (History/Political Science), (Life)
California Children's Center Teaching Permit, (Life)

PROFESSIONAL EXPERIENCE

TEACHER (Junior High) 1985-present
Los Angeles Unified School District

Johnson Junior High School, San Fernando, CA

- Taught Reading, Math, World History and American History courses.
- Served as Reading Department Chairperson/Coordinator from 1974-85.
- Coordinated and revised programs for basic reading, reading improvement and power reading.
- Developed three Power Reading Electives, intended to encourage and further develop reading skills of the average reader.
  - "Sports Appreciation-Reading"
  - "Mystery Theater-Reading"
  - "World Travel-Reading"
- Developed and coordinated a school-wide VCR program used in the classrooms for taping and broadcasting.

PROFESSIONAL ORGANIZATIONS

Member, American Federation of Teachers
Member, United Teachers of Los Angeles

PREVIOUS EMPLOYMENT HISTORY

Teacher (Pre-K-6), Murphy Street School Children's Center 1967-70

Teacher, Private High School—Functional Resume
Recent College Graduate with Related Work Experience

SCOTT WILLIAM EDWARDS

Current Address:
1234 Sabado Tarde #1
Goleta, CA 93117
(805) 966-1234

Permanent Address:
2220 Santa Ana Street
Ventura, CA 93004
(805) 682-0987

OBJECTIVE

A teaching position at a private school, teaching grades 9-12.

PROFESSIONAL PROFILE

- Financed education with experience as a teacher and counselor.
- Special talent for motivating people of all backgrounds.
- Work well under pressure situations maintaining a professional and concerned manner.
- Achieved the Dean's Honor List at UCSB 10 times.

EXPERIENCE

Teaching Skills

- Tutor math, biology, physics, general & organic chemistry to college students on a one-on-one basis as well as in small group sessions.
  - Deal effectively with students of all levels and learning abilities.
  - Strong ability to present subject matter in multiple context tailored to individual needs.
  - Outstanding ability to motivate uninterested individuals in required non-major subjects.
- Taught private and public swim lessons to children and adults.
  - Instructed individuals and groups from beginners to competitive levels.

Communication Skills

- Conduct educational presentations to groups of 25-150 elementary, junior and high school students throughout the Santa Barbara community.
  - Provide awareness concerning relationships with a disabled person in the community.
- Counsel and instruct disabled children and adolescents at the Santa Barbara Junior Wheelchair Sports Camp.
  - Effectively motivate campers to learn new activities including: tennis...basketball...swimming...track & field...weight lifting...archery
  - Provide continued support as a role model to handle real life situations.

EDUCATION

BA Degree, Biochemistry/Molecular biology
University of California, Santa Barbara
GPA: 3.8   Graduation: June 1990

EMPLOYMENT HISTORY

Private Tutor, Self Employed, Santa Barbara, CA — 1986-present
Instructor/Counselor, Santa Barbara Wheelchair Sports Camp — Summers 1987-89

MELANNIE P. PULLMAN
909 South Avenue
Memphis, TN 38126
(901) 774-4556

OBJECTIVE

A Special Education Teaching position

PROFESSIONAL EXPERIENCE

RUTLEDGE CITY COLLEGE, Memphis, TN — 1987-present

Essential Skills Instructor

- Assess students' individualized reading and writing skills and needs.
- Direct instruction in reading and writing skills.
- Supervise students in reading lab.
- Direct and supervise instructional aide's work in class and office.
- Evaluate student progress.

RHODES SCHOOL, Memphis, TN — 1982-87

Coordinator of Education (1985-87)

- Supervised and evaluated teachers and instructional aides.
- Coordinated student intake, assessment and class placement.
- Monitored and evaluated instructional program and curriculum guidelines.
- Developed and facilitated staff inservice.
- Reported to Board of Directors on education program implementation and new program development.
- Interfaced and consulted with public agencies.
- Facilitated transition from one administrator to another.

Special Education Day Class Teacher (1982-85)

- Directed instruction in academic and independent living skills for young adults with developmental disability, ages 16-22 years.
- Developed and implemented individualized educational plans.
- Monitor student progress and maintain student records.
- Coordinate community vocational experiences with agencies and school sites.

MEMPHIS RESIDENTIAL PROGRAM, Memphis, TN — 1976-84

Educational Consultant (1983-84)

- Developed and implemented inservice training program for independent living skills instructors.
- Evaluated independent living skills instructors' performance and classes.
- Provided ongoing consultation, resources and materials to instructors.

- More -

PROFESSIONAL EXPERIENCE (Continued)

Sensory Motor Program Supervisor (1981-82)
- Supervised staff therapists.
- Assessed and evaluated clients' needs.
- Designed and implemented behavioral goals and objectives for clients.
- Planned and conducted inservice training for staff and school faculty.
- Evaluated and revised program goals.
- Provided direct service to clients with developmental disability, ages 7-18.

EDUCATION

MA, Special Education, in-progress
University of California, Santa Barbara

BA, English, Penn State University, Univ. Park, PA, 1967

SPECIAL TRAINING

- Learning Handicapped Specialist Teaching Credential, Life
- Single Subject Teaching Credential, English, Life
- Community College Basic Skills Credential, Life

PROFESSIONAL AFFILIATIONS

- Association for Children and Adults with Learning Disabilities (ACLD) - California, Santa Barbara Chapter
- Council on Exceptional Children - Mental Retardation Division, Early Childhood Division
- National Down Syndrome Congress

EMPLOYMENT HISTORY

Substitute Teacher, Maricopa County Schools, Austin, TX — 1973-75
Res. Group Home Coordinator, Children's Industrial Home, Bellingham, WA — 1972
Special Education Resource Teacher
Camp Springs Elementary School Bellingham, WA — 1970-71
Special Education Day Class Teacher, Severely Emotionally Disabled
Edgemeade School, Seattle, WA — 1969-70

Telecommunications Sales Manager—Chronological Resume

JEFFREY LAZLOW
PO Box 1000
Hollywood, CA 90067
(213) 830-0003

JOB OBJECTIVE

A Sales Manager position with a Fortune 500 Company.

PROFESSIONAL EXPERIENCE

DIRECTOR OF MARKETING 1984-present

Los Angeles Cellular Systems, Los Angeles, CA

- Established and administered marketing, sales and telemarketing departments, resulting in 100+% increase in the customer base and a 40% increase in the number of authorized marketing Agents.
- Developed a sales and management training program for the direct sales force, telemarketing team and marketing agents.
- Successfully negotiated service contracts for Hughes Aircraft, GM Delco Electronics Corporate, the City of LA and US Coast Guard.
- Expanded marketing and advertising programs to include sponsorships in the LA Golf Open, the LA County Fair and LA National Horse and Flower Show.

MARKETING SUPERVISOR 1979-84

General Telephone, Orange, CA

- Successfully managed a dynamic sales team.
- Represented GTE in the sale and provision of network communications services to Long Distance, Cellular and Radio Common Carriers, resulting in sales of $4.4M in 1986-87.
- Exceeded annual sales objectives by 244% in 1986-87.
- Sales Person of the Year in 1987 - Access Services. Recipient of the prestigious GTE Winner's Circle, Circle 100 and Group Excellent Sales Achievement Awards.
- Successfully negotiated service contracts with Pac Tel Cellular, LA Cellular, Ventura Cellular and GTE Mobilnet Systems.
- Assisted in the development and sale of the Type 2A Tandem Access service arrangement for cellular and paging carriers.

REGULATORY COORDINATOR

- Liaison between GTE, California Public Utilities Commission (CPUC) and outside consumer organizations for all phases associated with rate applications and other regulatory filings.
- Coordinated all intracompany departments in the development, review and compilation of testimonies, exhibits, documentation and other information related to general rate increases resulting in rate case award of $192.6M for 1985.

EDUCATION

BS Degree - Business Administration, 1979
University of California, Los Angeles, CA

Telemarketing Sales Representative—Chronological Resume

WENDY MACGREGOR
27900 Roseridge Lane
Montecito, CA 93108
(805) 684-1669

Objective: Position in Telemarketing Sales

EXPERIENCE:

1988-present **SALES SUPPORT/CUSTOMER SERVICE**
Amvox Incorporated, Carpinteria, CA

- Develop marketing strategies, train, support field representatives for this manufacturer and distributor of voicemail systems.
- Administer 100 retail accounts with Kinkos, PakMail and Mailbox.
- Train management and staff; implement retail sales procedures and documentation, assuring smooth flow of business operations from installation through orientation of new customers.
- Resolve customer problems of technical and billing concerns in a timely manner to assure continued customer satisfaction.

1986-88 **SENIOR ACCOUNT REPRESENTATIVE**
Mini-Systems Associates, Santa Barbara, CA

- In charge of Colorado operations with major clients for this Aerospace Engineering Jobshop.
  - Honeywell...Rockwell Int'l...Contel Spacecom...Ford Aerospace ...Martin Marietta...numerous electronics manufacturers.
- Negotiate contracts to supply technical labor, monitor government contracts and track project dates.
- Research department heads and project managers extensive networking activities to increase manager contacts.
- Determine staff needs, job descriptions and arrange interviews; negotiate engineer contracts and all contract administration.
- Review all incoming resumes, network with engineers to find best candidates, verify background and job placement including engineer pay negotiation and travel arrangements.

1984-86 **LIFE & DISABILITY AGENT**
California Casualty & Life Insurance Company, Santa Barbara, CA

- Generated leads in telemarketing sales; worked closely with clients from the school districts, fire, police and highway patrol departments, University of California, Santa Barbara County.
- Planned, coordinated and set up custom packages for retirement, life insurance, annuity and IRA contributions and investments.
- Delivered policies, maintained billing and continued efficient customer service of all accounts.
- Achieved highest premium sold, 9 out of 16 months.

TV News Reporter—Combination Resume
Recent College Graduate with Related Internship Experience

CHLOE RAE KENNARD
30566 Spruce Street
Santa Barbara, CA 90103
(805) 569-2290

OBJECTIVE

A position leading to a career in Television News Broadcasting

EDUCATION

BA Degree, Law & Society, June 1990
University of California, Santa Barbara
Dean's Honor List: Fall 1987 GPA: 3.20

Study Abroad Program, 1988-89
Syracuse University, Madrid, Spain
Speak fluent Spanish

Extracurricular Courses:
Photography...Acting...Drama...Modeling

RELATED EXPERIENCE

KCTV, (COX) CHANNEL 19, Santa Barbara, CA — 1990-present
Studio Production/Camera Operation
- Received intensive hands-on training in all phases of studio production and camera operations including the teleprompter.

CENTRAL COAST MODEL & TALENT, San Luis Obispo, CA — 1989-present
Model, Actress, Personal Development Student
- Received training in print, commercial and runway modeling techniques.
- Developed effective communication skills, telephone and selling techniques, social etiquette, fitness & nutrition and makeup application.
- Gained valuable acting techniques for television, commercial, soap, sitcom and film.

ABC TV STATION, New York City, NY — 1989-90
Production Intern
- Received training in television production techniques during several airings of the Good Morning America show.

EMPLOYMENT HISTORY

Front Desk/Phone Sales, Nutri-System, Santa Barbara, CA — 1989-90
Law Secretary, P. Heckendorn, Lawyer, San Marino, CA — Summers 1985/87

TV News Reporter—Functional Resume
Recent Graduate with Internship and School Activity Experience

NATASHA LAKINSKI

Present Address
1345 Wisconsin Avenue
Washington DC 01003
(202) 470-0021

Permanent Address
Springfield Drive
Berkeley, CA 93902
(415) 234-9876

Objective: A position leading to a career in Broadcasting

EDUCATION: **BA Degree, Communication Studies**, June 1989
George Washington University, Washington, DC

Related Coursework
Interpersonal/Small Group Communication
Public Communication
Communication and Conflict
Rhetoric & Phonetics
Mass Communication
Persuasion

BROADCASTING EXPERIENCE: **PRODUCTION/REPORTER INTERN,**
Channel 22, Government Access, Fairfax, VA

1988-90

Studio Production
- Assisted production staff for a weekly talk show.
  - Operated cameras...floor directed...set-up lighting equipment.
  - Prepared sets before and in-between tapings.
  - Supervised camera operators during talk shows.

Field Production
- Researched/reported three 180 second news packages aired on public television.
  - Wrote and edited scripts; operated video cameras.
- Learned how to handle multiple assignments under highly pressured situations quickly and efficiently.

Talk Show Host
- Hosted weekly talk shows concerning the local community.
  - family issues...safety programs...recreational activities.
- Learned to speak with poise and confidence in front of camera.
- Gained valuable research skills, writing techniques and the ability to communicate effectively with professionals at all levels.

ACTIVITIES: **PRESIDENT**, University Advertising Club, 1987-88
In charge of coordinating and conducting weekly meetings. Organized guest speakers. Created a learning environment for students eager to learn about the advertising industry.

TV Post-Production Staff—Artist Resume
Recent College Graduate with Related School Project Experience

VERONICA BRICE
PO Box 2345
Santa Barbara, CA 93100
(805) 888-6789

OBJECTIVE

A Post-Production position in the Television/Film Industry.

PROFESSIONAL PROFILE

- Experienced in film production/post-production management.
- Highly organized, dedicated with a positive attitude.
- Strength in assessing people's needs and priorities.
- Outstanding ability to communicate with all types of people.
- Team player with proven leadership qualities.
- Ability to handle multiple assignments in highly pressured situations and consistently meet tight deadline schedules.
- Traveled extensively throughout Japan, China, Europe, Canada, Mexico and the USA.

EDUCATION

BA Degree, Motion Picture - Spring 1990
Brooks Institute of Photography, Santa Barbara, CA

PRODUCTION EXPERIENCE

- Gained valuable knowledge and skills working closely with director and producer in all phases of film production.
  - Produced, directed, wrote and edited films; mixed sound tracks for several small narrative and documentary film productions.
- In charge of post-production; completed projects while consistently maintaining tight deadline schedules and strict budget requirements.

FILM & VIDEO PROJECTS

- Producer - "Freedom," a 15-minute documentary on the homeless.
- 1st Assistant Camera - "Circles," a rock style music video.
- Head Editor - "The Third World," a 15-minute documentary on Indonesia.
- Script & Post-Production Supervisor, "Non Compos Mentis," a 15-minute dramatic short. Psychological heart-beating thriller.
- Assistant Camera/Editor - "The Long Summer," aired on NBC Summer 1989; a documentary about a sporty homebuilt airplane.
- Producer - "Rhythms," an animated 3-minute music video.

REFERENCES & PORTFOLIO

Available upon request

EDWARD J. MILLER
PO Box 9002
Solvang, CA 93463
(805) 688-2345

Objective: An Administrator in the Thoroughbred Industry.

PROFESSIONAL PROFILE

- 20 years experience in the Thoroughbred Industry; demonstrate superior client relations, horsemanship & management.
- Highly organized, dedicated with a positive attitude.
- Rapidly analyze/recognize industry problems & opportunities.
- Excellent written, oral and interpersonal communication skills.
- Deal with clients in highly diplomatic and professional manner.
- Gained valuable business and personal contacts throughout the Thoroughbred industry.

PROFESSIONAL EXPERIENCE

<u>Business Administration & Management</u>

- Develop & implemented programs to improve operations & produce profits.
  - Established an effective budget program for international and domestic corporations with multi-million dollar gross revenues.
  - Increased computer usage by 70% to maximize time management efficiency.
- Reduced overhead by 35% within first year of employment.
- Service multiple assignments in highly pressured situations, maintaining a positive attitude and consistently meet tight deadline schedules.
- In charge of hiring, supervision and delegation of assignments to 35-50 farm personnel.

<u>Client & Public Relations</u>

- Liaison between clients and farm divisions to provide information concerning status of their bloodstock.
- Interface with clients to interpret needs and priorities. Advise clients in a professional and concerned manner, securing their trust and confidence.
- Represent company on extended sales trips; meet with clients, promote good will and present farm services.
- Demonstrate poise and competence as a professional business representative in any social or business situation.

<u>Equine Marketing, Sales & Promotions</u>

- Market and purchase bloodstock for breeding and racing for the following: Yearling...breeding stock...and two-year-olds in training
- Demonstrate excellent sales ability with thorough knowledge of conformation and strong pedigree research.

- More -

PROFESSIONAL EXPERIENCE (Continued)

- Developed successful marketing strategies to promote stallions and farm services through trade magazine advertising and creative video presentations.
- Coordinated and developed $1.5M equine science center focusing on curriculum and facilities; maintained strict budget requirements.
- Conducted equine seminars and educational programs at tradeshows nationwide including the International Thoroughbred Exposition & Conference.

EDUCATION

MS Degree, Animal Science, Equine preference
Sul Ross State University, Alpine, TX, 1970

BS Degree, Animal Science; Minor: Biology
Sul Ross State University, Alpine, TX, 1966

EMPLOYMENT HISTORY

General Manager, Thoroughbred Farms, Solvang, CA 1984-present
Manager-Equine Division, Little Rock Valley Farms, Little Rock, AK 1980-84
Equine Marketing Research & Development Consultant, Louisville, KY 1970-80
Equine Science Instructor, Sul Ross State University, Alpine, TX 1966-70
Marketing Agent, The Old Mill, Alpine, TX 1976-78

Trade Show Manager—Functional Resume
Housewife/Mom Re-Entering the Workforce with Prior Experience

SUSIE M. MCDOWELL
1039 Beacon Hill
Boston, MA 02115
(619) 284-5551

OBJECTIVE

A Trade Show Management position for a National Magazine

EDUCATION

BA Degree, Graphics Art, 1988
Boston University, Boston, MA
Microcomputer Paste-up, Layout, & Design;
The Art of Interviewing; Travel Writing.

Amherst College, Amherst, MA, 1984
Journalism: Advanced Magazine/Specialty
Copywriting-Editing; Photography.

PROFESSIONAL EXPERIENCE

Writing, Editing & Production

- In charge of editing and coordinating the publication of corporate newsletter with a circulation of 4,000.
  - Developed story board and delegated selected articles to staff experts.
  - Selected artwork, took photos and produced layout for newsletter.
  - Coordinated projects with graphic designers, typesetters and printers meeting strict deadline schedules and budget requirements.
- Wrote, edited and produced promotional materials: letters...ads...news releases...brochures...directories...manuals...mailers.
- Three year member of the Boston Ad Club.

Trade Shows, Special Events & Meetings

- Coordinated and supervised national and regional trade shows for a multi-million dollar computer software company.
  - Developed/distributed materials that created interest, excitement and promoted sales.
  - Coordinated the entire set up: selected booth space, arranged staffing, chose graphic designs, lighting and furnishings.
- Organized special events and national training meetings.

EMPLOYMENT HISTORY

International Travel, Studies & Research	**1989-91**
Graphics/Editorial Manager, Boston<u></u>ian Magazine, Boston, MA	**1984-88**
Corporate Communications Supervisor, COMTECK, Amherst, MA	**1979-84**

Trust Administrator—Functional Resume

CHERYL ALLORY JAMES
59 Martinella Drive
Montecito, CA 93108
(805) 966-0845

Objective: Trust Administrator

EDUCATION

Certified Financial Planner, 1990
College of Financial Planning, Denver, CO

Paralegal, Certified: 1982
The Institute of Paralegal Training
Philadelphia, PA

BA, Psychology/Business Administration
University of Arizona, Tucson, AZ, 1980

PROFESSIONAL EXPERIENCE

Trust Administration & Marketing

- Managed 180 accounts with total market value of $150M; revenues of $1.4M. Living...Testamentary...Conservatorship...Unitrusts...Agency...Custody.
- Launched intensive Cohen-Brown marketing techniques including financial profiling of existing client base, branch contact and organizing seminars.
- Organized highly successful in-house marketing campaigns that created excitement, promoted sales and generated new business for the bank.
- Conducted a week-long training seminar on new Trust Aid procedures for our updated in-house computer system.
- Prepared discretionary requests and monitored investments, distributions, terminations and sale of personal property.
- Portfolio manager for accounts fully vested in Common Trust Funds.
- Gained valuable business contacts through interbank communication and corresponding with attorneys, brokers, accountants in the trust industry.

Probate Paralegal

- Responsible for file management and factual investigation.
- Discovered, collected and distributed assets.
- Prepared and processed pleadings, federal/state estate, gift and inheritance tax and income tax returns, probate accountings and narrative descriptions.
- Interfaced with secretarial, word processing, accounting and other support departments.

EMPLOYMENT HISTORY

Trust Administrator, Wells Fargo Bank, Santa Barbara, CA	1987-present
Trust Administrator, Union Bank, Los Angeles, CA	1985-87
Probate Paralegal, Sheppard, Mullin, Hampton, Lyne, CA	1983-85
Probate Paralegal, Rooks, Pitts, & Poust, Chicago, IL	1982-83

RENEE LANDSBURY
3456 Berry Avenue
Two Harbors, MN 55616
(218) 824-4590

Objective: An Administrative Trust Assistant position

PROFESSIONAL PROFILE

- Extensive company training in Trust Administration.
- Work well under pressure with the ability to service several transactions simultaneously.
- Resourceful; skilled in analyzing and solving problems.
- Highly organized, dedicated with a positive attitude.

OFFICE SKILLS

IBM PC computer, Multimate and Word Perfect word processing, data entry, calculator...purchasing, excellent phone skills, payroll, accounts payable, billing, outstanding customer relations...filing. Typing Speed: 50 wpm

PROFESSIONAL EXPERIENCE

Administrative/Secretarial

- Executive assistant for the president of a major security corporation with offices nationwide.
- Assisted the vice president for a busy Trust Department.
- Processed probate and conservatorship accounts.
  - Maintained trust account dividends, stocks, bonds; monthly billing and employee household payroll.
  - Notified creditors of deceased, meeting tight deadline schedules.
  - Audited estate inventory along with the trust officer and appraiser.
  - Distributed assets to family members and charities according to the Will.
- Composed/typed daily correspondence and memos on the word processor.

Customer Relations/Management/Sales

- Provide assistance to customers in an efficient and friendly manner.
- Possess professional phone skills with excellent customer relations under highly pressured and sensitive situations.
- Built a personal customer base through outstanding customer relation skills and sales ability.

EMPLOYMENT HISTORY

Trust Assistant, Treasury Bank and Trust, Inc., Duluth, MN — 1989-present
Executive Assistant, Two Harbors Bank & Trust, Duluth, MN — 1985-89
File Clerk, Mid Western Bank & Trust, Duluth, MN — 1984-85

Urban Development Counselor—Functional Resume
Recent College Graduate with Related School Activity Experience

LISA LENNON

Current Address
6661 Shannon Place
Santa Barbara, CA 93103
(805) 967-0869

Permanent Address
11th Avenue
Bellingham, WA 99353
(202) 382-4587

OBJECTIVE

A growth-oriented Urban Development position

EDUCATION

BA Degree, Sociology, December 1989
University of California, Santa Barbara

RELATED EXPERIENCE

Communication Skills

- Educate the Greek community and the entire UCSB campus to promote racial awareness and cultural sensitivity.
  - Received intensive professional training to facilitate programs.
- Speak with poise and confidence in front of large/small groups of people.
- Interfaced via phone with clients worldwide for a large financial institution.
- Learned to maintain a highly professional and concerned manner under sensitive situations.

Organization & Administrative Skills

- Established procedures for GRACE as part of a 20-member team.
- Planned and supervised daily activities for 20 children ages 6-7 at a cultural day camp in Seattle, WA. Oversaw associate counselors.
  - Created programs focusing on a wide range of cultures each week.
- Coordinated a large Philanthropy event for the American Cancer Society and Diabetes Foundation. In charge of ticket distribution and sales.
  - Successfully promoted fundraiser through local business sponsorship.

HONORS/ACTIVITIES

Excellence in Public Relations Award
Executive Planning Committee, Philanthropy
GRACE Rep., Cultural Awareness Program

EMPLOYMENT HISTORY

Assistant Bookkeeper, Wells Fargo Asian Bank, Seattle, WA — Summer 1988
Head Counselor, Friendship Day Camp, Seattle, WA — Summer 1987

Varsity Water Polo Coach—Combination Resume

KARL E. BLUM
5555 Lili Drive
Goleta, CA 93117
(805) 967-0000

Objective: Varsity Water Polo Coach

PROFESSIONAL PROFILE

- 7+ years experience in Water Polo Coaching.
- Highly organized, dedicated with a positive attitude.
- Special talent for assessing team needs and priorities.

EDUCATION

BA Degree, Physical Education, 1985
University of California, Santa Barbara

COACHING EXPERIENCE

Water Polo Coach Experience

- Recruit, train and supervise 20 Freshman for the UCSB Junior Varsity Water Polo Team.
- Teach basic swimming skills and fundamental tactics of the game, focusing on coordination, team work and safety standards.
- Set up scheduling and plan practices for all players. Referee scrimmages.
- Assisted a Youth Enrichment Through Sports clinic at the NCAA Water Polo Championship.
- Assisted coaches at two high schools with programs of 20-40 players.
- Developed excellent rapport with thorough game knowledge and the natural ability to gain trust and respect of players and fellow staff members.

Lifeguard Experience

- Supervise beach activities throughout the entire Santa Barbara County.
- Received special training in Water Safety Instruction...First Aid...CPR.
- Deal in emergency situations quickly and efficiently while maintaining a highly professional and concerned manner.

ACTIVITIES

Team Captain/Member, UC Santa Barbara Water Polo, 1984-85
Athlete of the Year, University of California, Santa Barbara, 1984
Team Captain, UCSB Water Polo Team, 1983

EMPLOYMENT HISTORY

Jr. Varsity Water Polo Coach, UC Santa Barbara	1985-present
Pool Lifeguard/Maintenance, UC Santa Barbara	1983-84
Assistant Water Polo Coach, San Luis Obispo High School	Summer 1983

EUGENE H. RAINIER
PO Box 999
Los Altos, CA 94022
(415) 494-1111

Objective: A Wholesale Manufacturer General Manager position.

EDUCATION

University of California, Santa Barbara
BA Degree, Business Administration, 1976

PROFESSIONAL EXPERIENCE

ROCKHOPPER FISHING TACKLE WHOLESALERS — 1980-present
General/Finance Manager

Project Management

- Built the foundation of a successful wholesale manufacturing business.
  - Established a computerized billing and payroll system resulting in a more efficient and streamline operation.
  - Developed effective policy and procedures to ensure quality control and meet strict deadline schedules on a daily basis.
  - Established procedures resulting in more efficient mfg. productivity.

Administrative Skills

- Purchase raw materials and equipment for a wholesale manufacturing co.
- Monitor distribution of products throughout Southern California.
- Prepare bookkeeping and determine quarterly sales forecast.
- Hire, train and supervise employees.
- Work on multiple projects in highly pressured situations while maintaining a positive attitude.

Customer/Vendor Relations

- Locate qualified vendors and negotiate contracts with clients.
- Developed a large personal customer base through excellent customer service, thorough product/industry knowledge and word-of-mouth.
- Conducted a presentation on Southern California Saltwater Fishing as a Guest Lecturer at UCSB in Winter 1989.
- Communicate effectively with and all levels of professionals.

Youth Counselor—Chronological Resume

CHLOE GRAHAM CRAWFORD
PO Box 123
Goleta, CA 93117
(805) 968-7776

Objective: A Youth Counselor position for ages 6-17.

PROFESSIONAL EXPERIENCE

SPECIAL EDUCATION TEACHER 1988-present
Foothill Elementary School, Goleta, CA
- Teach children ages 5-10 with learning disabilities.
- Lead reading groups and worked one-on-one providing individual tutoring.
- teaching methods focused on the total growth and needs of children: social...emotional...intellectual...creative...physical behavior.

TEEN DIRECTOR/RECREATIONAL SUPERVISOR 1982-88
Goleta Valley Girls Club, Goleta, CA
- Implemented, organized and developed original programs including classes in arts & crafts, cooking, fishing, camping, sports activities and fund-raising events.
- Liaison and mediator between teens and staff members.
- Conducted regular problem solving meetings.
- Established strong interpersonal relationships through counseling individuals with concerns on family and peer relationships.
- Learned to work on multiple projects simultaneously in highly pressured situations while maintaining a highly professional and concerned manner.

YOUTH COUNSELOR 1976-82
Pilgrim Pines, Yucaipa, CA
- Counseled and supervised cabins of 10 campers, ages 6-17.
- Assisted camp director in organizing daily activities.
- Lead small discussion groups focusing on interpersonal relationships.
  - Helped resolve personal conflicts between campers.
- Acting liaison and mediator between campers and administration.

CAMP DIRECTOR Summer 1975
Amy's Week, Goleta, CA
- Set up and coordinated a one-week day camp program for 8-10 youths, ages 5-10. Organized field trips...arts & crafts...cooking...self esteem program
- Worked closely with parents to meet their needs, demonstrating leadership skills.

EDUCATION

BA Degree, Childhood Development, 1975
Emphasis: Special Education
University of California, Santa Barbara

Index to Resume Samples by Job Title